CW01665664

Journey to Freedom Series

BUILDING ON THE ROCK

Commendations and Testimonies

JOURNEY TO FREEDOM

"If you are serious about wanting to experience the deep truths of God in your life, then this is possibly the most relevant and pertinent tool of ministry I have discovered. It is insightful, challenging, and informative. I heartily endorse this tool of transformation. And now I challenge you to read it and prepare for change!"
Alistair P. Petrie *Executive Director – Partnership Ministries*

"It is an inexpressible relief and joy to discover daily teaching from the Word of God which embraces the breadth of Christian teaching, and whose depth, by the convicting and instructing power of the Holy Spirit, reaches the nooks and crannies of the reader's heart. This comprehensive teaching about the ways, works and words of the living God, always invites us deeper into intimacy with Him. It is personal and practical, pastoral and prophetic, encouraging and educating, appealing and revealing. It is Christ-centred, Holy Spirit empowered and inspired. I love it! I need it! I'm going to use it! So should you!"
Stuart McAlpine *Pastor, Christ Our Shepherd Church, Capitol Hill, Washington D.C.*

"The church is starving through lack of teaching that connects us to Christ and builds our foundation in Him. This is why I am so thrilled with *Journey to Freedom*. It is a marvellous discipleship tool that can inspire you in your walk with God and help you overcome every personal struggle. I hope you can make this part of your daily devotions. It is strong meat that boosts your spiritual diet!"
J. Lee Grady *Director, The Mordecai Project and former Editor, Charisma Magazine*

"Down-to-earth lessons in the reality of our lives, with desperately needed spiritual answers. They teach us how to apply the blood, cross and resurrection of our Lord Jesus Christ to transform us from weakness to strength, incapacity to capability, misery to blessedness."
John Sandford *Co-Founder of Elijah House Ministries*

"*Journey to Freedom* presents an amazing array of information that is at once biblical, practical and comprehensive. Discipleship is generally a lost art in the church today. So, to find a guide like this, covering the simplest truths of the faith to the deepest and most profound is like discovering buried treasure – simply outstanding!"
David Kyle Foster *Director, Mastering Life Ministries, Franklin, TN and Producer of Pure Passion TV Channel*

"What an incredible opportunity for the body of Christ to help people grow into strong, mature Christians. Simple, understandable and yet profound teaching that anyone interested in finding fullness in the Lord can easily access. The materials are presented in a practical way with opportunity for personal application. An incredible opportunity to learn the ways of the Lord."
Ruth Ruibal *President, Julio C. Ruibal Ministries, Colombia*

"Consecutive, practical Bible teaching in a straightforward and understandable way – pastoral in content and personal in application. It is designed to engage us where it finds us but not to leave us as we are. It will stimulate the mind; stir the emotions; strengthen the will; and nourish the spirit. My concern is not just to commend it to you, but to plead with you to take a look for yourself with a view to making a new discipleship commitment to our Lord Jesus."
Rev. Jim Graham *Former Pastor of Gold Hill Baptist Church and Director of External Ministries.*

"As I read through the teachings, I was drawn into the spiritual journey toward wholeness that is offered by *Journey to Freedom*. Peter Horrobin's insights into God's purpose in creating each of us are powerful and he is anointed with God's desire to call us to lives that are healed of sin and its consequences. I was reminded of the scripture *'And do not be conformed to this world, but be transformed by the renewing of your mind, so that you may prove what the will of God is, that which is good and acceptable and perfect'* (Romans 12:2)."
Rev. Peter Tsukahira *Co-Founder and Director, Or Ha Carmel Ministry Centre, Haifa, Israel*

TESTIMONIES

from some of those who applied the *Journey to Freedom* teaching in their lives when first published on-line as Ellel 365.

"I weep with gratitude for what God has done for me."

"Ellel 365 has changed my life forever. These past twelve months have been the most fulfilling and exciting experience I have had in my walk with the Lord."

"My relationship with God is going from strength to strength – I just love it."

"Ellel 365 has been a lifeline – it held me safe while Father God touched the broken places."

"I so long for everyone to experience what I'm now experiencing."

"Ellel 365 is the most important thing I've ever done – it's reality!"

"Ellel 365 has been truly LIFE TRANSFORMING –
and I still have a way to go!"

*"In faith, honesty and obedience my heavy burden was lifted,
I was set free – what joy!"*

**"The relief from the hold of sin was wonderful –
worth every pain and all the tears I've shed!"**

*"Now I know I have a FATHER in heaven. The lie of the enemy
has been broken."*

"The teaching is extraordinary and beautiful. It all makes perfect sense. I'm amazed at the things I am learning – I wish I'd had this when I first became a Christian."

"Thank you from the bottom of my very grateful heart!"

"My formerly derailed destiny in life is being put back on the fast track!"

"This journey becomes more exciting every day. I have dealt with so many issues in my own life."

"Ellel 365 is challenging and provoking – God is using it to wonderfully transform my life."

"Inspired and inspirational. The teaching is astounding and has opened up a whole new experience for me in my Christian journey."

"I now believe I have a destiny and a future which I didn't have before – miracles DO happen!"

"Excellent and brilliant foundational teaching for every Christian."

Book 1

Journey to Freedom Series

Personal Transformation – One Step at a Time

BUILDING ON THE ROCK

Peter Horrobin

Founder of Ellel Ministries

Understanding the Gospel and Living it Out

Sovereign World

Published by

Sovereign World Ltd
PO Box 784
Ellel
Lancaster
LA1 9DA
United Kingdom

www.sovereignworld.com
Twitter: @sovereignworld
Facebook: www.facebook.com/sovereignworld

Published July 2018

ISBN 978-1-85240-742-1

British Library Cataloguing-in-Publication Data
A catalogue record for this book is available from the British Library.

Cover designs by Paul Stanier of Zaccmedia
www.zaccmedia.com

Printed and bound in Great Britain by Bell and Bain Ltd, Glasgow

CONTENTS

PREFACE TO JOURNEY TO FREEDOM

"If you abide in my word, you are truly my disciples and you will know the truth and the truth will set you free." John 8:31

In 30 years of ministry, I have witnessed first-hand, and on many occasions, how the Lord has brought deep healing, restoration and freedom to even the most hurting and broken of people. *Journey to Freedom* contains the life-transforming keys that God has given us in His Word, which will enable you to enjoy personal transformation and freedom, one step at a time.

The original edition of *Journey to Freedom* was published on-line under the title *Ellel 365* – providing a whole year's teaching and training in 365 daily units. The material has, therefore, been thoroughly tested and used by thousands of people across most of the nations of the world. There are many wonderful stories of how God used these daily lessons to transform and heal people's lives, as they joined in the adventure of faith that is at the heart of *Journey to Freedom*. A new, updated, on-line edition of *Ellel 365*, also under the *Journey to Freedom* title, is being prepared simultaneously with the books.

While thousands of people have enjoyed reading the lessons of *Ellel*

365 on-line, there is still a large body of people who prefer the enjoyment of being able to hold a traditional book in their hands. These volumes, therefore, have been produced in response to popular demand. Whether you are studying *Journey to Freedom* on-line or reading it as a series of books, it is the same God who will be there with you and for you along the way – on a journey which is both a pilgrimage and an adventure.

This is a journey through which God can transform your life one step at a time, as you understand and apply each chapter's scriptural teaching. I don't write these words lightly – I believe them with every part of my being. I KNOW God changes people's lives, I have seen it happen! I KNOW He brings healing and freedom to those who are struggling. I KNOW God is interested in every detail of our lives. I KNOW He wants to set us free from the holds of the enemy. And I KNOW He wants to see you living in the destiny He has prepared for you.

We serve a truly awesome God who is as real and active today as He was in all the stories we read in the Bible (Hebrews 13:8). I am looking forward to sharing some of these with you. They are powerful testimonies to what the Lord has done in people's lives, as His truth has become established in their hearts.

Many have been set free from long term physical and psychological conditions, addictions and generational curses. Deep wounds of abuse and rejection have been healed by our gentle Father God. Identities that have been crushed, and sometimes burdened with guilt and shame, have been restored and relationships have been healed and repaired.

People have been healed from the consequences of deep traumas. Wounds have been touched by the Lord and the holds of the enemy have been broken. The fruits of bitterness have melted away through love and forgiveness. Debilitating fears have been discarded and replaced with courage and trust – so many beautiful stories of life-transformation, by a God who cares passionately for you and for me.

STRONG AND LASTING FOUNDATIONS

All buildings need strong and lasting foundations. Without these buildings will have a limited life and could collapse dangerously. In a similar way our lives need to have strong and lasting spiritual foundations. With good foundations in place a building will fulfil the purpose for which it was built. And when our lives are built on solid foundations we are able to enter into the calling and destiny that God has reserved for each one of us. *Journey to Freedom* will help you establish such foundations as a preparation for all that God has for you in the rest of your life.

I am excited and envisioned about the faith journey we're embarking on together. A wealth of vital material is going to be available to you. And you will be able to make this journey at the pace that is just right for you, with the freedom to move on from one chapter to the next whenever you feel ready. But may I encourage you to begin at the beginning – and not to miss out any of the chapters. Each and every one contains vital life-giving material.

It may be tempting to flick through the book and dip into later chapters, especially on subjects you have a special interest in, but you can't construct a safe building without the foundations being in place. And the foundations which will be built into your life through the early chapters of the book could be of critical importance to you.

The most genuine and lasting works of personal transformation that I have witnessed, have usually come as part of such an ongoing pilgrimage with the Lord. This is how the Holy Spirit normally works in our lives in order to establish godly order – one step at a time.

For many of us the struggles in our lives aren't going to be fixed in a day. We may cry out *"Heal Me, Lord"*, but for most of us God doesn't heal us dramatically or through an instant transformation. He heals us by carefully and tenderly working deep in our hearts, in the hidden areas that we may have tried so hard to ignore or discard. When our Heavenly Father brings His truth into our innermost being, He establishes those strong and lasting foundations, through which He brings stability, deep healing and wholeness.

Many of the people I meet and pray with come to our Centres because of the unwelcome fruit they see in their lives, such as depression, relationship breakdown, sicknesses, financial crisis or ruin, insomnia, addictions, pornography or obesity and many more different problems that Christians can struggle with.

This causes them to cry out to the Lord for healing of the symptoms, but the real problems usually go a whole lot deeper. What is the real cry of their heart? It's things like sadness, despair, fear, anxiety, sense of failure and unworthiness. It's feeling guilty and unfulfilled. It's anger, loneliness, the cold wall of self-protection, inner brokenness, hopelessness and lack of identity. It's not having a reason to live.

As a human being I may be an expert at covering up my struggles. I may try and function normally and ignore the inner limping which has become part of my everyday life. But the Lord longs to repair deep areas of our heart; not just deal with the fruit seen on the surface – not just what I'm struggling with today.

Jesus said, *'If the Son sets you free, you will be free indeed.'* (John 8:36) Unless He heals the foundation of our lives, we can never really become the people He created us to be and enjoy the blessing of being that person!

TRUTH AND REALITY

On each stage of this journey, as you read and take in one chapter at a time, I believe the Lord will be building new foundations of truth and revelation into your heart. We will start at the beginning and look with reality, not condemnation, at who we are in God and our relationship with Him. We will learn much from the lives of others as we absorb the invaluable lessons contained within God's word.

Journey to Freedom isn't a Bible study aimed at making us more knowledgeable Christians – the heart of this journey is to learn how to apply the truths of God's word and His character deep into our own being. Then He can transform the hidden depths of who we are into the beautiful creation He intended us to be. It's all for His glory and not for ours. My prayer is that by the enabling power of the Holy Spirit you will have the courage and the willingness to allow the Lord to shine His truth into every area of your being.

It's so easy to hide the true motives of our hearts, and even to deceive ourselves! But it's only as we are real before the One who created us, that we can fully allow Him to make that essential difference to our lives. Psalm 51:6 (NKJV) says *'You desire truth in the inward parts, and in the hidden part you will make me to know wisdom'*, and Jesus Himself said, *'Then you will know the truth, and the truth will set you free.'* (John 8:32)?

So at the very beginning of your *Journey to Freedom* may I encourage you to commit your life afresh to the Lord and give Him permission to shine His light of truth deep into your heart:

Father God, thank you so much for who you are, for your love and for your desire to restore my life, so that I can walk in the destiny prepared for me from the very beginning. I pray that you will show me the areas where I have been hurt and need healing. Help me to see the places where I have got it wrong and need forgiveness and restoration. Help me to give you first place in every area of my being as I learn how to apply the truth of your Word in my life. I invite you to be Lord of every area of my being. In Jesus' Name, Amen

ON A PRACTICAL NOTE

The original *Ellel 365* programme contained five teachings each week, followed on the sixth day by a review of all that had been covered in the previous five days and, on the seventh day, there was a devotional reading to round off the week.

The structure of the original material has been retained in this printed version of *Journey to Freedom*, so that you can follow the same weekly pattern through a whole year. Alternatively, you may prefer to work through the book at your own speed, either slower or faster, to suit your own personal situation. Each week's teaching of the original Ellel 365 is now referred to as a *'Stage'* in this book form of *Journey to Freedom*.

But whatever pattern you choose may I encourage you to persevere. Some of the most profound testimonies from *Ellel 365* were from people who did just that, and at the end of the journey were totally amazed at all that God had done. I passionately believe in the God of miracles – but I also recognise that some miracles take place over a period of time! And when I see now, the extraordinary transformation that God has wrought, one step at a time, I stand amazed at the way the God of miracles has been at work.

I would love to hear what God does in your life on your own *Journey to Freedom*. You can share your testimony by writing to me at peter.horrobin@ellel.org. I will look forward to hearing from you.

Peter Horrobin
Ellel Grange
June 2018

STAGE 1

My Life in God's Hands

God is my security – I can totally trust and depend on Him

Stage 1, Chapter 1

THE "GOD BOX"

PERSONAL NOTES

TO BEGIN AT THE BEGINNING!

All of us had a beginning. None of us have memories of the precise moment we were conceived, but it was at that moment God gave YOU life and your earthly pilgrimage began.

God breathed into you His breath of life (your human spirit) and you became a living soul (Genesis 2:7). The physical cells began to divide and you started to grow. Your spirit, soul and body were all present from those earliest moments – they are what makes you a human being.

On your 'birth-day' you began life separated from your mother. From babyhood you progressed through a time of being cared for as a child, and eventually you grew into adulthood. The years passed and you became the person you are today.

Although you are a unique creation in God, what you look like physically was influenced by your family's genetic history. The person God created you to be (the person living within your body) has also been influenced by the many experiences of your life from the time of your birth.

PERSONAL NOTES

What you have chosen to do, the way others have treated you and the way you have responded to these events have all contributed to moulding you into the person you now are. Our physical appearance bears the impression and scars of life's events – both the good and the bad.

When I have to wait at an airport or a railway station, I look at the faces of people passing by. Some are happy, others sad, and it's easy to see the emotional and spiritual scars that people are carrying. The face was designed by God to express our feelings and it shows the consequences of what we have been through.

The majority of people make their way through life without any knowledge of God, and how He could help and heal them. But this was not God's original intention.

GOD'S PLAN FOR THE HUMAN RACE

God intended that children should learn everything about God and what it means to live a godly life from their parents. That way all children would be brought up in the nurture of the Lord (Ephesians 6:4 & Proverbs 22:6). They would also learn how to live as a human being in the very best way possible.

In this way learning about the knowledge of God would be part of everyday life from day one onwards. Growing up would be a good experience and, little by little, children would learn about the nature and ways of God from Mum and Dad (Deuteronomy 6:6-7), because their parents had learned the truth about God from *their* parents, and so on down the generations. That was and is God's ideal.

God's plan was that human beings should grow up to enjoy every aspect of their humanity, in a loving relationship with the God who had made them, and in loving relationships with each other.

THE REALITY

But reality tells us that the world is now very different from the ideal that God originally intended. We only need to see the headlines in one issue of any national newspaper to see, for example, plenty of evidence that lives are not being lived according to God's intentions. In many places normal family life has almost disintegrated. Something has gone seriously wrong.

We see violence, stealing, ungodly sexual relationships, war, drugs, betrayal and a thousand and one other things that God did not plan or intend for us. We are now seeing some of the evil things prophesied in the Word of God being fulfilled before our very eyes, even to the extent that evil is being called good, and good is being called evil (Isaiah 5:20).

In most countries of the world, scriptural morality is no longer an acceptable basis for law, and every flavour of occult or perverted sexual activity is acceptable for both entertainment and even personal involvement. A large percentage of the films being produced by the movie industry are about horror, demonic power and explicit sex. Tragically this is what the deceived heart of man wants to watch. All of this simply confirms that the world is in an unholy mess, and is a million miles away from what God planned or intended for us.

It will be important for us to see how the world got into its present mess and then to understand that God really does have an amazing rescue plan for humanity (Isaiah 61:1-4 & John 10:10). We will then discover how He wants to heal and restore each one of us personally, so we can walk in the wonderful destiny He has planned for us all (Joel 2:25-27, Jeremiah 29:11).

GOD'S JIG-SAW PUZZLE!

A jig-saw is a simple puzzle, made up of many different pieces, and which can be enjoyed by children and adults alike. A jig-saw usually comes in a box, with a picture on the lid, showing the completed jig-saw. The picture on each piece is a tiny part of the whole.

God has revealed Himself to mankind in the most wonderful of pictures. Within Scripture the revelation began in the Garden of Eden and is concluded with images of Heaven in the book of Revelation. From Genesis to Revelation we see an amazing picture unfolding of foundational truth about God and man.

Each truth is like a piece of an incredible jig-saw. Put them all together and you have an amazing understanding of the nature and character of God and of what God's best is for mankind.

PERSONAL NOTES

PERSONAL NOTES

OUR "*GOD-BOX*"

The *God-box* is the name I have given to the 'spiritual container', into which we put all the bits of spiritual knowledge we acquire on life's journey. Ever since we were conceived we have been learning new things and putting pieces of spiritual understanding into our *God-box*. They are like pieces of a jig-saw.

But everyone has had different parenting and different life experiences, so everyone's *God-box* is filled differently. As a result, no two people can ever be in full agreement about what they think about God, if their only source of knowledge is their own life-experience! The pieces of jig-saw in their personal *God-box* will never be the same as anyone else's.

That's why, for example, there are so many different religions in the world. They are all different because each one is an expression of *man's* attempt to find God, based on their own accumulated knowledge and experience, which will always be incomplete and inadequate.

As a child I loved doing jig-saws, but a puzzle with pieces missing could never be completed. It was so frustrating and disappointing not to be able to complete the picture. Lack of sufficient knowledge and spiritual understanding is a problem we all face. If we try and depend on our own understanding (Proverbs 3:5-6) we will always have an inadequate knowledge of the truth about God. There will be important pieces missing from our *God-box* – and we will not be able to complete the picture of truth about either God or man!

EXTRA PIECES!

One day I came across a particularly difficult jig-saw that had some extra pieces. The extra pieces looked as though they were part of the picture on the lid of the box, but they didn't actually fit anywhere in the puzzle!

They had been deliberately added by the manufacturers to make the jig-saw even more difficult! If you did put one of these extra pieces into the jig-saw it made the rest of the jig-saw impossible to do!

This illustrates the sort of difficulty we all face when trying to understand the truth about God. From the moment we were conceived we have been acquiring many different pieces of information about life and have been putting these into our *God-box* like pieces of a spiritual jig-saw puzzle.

Some of them have been true, but, sadly, many of those bits of spiritual understanding have been false. Because God has inbuilt in us to believe that whatever our parents believe or demonstrate to us, is right (the truth), and because our parents are God's intended role models to show us what He is like, we instinctively believe that everything we have put in our *God-box* must be true!

I once prayed with a lady who had a terrible problem believing that God was a Father who loved her. I later found out that her human father had regularly beaten her. As a result she believed that all fathers are cruel – including Father God.

Some people have difficulty praying. They cannot really believe that God has time for them! Many such people had fathers who were too busy with their own lives and never had time for their children. So the message in their *God-box* says *'God doesn't have time for me either.'*

And then again, many people have been introduced to various occult practices, or beliefs associated with one of the many false religions. Experiences like this have the effect of sowing lies into our *God-box*. Young children cannot differentiate between the good and bad pieces of information they have received from significant adults in their lives. It's all 'truth' to them!

THE REAL SITUATION

The fact is, all of us have had truth and error, good and bad, poured into us throughout our lives and most human beings are, as a result, very confused. We can have huge gaps in our understanding of real truth. And we can have many *'extra pieces'* of spiritual knowledge that are nothing whatsoever to do with God! Our image of God has been distorted by our experiences in life.

It's important that we take a hard look at ourselves in this respect, and let God show up any areas of unbelief or wrong belief that might have been influencing our relationship with God and standing in the way of our growth or healing (Psalm 51:6; Psalm 139:23-24).

PERSONAL NOTES

PERSONAL NOTES

GOD'S ANSWER

The answer to this seemingly impossible problem lies, ultimately, in Jesus. **For one of the reasons that Jesus came, was to show us what Father God is really like** (John 14:7-11).

It was as if the human race had been trying to make all their jig-saw pieces into a picture – but it made no sense. They couldn't tell truth from error. They needed a picture to look at, which they could use to compare with the pieces in their *God-box*, so they could get rid of the ones that didn't fit into the puzzle.

Jesus is the picture we need. We can model our lives on Him and the more we become like Him, the more effective and blessed our earthly and eternal lives will be (2 Corinthians 3:18). The progressive revelation of Scripture finds its total fulfilment in Jesus (Luke 4:21). He is the ultimate gift of God to the human race (John 3:16). *It is so very important that we truly know Him as he really is – for He is the key to all healing and to finding our destiny in God* (John 10:10).

As you take one step at a time, on your own personal *Journey to Freedom*, you will see that not only did Jesus come to save us from the consequences of sin (1 Timothy 1:15), but He also came to show us by example the nature and character of God (John 14:6-11), and to teach us how we can have a healed and restored relationship with the Father (2 Corinthians 6:18).

SUMMARY

Our life was a gift of God, but through the years we have all developed a distorted view of the nature and character of the God who made us. How much we must be missing out on as a result! To get back to a right understanding of God, we will need to identify and deal with those things in our beliefs that are not of God and complete the picture of truth as we look at Jesus.

PRAYER

Thank you, Lord, for the privilege of being part of your creation. As I start moving forward, one step at a time, help me to appreciate all you have provided for your children, and to desire to love and serve you all my days. In Jesus' Name, Amen

Stage 1, Chapter 2

MY LIFE – MADE FOR LIVING

For many years I have enjoyed restoring old cars. My heart seems to beat just a little bit faster, when I see a grand old car of days gone by still on the road. I have had many wonderful adventures with cars bearing names that many of you may have never heard of, such as Riley, Lagonda and Alvis.

Even today I have a car in the garage which is older than I am! But very few people would be able to drive it! Not because it's hard to drive, but because no-one has taught them how to start the engine. You can't just jump into the driver's seat and turn the key – there isn't one! There are a few basic steps that must be carried out before the engine will burst into life. Without knowing these basics, the car is useless.

GOD'S ORDER FOR LIVING

In a similar way, many people today have never learnt the basics of God's order for living. As a result, they are unable to do what God intended for their lives or discover that their life really was made for living!

PERSONAL NOTES

PERSONAL NOTES

So, in these early sections of our *Journey to Freedom*, I am putting some really important foundational principles in place. Many years of experience of ministering to people right across the world, have proved time and time again how important this is.

What is obvious to some people is not obvious to others. And for many people a reminder of vital foundations has been the key that opened the door of miracles in their life.

I well remember a man, who had two theological degrees, telling me that it was only when we went through these foundations together that he really understood what the cross was all about. And that changed everything for him!

YOU ARE A MIRACLE!

Take a look at your hands and marvel at the way they are made. The fingers and the joints are perfectly designed to carry out all the essential tasks of life. Imagine what eating would be like if you had no hands to prepare the food, to pick it up or to put it in your mouth!

Then run the end of your fingers gently over different surfaces. Your fingers are so sensitive that even with your eyes closed you can tell what you are touching.

Now take a deep breath and thank God for the oxygen in the air. Imagine what's happening in your lungs as the oxygen crosses into your blood stream and is carried to every part of your body, bringing life to all your vital organs. Without oxygen you would quickly die.

Every part of your body has been carefully designed by an incredible genius – the one we call our loving, Creator God. As the Psalmist said, '*I am fearfully and wonderfully made!*' (Psalm 139:14).

With your eyes you can see. With your ears you can hear. With your nose you can smell. And with your tongue you can taste. Every one of your senses is a miracle of operational genius. And with your mouth you can speak and eat as well.

Your digestive system processes food, extracts the goodness, stores energy as fat and eliminates waste. Your legs, arms, muscles and bones help you get around and do things. And at night everything shuts down for seven or eight hours to allow your body to rest, so you can recover your strength for a new day.

Yes, you are a miracle and your body is the most amazing of machines. But you are more than a machine!

PERSONAL NOTES

MORE THAN A MACHINE

I'm typing these notes on a computer – with those amazing fingers God gave me! The computer is also a marvellous machine, but it doesn't do anything unless I correctly set up the operating programs and type instructions on the keyboard or click my 'mouse'.

A computer, like any other machine, requires an operator to use it according to the maker's instructions. Without an operator the computer will sit on the desk and produce nothing! And if you don't know how to obey the instructions, even the most expensive computer will cause you endless frustration as it refuses to do what you want. I know – from hard experience!

In a similar way, you're the operator of the machine called your body and unless you give your body some instructions it will lie there, like an unused computer, doing nothing. An unused computer has great potential but it produces absolutely nothing!

Machines are also made to be used in a certain way. If you misuse a machine you will quickly damage its operating mechanisms and before long it will become useless. And in the same way, if you misuse your body, the time will come when it will cease to function properly and life will come grinding to a halt.

The computer was designed to be highly productive when working together in harmony with its operator. There seems to be no limit to what can be done from the keyboard. I have just written an important letter to a friend and sent it by e-mail. Then I ordered a birthday present for my grandson from an online store. After which I looked at a news website to see what's happening around the world.

This one machine, correctly programmed and operated, achieved all of these different things in a matter of minutes! But I had to give the computer the correct instructions and tell it what to do.

Your body was designed in a similar way to be highly productive. I have already done many things today with my own personal machine – my body! After a night's sleep I got my body out of bed, then together we went and took on some fuel (breakfast), before taking the dog for a

PERSONAL NOTES

walk. After which I sat down at the computer to do all the things I told you about. My body and I worked together as a unit to achieve all that I had planned for the day.

SO WHO ARE YOU?

While most people will recognise you by the shape of your body, you are more than your body.

A day will come when your bodily machine runs out of its capacity to cope any longer with the pressures of daily living. Your machine will then cease to function and the world will say you have died. But nothing could be farther from the truth! You do not die when your body ceases to function.

When you reach that point you will discover first-hand that your body is, in reality, only a machine, a temporary home, and that you have moved on to a different realm of existence.

There is life after death – as Jesus proved to us when He was raised from the dead. Our soul and our spirit will continue to live beyond the grave.

But the nature and quality of that life will be directly related to the choices we have made while living here on earth (1 Corinthians 3:12-15, Matthew 6:19-20).

Later we will look more closely at the nature of both God and man. We will learn more about how God intended our soul and spirit to work together in harmony within our body, so that we can be the people God intended us to be.

LIFE IS FOR LIVING – TO THE FULL

You are a person in your own right. Your earthly body is a temporary home – not an eternal residence. Here on earth you and your body are inseparable. Your body gives you visible identity and your body also enables you to function as a human being on planet Earth. And God has created you for a purpose – He *loves* YOU. You are special to Him. You are made for living!

But what does that mean? It certainly means more than just functioning as a machine. For Jesus said, *"I have come that you might have life – and have it to the full"* John 10:10. Jesus certainly wasn't talking about mere existence.

To fully understand this we will need to understand just why the world is in such a mess. For Jesus came to rescue us from the mess that man had got himself into, because of his sinful choices (John 3:17). Those choices have produced a harvest of pain, bitterness and suffering, arising out of man's rebellion against the God who created him for a purpose.

How can we live life to the full when we're so held back by the chains of ungodly choices, made by both ourselves and others and also by our ancestors? These are important questions, which we will need to address.

Yes, we can look forward to eternity in heaven, and that will be a wonderful escape from the hardships of life on earth. But I don't think that's all Jesus was referring to when He talked about giving us the opportunity to live life to the full.

You are made for living – here on earth as well! But you also have an enemy, the enemy of souls. Satan does not want you to enter into the blessings God has prepared for you. Satan wants you to be spiritually dysfunctional and never know the joy of real life. (John 10:10a) God has a better plan for your life! (Ephesians 2:10).

Before man sinned he was able to enjoy the fullness of life in fellowship and relationship with God. But because of sin man became separated from God (Genesis 3:8-10). Fullness of life means living in relationship with our Creator (Ephesians 3:17-19). Outside of God we can never live life to the full. Our potential will always be limited by that breakdown in relationship with the One who made us.

We may be able to use the gifts and abilities that God gave us, but outside of a restored relationship with God the damage caused by sin can never be healed. And no matter how successful a person might appear to be, outside of God that success will never satisfy the desire of the human heart for relationship with our Creator.

Yes, living life to the full means living life in a restored relationship with Father God and then discovering how he transforms us from the inside out. That way we can become the children of God He planned from the beginning. Only in that place will we truly know the joy of the Lord and that joy will become our strength for daily living (Nehemiah 8:10).

PERSONAL NOTES

PERSONAL NOTES

Today is a good day for you to decide to give God first place in every area of your life. As you travel step by step on this *Journey to Freedom*, allow Him to restore you to be like Him.

SUMMARY

God intended our lives to be more than mere existence. We were made for a purpose and God wants to see us restored to a right relationship with Him so that we can enter into the fullness of Life. Satan, the enemy of our souls, would want us to look at the mess and give up. God wants us to see Him and look up! 'Jesus is the Way, the Truth and the Life!' (John 14:6)

PRAYER

Help me, Lord, never to forget that you made me for a purpose. I pray you will show me how to start living life to the full and discover my true potential in God. In Jesus' Name, Amen.

Stage 1, Chapter 3

MY PLACE IN GOD'S WORLD

THE NEXT STEP ON OUR JOURNEY

We are now turning our attention to the personal place God has for us in the incredible universe He created.

When I take our dog for a walk on a dark night, and look up at the painted ceiling of stars above my head, I really understand what the Psalmist must have been feeling when he saw the same stars and said, *'What is man that you are mindful of him, the son of man that you care for him?'* (Psalm 8:4)

He couldn't get his head round the fact that the God who made all the created realms claimed to know and love him personally!

The universe itself is so vast that it is beyond measuring. That is not just a statement of Scripture (Job 11:7), but a scientific fact. As soon as man finds a way of measuring the distance to the farthest known heavenly body, astronomers discover a new way of detecting the existence of things even farther out. The edge of the universe doesn't seem to exist. It is without limit! And you cannot measure the size of something that has no limits or boundaries!

PERSONAL NOTES

PERSONAL NOTES

It is hard for us to believe or understand that the Creator of this immeasurable Universe can care about the individual life of any one human being! Or, that the prayers of any one individual can be heard by a God who currently has over six billion children on Planet Earth!

Yet Scripture tells us that not even one sparrow falls to the ground without our Heavenly Father knowing! (Matthew 10:29). Jesus then urges us, in verse 31, to remember that we are worth more than many sparrows.

If something you own is very valuable you really care about it. You look after it, you protect it and you insure it. But all your treasured possessions count as nothing when compared with the value of the life of someone you really love.

If your house was burning you wouldn't even think about rescuing the furniture, when someone you love was still inside. You would care far more about the person than any of your possessions.

WHY DO YOU FEEL LIKE THAT?

The reason we care about the people we love is that God created us to be like Him! He cares about the people He loves (1 Peter 5:7). He didn't create a race of alien creatures with whom He had nothing in common.

Genesis 1:26 says that we are made in His image and in His likeness. That means the appearance (the image) of human beings is a reflection of the appearance of God. Or, to put it the other way round, the Son of God (Jesus) looked like a man and He was the image of His Father.

But we are also made in His likeness – which means that we are like Him in terms of our nature. Scripture tells us that God is love. If, therefore, we are made to be like God, it must also mean that a capacity to love will be found at the heart of every human being, irrespective of whether or not they choose to believe in Him or love Him back.

That's why unbelieving parents are still passionate about loving their children. And why all unbelievers are still capable of great acts of personal sacrifice, which are often seen as an expression of great love. People may behave very badly and even do evil things, but you cannot totally eliminate love from the heart of man or the capacity to respond to love from others. It's how God made us.

PERSONAL NOTES

I recently visited the home in which I was brought up as a child, just after the Second World War. Times were hard and my parents had very little to live on. But as I walked round that house I was reminded of hundreds of things that Mum and Dad did for me – often very sacrificially – just because they loved me.

BECAUSE THEY LOVED

Because my parents loved me, they cared for me. That meant they wanted what was best for me as I grew up. They wanted to help me find my place in the world. They were careful to encourage me in the things I enjoyed. They saw the things I wanted to do and was good at, and then tried to help me learn about those things and get better at them.

My mother would play the piano for a boys' Bible class that was held in our house. Long before I was five years old I would sit at the piano and try and copy her, but I could only make a joyful noise! I really wanted to be able to play like she did. But I needed training.

So, at considerable personal sacrifice for them at that time, they paid for me to have piano lessons from Miss Duxbury, an elderly lady with a very kind heart. I learnt enough to enjoy playing hymns and choruses and as I grew up I developed a life-long interest in Christian music, which led to the compiling of hymn and song books, such as *Mission Praise*. Without their love and care for me as a child, I couldn't have done such things as an adult.

I realise that not everyone experienced the same love and care that I was privileged to have, and that for many people their early childhood days were far from happy. But the good news is that God understands exactly what our experience has been and He longs to heal and restore us.

As we journey together I know that many people are going to discover God to be their healer as they enter into a living experience of His love and care. I have seen it happen so many times and I know God can do this for you too.

GOD HAS A PLACE FOR YOU!

Every human being is different. We are all made in the image and likeness of God, but our gifts, interests, abilities and opportunities are all totally

PERSONAL NOTES

different and utterly unique. Earlier we used the illustration of a jig-saw puzzle in which every single piece is different, yet when all the pieces are in their place a complete picture is made.

Each of us is like a unique piece in God's jig-saw puzzle. In His providence He has equipped us for life and He rejoices when we find the place He has prepared for us.

Sadly, many people have never had the loving care from human beings, that would have helped them discover that best place for them in God's world. Others have been hindered by their own ungodly choices or the awful consequences of violence, war, famine, accident, trauma or tragedy.

Does that mean God doesn't love them? Far from it! If you have a child who is hurting, you will pour all the love you can into that hurting child to bring hope, healing and restoration. We are like God in that respect. So if a human being would want to respond like that, how much more would Father God want to respond in a similar way for all His children? (Matthew 7:9-11, Luke 11:11-13).

Many times we have ministered to older people who were never given opportunities to discover their creative gifting in their youth. So often we have seen God heal their past and restore them in the present through discovering the joy of creative expression. The door of their destiny has been unlocked by love!

HEALED FOR A PURPOSE

These teachings have been deliberately planned as a journey and not just an aid to gaining more head knowledge! It is a journey of discovery – to discover the truth about both God and yourself and then walk forward into God's plans and purposes for your life.

Healing is far more than getting better after some physical sickness. It is seeing God restore what has been damaged in the past, in such a way that we are able to know God's fulfilment for our lives in the present, and then walk into the future that He has for us (Jeremiah 29:11).

God created you for relationship with Him – but He also created you to enjoy living in the purposes that He prepared for you in advance – His providence (Ephesians 2:10). When we are being the person God made us to be and doing the things God made us to do, the joy of the Lord is released through our hearts. Life cannot be boring when you are at the centre of God's will for your life.

Over the years we have helped many people face the reality of their past and see God bring amazing healing into their present. But then, the greatest joy has come when we have seen those people begin to grow in their giftings and find the unique place that God had prepared for them.

I just love that wonderful promise from Joel 2:25, where God says *'I will restore to you the years that the locust has eaten.'* The locust devours, but God promises to give back in abundance when we have a right heart before Him. I am sure many of you will come to experience the blessing of this amazing promise as you journey through the pages of this book, You really can trust the God who loves you so much He made the whole universe for you to enjoy!

SUMMARY

God loves you and cares about you. Just as Jesus promised that when He went back to heaven, He would prepare a place for us there (John 14:3), He also wants us to discover the place He has for us here, as we respond to His loving care and receive His healing.

PRAYER

Help me, Lord, to lift up my eyes and not only see the extraordinary wonders of Your creation, but to realise that You care for every single human being, even me! Thank You for the miracle of Your love. In Jesus' name, Amen.

PERSONAL NOTES

Stage 1, Chapter 4

MY DESTINY IN GOD'S HANDS

PERSONAL NOTES

MEN AND WOMEN OF DESTINY

I really enjoy reading the stories of great Christian pioneers and leaders, especially of people who have believed for the impossible and obeyed God, rather than listened to the doubts of men and done nothing!

In the eighteenth century William Carey went to India and translated the Scriptures into many different languages. In the nineteenth century, Hudson Taylor founded the *China Inland Mission* and took the Gospel into mainland China; Charles Cowman founded the *Oriental Missionary Society*, and opened up an amazing work in Japan before the first World War. And in the twentieth century Jackie Pullinger took the Gospel and ministered healing to the drug addicts of Hong Kong.

There are many, many others – some famous and the majority largely unknown, but, nevertheless, very precious saints who did amazing exploits, in obedience to God's call on their lives.

Reading their stories will encourage and strengthen you in your own Christian pilgrimage. They are stories of ordinary men and women who discovered their destiny and became agents of change for the

PERSONAL NOTES

Kingdom of God. They were envisioned by God, they responded with an uncompromising *'Yes'* and history records the testimony of their achievements.

BUT WHAT ABOUT ME?

I can hear some of you saying that the stories of such famous people are wonderful, but *"I could never do what they did!"* That is both a true and a false statement at the same time!

It is true, in that God never calls any of us to do exactly the same things as anyone else. For every single one of us is totally unique. We have different looks, different gifts, different abilities and different destinies.

But it is totally false for you to think that you could not apply the same Kingdom principles in your own life and fulfil your destiny in God! You can – and I have prayed that as we make this amazing journey together you will see the fruit of doing just that in your own life. We all have the potential to do great things in the Kingdom of God, as we enter into the destiny He has prepared for us. (Daniel 11:32)

But let's not worry about becoming great in man's eyes, it is only God's measure of greatness that matters! (Galatians 1:10) You don't have to become a famous pioneering Christian, or have your name up in lights at some big meeting, to be considered great in the Kingdom of God! All you have to do is be obedient to the vision God gives you – however large or small that is. (Proverbs 29:18, John 14:21}.

My guess is that when the books are finally opened in Heaven (Revelation 20:12), that there will be many, many people who were totally unknown on earth, who will be considered great in Heaven, because of their simple faith and steadfast obedience (see also, Hebrews 11).

SO WHAT ACTUALLY IS DESTINY?

Sometimes people will come up to me at the end of a meeting and say something like this: *"I would like some of your anointing, will you pray for me?"* I understand the desire of their heart but generally I respond this way, *"I can't actually pray like that, because you can't live my life and I can't live yours. But I'd be glad to pray that God will give you His anointing for your life."*

Anointing and destiny are very closely linked, but they are not the same as gifting. It was the shepherd boy David's destiny to be the next King of Israel after Saul. He needed many gifts to fulfil the task. No doubt there were many other people in Israel who had similar gifts, but it was only David who had the destiny calling of kingship.

As soon as the Lord confirmed to Samuel that it was David who would be the next King, he took a horn of specially prepared oil and poured it over David. From that day on the Spirit of God rested on David (1 Samuel 16:13).

David was being prepared for his destiny. He had been anointed anointed for the particular task (his destiny) that God had prepared him for. And the primary anointing David needed, therefore, was the specific anointing that was relevant to his future role as King.

FINDING MY DESTINY

The need to be valued for who we are, and to have a purpose in life, is fundamental to every human being. Life without a purpose is meaningless. We all need a destiny to walk in.

I first invited Jesus into my life at the age of nine. It was the best decision I ever made. At that moment I knew for certain that my eternal destination had changed – Heaven was now to be my future home. But I also knew that my earthly life would now have a purpose that was unique to me.

I began to pray for God to show me what He wanted me to do. While there were lots of things I was interested in, I was always thinking about some form of Christian ministry. My destiny was rising to the surface of my life. Without fully realising what was happening, I was beginning to understand what God had planted deep into my spirit – even before I was born.

This was Jeremiah's experience and testimony. This is what God said about him: *'Before I formed you in the womb I knew you, before you were born I set you apart. I appointed you as a prophet to the nations.'* (Jeremiah 1:5).

As Jeremiah matured into a man of God, he connected with what God had already spoken into his being. He was discovering what God had made him for – he was discovering his destiny.

The picture on the front of a packet of seeds is never of the seeds in

PERSONAL NOTES

PERSONAL NOTES

the packet! It's always of the plant in full bloom! The destiny of each seed in the packet is shown on the picture.

It's a bit like that with God – He sees the destiny on the 'packet' which contains the seed of our life. Little by little we become aware of what God has in store for us, as we grow in Him and mature as disciples of Jesus.

Psalm 139:13 tells us how God created our innermost being and knit us together in our mother's womb. It's not just Jeremiah who had a destiny! God has had His hand upon each one of us since those very earliest of days and has longed to see us, as His children, take the place in life for which He has prepared and equipped us. (Ephesians 1:4-5, 1 Corinthians 2:7-9).

Later on we will see how Satan tries to rob us of our destiny and prevent us from fulfilling our calling in God. But we will also learn how to overcome the enemy!

GOD'S STRATEGY FOR YOUR DESTINY

God's fundamental desire for each one of us is that we should first find our eternal destiny in a restored relationship with Him, and then begin to walk in our earthly destiny as citizens of the Kingdom of Heaven.

I was brought up hearing stories of two young women, Phoebe Lewsey and Ida Whittle. They both loved the Lord and sensed His call on their lives to bring hope and healing to children with leprosy in Northern Nigeria. They sailed for Nigeria in faith. There they established the work of the *Albarka Fellowship* in Kaduna.

They were unknown to most of the Christian world, but in their faithfulness to the vision God had given them, they experienced extraordinary protection and provision, saved the lives of hundreds of children and Ida experienced personal miraculous healing from advanced cancer.

One day there will be a roll-call in heaven of the lives that were transformed by the power of God through their ministry. They were living in their destiny. Today many of those children (and their children!) are now serving the Lord in different parts of the world!

Scripture tells us that without vision people are perishing (Proverbs 29:18). Vision brings life and hope, purpose and fulfilment of destiny – both to ourselves and everyone whose life is touched by ours. It is important, therefore, that believers should really look to God to envision them for their lives. For when we are living in the visions that come from God, we will know the greatest joy possible as we serve Him.

As unique individuals, God calls us to a unique destiny in our lives with Him. Whilst some are called to the 'big' things, others are called to smaller tasks. When the roll call of Heaven takes place God won't be looking first for those that have achieved big things, but for those who were obedient to whatever was asked of them.

AND IT'S NEVER TOO LATE FOR YOU!

Some of you may be thinking that because the early days of your life were a long way from ideal or you have really got messed up along life's journey, for a variety of possible reasons, that you no longer have a realisable destiny, or that God can no longer use you. If that is what you believe, you are believing a lie.

This is what Satan wants you to believe, for he is a destiny robber. His strategy is to so interfere in your life that you never realise the potential God has stored up for you. The good news is that Jesus overcame Satan at the cross – so with Jesus as your helper there is an answer to even the very worst of situations. Later on we will discover God's answers for the issues that may be holding you back in your life.

You may not be able to start life again at a young age, but God is the great Redeemer. Not only did He redeem us from the consequences of our sins, but He redeems our lives from the pit. He is the one who can restore the years that the locust has eaten. He is the one who can take the humble offering of our lives, at whatever stage we come to that point of absolute surrender to Him, and build something precious in time, that will last throughout eternity.

All God asks of us is our availability and our obedience. He will then take whatever abilities we may have and as they are used for Him will multiply them in the service of the King.

I pray that as you walk this exciting journey, God will clearly show you His best for the rest of your life and then, as you walk in obedience to His vision, He will give you the joy of being fulfilled in the service of the King!

PERSONAL NOTES

PERSONAL NOTES

SUMMARY

God not only loves and cares for each one of us, He also has a purpose for each one of our lives. When we are living the life that He planned and purposed for us, we will know His joy flooding our heart as God's eternal purposes are being fulfilled through us. We are children of destiny!

PRAYER

Help me, Lord, to discover the plans and purposes that You have for my life using the gifts and abilities You have given me. I want to discover my destiny and fulfil the vision You have for me. In Jesus' Name, Amen.

Stage 1, Chapter 5

MY SECURITY IN GOD'S LOVE

MY SECURITY IN GOD'S LOVE

Each step of our journey together will put something more of God's amazing truth into our understanding – or, to use the illustration that we began with – into our *God-box*. The more truth there is in our *God-box*, the better equipped we'll be for living the life God has given us, and fulfilling our destiny in Him.

So far, we have established that our lives are precious to God and that what we do with them really matters – both to us and to Him. We know that God created the world for His people and He rejoices when we find our place in it and discover our destiny.

We are turning our attention now to the deep inner need we all have for security in the very core of our beings.

THE WORLD AS IT IS

We're living in a world which is increasingly insecure, especially at the personal level, and particularly for children.

PERSONAL NOTES

PERSONAL NOTES

Security and love are inextricably bound together. The traditional family, as God's strategic plan for putting the security of love into the heart of every human being (Ephesians 3:14-15, Psalm 68:5-6 & 127:3-5), is steadily being undermined by the collapse of morality in both society and government. As a result we are now growing generations of children who have no secure family anchor. They are having to fend for themselves, emotionally and physically, and learn how to be independent, far earlier than God ever intended.

The break-up of so many families, and the consequential absence of fathering, has removed much of the security that God desired children to enjoy within the safety and covering of a family. This is true for families all over the world.

Today, people are being forced to behave as if they're 'grown up', long before they are ready to take on the responsibilities of adulthood. Sadly, the very word 'adult' no longer means a mature man or woman, but is a description of what level of pornographic material people are looking at! And, even as I write this, a new report has revealed that all the sexual awareness teaching, which was designed by ill-informed governments, at great expense, to reduce teenage pregnancies, has more than doubled the incidence of teenage pregnancies in the groups involved!

We have fallen a long way from God's ideal. But this is the world as it is. Some of you may have been affected by these very issues. I am not drawing your attention to them just because I feel strongly about what is happening in the world, but because the Gospel has to be made relevant to real people in the real world as it is. God is intensely interested in today's generations – from the young to the old, and everyone in between.

REAL ANSWERS FOR REAL PROBLEMS

The issues of life leave behind a legacy in the heart. And unless we have answers that will satisfy the deepest longings of the human heart – which usually lie hidden beneath the external behaviour of those who are hurting – then the Gospel is not good news for all, but only for a chosen few.

People are hurting because of what has happened to them in the past – and perhaps, even you are one of them, and you are wondering what God can do for people with considerably less than perfect parenting? I want to assure you that there is no situation so bad that God cannot heal and no person so damaged that God isn't concerned for them.

I passionately believe that the Gospel is good news for all – for you, for me and whomever God leads us to on this planet full of people – all of whom are loved by our Creator. I am praying you will want to share this good news with as many others as are open to receive it.

But if we are to share it with others – we must, first, be willing to receive it for ourselves and allow Him to so work it into our lives that, as Paul prayed and longed for, we will grow up into maturity in Christ Jesus (Ephesians 4:13).

Journey to Freedom is not just a training course to help you understand the truth of God's Word in your head – but a dynamic experience of learning how to apply those wonderful truths, first in your own life and then, following in the steps of Jesus, as a servant to others.

WHAT HAPPENS WHEN WE NO LONGER KNOW THE SECURITY OF LOVE?

Security is a fruit of love. Without love there can only be insecurity, and insecurity breeds fear. It's no surprise, therefore, that the Scripture tells us *'perfect love drives out fear'* (1 John 4:18), because, when we have really begun to understand the perfect and totally selfless love of God, we know we can also begin to trust Him and depend on Him in every area of life (Ephesians 3:16-19). There is then nothing to be afraid of. We are liberated from the bondage of our past into the freedom which is the inheritance of God's children. (Romans 8:14 17)

Fear, however, promotes independence and the need to control one's circumstances and environment. Independence makes people put up walls of self-defence. A need to control, limits life to those experiences we can be in charge of.

For many, the need for self-defence forces them to retreat into an artificial fantasy world, where they are in charge and where they find some comfort, but sadly it is only false comfort and does not last. It can be a world containing anything from movie-addiction to religion; from dependence on music or computer games to addiction to food, pornography or sex, and anything which can form a seemingly 'secure' distraction from the realities of life.

PERSONAL NOTES

PERSONAL NOTES

Immorality has become the norm for the growing generations, not because they particularly want to be immoral, but because they don't know anything different. Parents and governments no longer have any moral boundaries of their own. When there is no longer any respect or holy fear of God, they no longer have a spiritual motive for disciplined love, which provides security through putting in firm and healthy boundaries for the next generation. (Proverbs 22:6 & Ephesians 6:4)

The old saying is very true – *the hand that rocks the cradle will one day change the world*. But if the hands that are rocking the cradle no longer know God, have no respect for Him, and cannot understand how to really love their offspring, then the sands of time are running very fast through the hour-glass of destiny. This is our world!

SO IS THERE ANY HOPE?

This is a good question! For it would be so easy to look at all the bad things and decide to give up on wanting to make a difference in this world for the Kingdom of God. So let me give you an example of what can happen.

The eighteenth century was a very violent and rebellious era in England. But in spite of all the bad things one could point to, hope for the nation came in the form of a man with a message, John Wesley.

He was one of the greatest evangelists the United Kingdom has ever known. In the eighteenth century he changed the face of society through his determined preaching and Holy Spirit anointing. It turned the face of the nation away from violence and rebellion and laid the foundation for many of the good things that developed in the Victorian era of the nineteenth century.

His mother, the *'hand'* that rocked his cradle, was a woman of extraordinary godliness and passion, praying with all her fourteen children individually, every day, and trusting that they would grow up to love and serve the Lord. They did!

John never forgot the influence of his mother on his life and there are countless millions in eternity who will one day give thanks to God for John Wesley's mother! Even Hudson Taylor, the extraordinary founder of the China Inland Mission, will be one of them. He was a second generation fruit of Wesley's life and preaching! His life was used by God to transform the lives of others. There is no-one beyond hope.

PERSONAL NOTES

Over the past thirty-five years I have been privileged to see how God can transform the lives of even the most hurting of people. Many of whom never knew the love and security of loving parents – but came to know a loving God. God then sent His agents to minister salvation and healing into their lives. Some of those people who received help are now some of the most whole people I know! God has truly healed them through love and has given them back *'the years which the locust has eaten'* (Joel 2:25) and equipped them with a heart of love for others.

I am only writing this because I want the whole Body of Christ to know these wonderful truths, be empowered by the Spirit of God to take this message to His Church and, through His Church, to the world, where they live. I want people to regain an understanding of the security that comes through love. I want them to understand that hope and healing flow from the cross to all who will come to Him.

There is hope! Will you join with me in being willing to let the God of Truth change you so that the Truth of God can change others?

THE SECURITY THAT IS A FRUIT OF LOVE

Security is both a feeling and a factual reality. In children the feeling of security is an emotional response to being loved by those who are responsible for them. Their physical security is the actual protection that is put in place by those who have the responsibility to love and care for them.

Our eternal security as a child of God is guaranteed by the love of our Heavenly Father. John expressed it perfectly in one of the most well-known verses in the whole of the Bible (John 3:16) when he said, *'For God so loved the world that He gave His one and only Son, that whoever believes in Him shall not perish, but have eternal life'*. The sacrifice of Jesus was the ultimate demonstration of love. It was also the ultimate guarantee of eternal security. What an amazing promise these words contain.

But if you are one of those people who, even today, is living in the aftermath of rejection, betrayal, abuse, disloyalty or other nasty experiences of childhood, don't fall into the trap of thinking that because your own upbringing was so hurtful that you will always be suffering as a result. That is a lie from the pit of hell. As we journey together you will see how the Lord can heal and restore you from whatever mess the

PERSONAL NOTES

enemy has made in your life and give you the security of His love. You will certainly find it helpful to read of God's heart to heal in Isaiah 61 and Psalm 91.

Yes, we do live in a fallen world. Yes, Satan is the god of this world and yes, life can be tough as a result. **But** fear not, Jesus said, *'I have overcome the world'* (John 16:33).

What truth! What promises! And what a Saviour!

THE ONWARD JOURNEY

Next we will be looking in greater depth at some of the vital foundations that must be in place in our lives in order for us to be strong in Him.

I am so looking forward to hearing some of what He is going to do in and through you in the years to come as a result of our travelling together on this exciting journey.

SUMMARY

Security is a fruit of love. When we are loved we feel safe. When we truly know the heart of God and have experienced His love, then there is no limit to what God can do in and through our lives!

PRAYER

Thank You, Lord, for Your great love. I want to know the security that comes from knowing You. Help me Lord to forgive those who were responsible for all insecurities in my own life. Help me to grow in the knowledge and understanding of Your Love, so that there will be no barrier to me fulfilling Your destiny for my life. In Jesus' name, Amen.

STAGE 2

Vital Foundations

Poor foundations make buildings unsafe.
Poor spiritual foundations make
real life impossible

Stage 2, Chapter 1

ETERNITY IN THE HEART OF MAN

The foundations of a big building are never visible, but unless they're there, the building will collapse. We are now looking at the need for solid spiritual foundations relating to our knowledge of God and the life He has given to each one of us.

PERSONAL NOTES

TESTING DAYS

The days in which we're living are both very exciting and very challenging. World events are moving so fast it's hard to know where to focus one's attention! And in many parts of the world it's getting harder to be a Christian – even in our western nations personal faith in Jesus Christ is ridiculed at every level of society.

A British TV presenter recently spoke of how difficult it was for him as a Christian to even mention his faith in the work environment. It was OK to talk about anything else – but not his Christian faith. And I know that some of you reading this will be in countries that are much more hostile than this to the truth about Jesus.

PERSONAL NOTES

A major advertising campaign in the UK, funded by atheists, put 800 advertisements on the sides of many of our buses. The slogan said, in very large letters – ***'There is probably no God'*** and was followed by words which encouraged you to go out and enjoy yourself, without fear of God's judgment.

The assumption behind the campaign was that the very idea of God offends the intellect and restricts the enjoyment of life. It's assumed that anyone who believes in God can't enjoy themselves! Atheist interest groups in other countries also developed similar campaigns.

ETERNITY IN THE HEART

The strange thing is this. The creative gifting that dreamt up this campaign against God and, especially, against Christianity, came from God in the first place! This is how the writer of Ecclesiastes summed it up: *'He has also set eternity in the hearts of men; yet they cannot fathom what God has done from beginning to end.'* (Eccles. 3:11). Men who profess to be clever aren't clever enough to recognise where their ability came from!

And in the book of Job we read a similar thought: *'But it is the spirit in a man, the breath of the Almighty, which gives him understanding'* (Job 32:8). Without the breath of the Almighty, man could have no understanding about anything!

The creative process, the ability to think and develop ideas and products, the artistic genius that creates a great painting or a wonderful book – they all come from the Almighty. Without God, even atheists wouldn't be able to do anything!

Because it's the Spirit of God that gives life to man (Genesis 2:7 & Acts 17:28) and it's the breath of the Almighty that gives him understanding, there's a deep recognition of eternal things in the heart of every human being – for God Himself is eternal – He has no beginning or end. The timelessness of eternal existence is part of our make-up and prompts people to believe that we must have come from somewhere and there must be an after-life and that death can't be the end.

PERSONAL NOTES

DEATH IS NOT THE END

If there was nothing of the eternal God in the heart of man, then there would be no reason for anyone to be concerned about what follows death or any reason to fear it. They may not relish the process of dying or want to leave everything and everyone behind, but if there was nothing on the *'other side'*, eternal destiny would not be an issue.

I was once on a plane that filled with smoke. The effect was instantaneous – people began to cry out to God and pray! Thankfully, for us all on the plane, the problem was soon rectified. When a US Airways plane plunged into the Hudson River, by New York City, the passengers, every one of whom was amazingly rescued from the icy waters, were all saying *"we began to pray"*. There's only one reason for this – they were facing the prospect of premature death and an earlier than expected appointment with their Maker! That element of eternity in their hearts immediately reminded people that there is a God.

The instantaneous reaction in the heart of man, when faced with the possible sudden termination of human life, is to respond to the breath of God within us. Perhaps it's because, as the Bible tells us, the spirit returns to its Maker at the time of death (Ecclesiastes 12:7). At that moment people are instantly aware of God, from whom their spirit came and to whom it could be about to return!

THE EVIDENCE OF GOD IN THE CHILDREN OF MEN

If something of the eternal nature of God is present in every human being, then we should expect to see some evidence of His character present in the whole of the human race. Of course, it's in Jesus that we have the one and only complete demonstration on Planet Earth of the true nature and character of the God who made us all (John 14:8-11).

We will be looking much closer at the life and ministry of Jesus later on, but for now let's focus on just two things that were pre-eminent in His life – ***love*** and ***sacrifice***. Is there any evidence that love and sacrifice are present in humanity as a whole, not just in the lives of believers? Love and sacrifice are obviously closely inter-related, but yet very different from each other.

When you see a young couple looking into each other's eyes, you don't need anyone to tell you they've fallen in love with each other –

PERSONAL NOTES

love pours out of their every expression of word, affection and touch. They don't have to be believers to know the reality of love. When people love each other like this, they're willing to sacrifice all sorts of things as an expression of their love for each other.

When you see a mother cradle her new-born baby in her arms for the first time and look down at this precious bundle of life, she doesn't have to be a believer to be overwhelmed with love for this fruit of her womb. And when her child has a need and the mother only has enough resource to meet either the need of the baby or her own personal wants, it's a joy for her to sacrifice her own desires so that her child won't go without.

I could give you many more similar examples, and you could probably come up with more as well, showing that the characteristics of love and sacrifice are evident in all the children of men. Eternity (the very nature of God Himself) truly is in the heart of man. It is the presence of God in man, that makes man want to seek after God.

THE SEARCH FOR GOD

The search after God has been an ever-present reality for the human race since the very beginning of man's existence on the earth. Every people group that has ever been researched by anthropologists has been found to have developed their own religious beliefs and religious practices, in an attempt to find God for themselves.

Amazingly, there are now well over three thousand identifiable religions. They all believe and practice something different from each other. The only factor common to all religions is that they're all different from each other, yet all claim to be true!

It's extraordinary to me that in an attempt to bring peace and harmony, organisations such as the United Nations can support the beliefs behind all the world's religions as if they are all true! In reality, each religion is saying very different things, many of which contradict each other. The obvious fact is that either one is true and all the others are wrong, or all are wrong. But they can't all be right!

Ever since man cut himself off from fellowship with his Creator in the Garden of Eden, fallen man has been searching for an answer to the reason for his existence. For in the heart of every human being is a huge question mark, put there by God Himself, to encourage an awareness of the ,existence of God and to cause man to seek after him.

The problem is, however, that all the other world's religions are versions of man's attempt to discover God. The fundamental difference between the Judaeo-Christian faith and all the other world's religions is that this is the story of God seeking man, not the other way round! Additionally, in all other religions, works of human effort are required in order to earn acceptance by their 'god'. Whereas, the only true God accepts and loves us from the outset and nothing we do can change His intrinsic love for us! (Romans 8:38-39).

ONWARD CHRISTIAN SOLDIERS!

Throughout our journey together we will be discovering what God has revealed to us about Himself and this world, and how we can enjoy fellowship and relationship with Him. He's the only One who truly understands who we are. He longs for us to know the depth of His sacrificial love for us, so that we can enter into all that He has planned and purposed for our lives.

There is a God in Heaven who truly loves you. Who knows what He is going to do in your life in the months to come?

SUMMARY

Eternity is in the heart of every human being. It's the very breath of God that gave each one of us life. God sought us out to enjoy fellowship with Him and longs that we should know Him.

PRAYER

Thank You that the desire in my heart for relationship with You was put there by You in the first place. I'm amazed by Your love for humanity and long to know You better and better day by day. Help me to get these foundations firmly in place so that the building of my life will be strong for the rest of my days. In Jesus' name, Amen.

PERSONAL NOTES

Stage 2, Chapter 2

THE FATHER'S HEART FOR YOU AND ME

Having established together that something of the heart of God is in the heart of every man and woman, we are now moving on to look at a second vital foundation for secure living – knowing that God, as the ultimate Father of the whole of the human race, is the very best of fathers.

Let's begin with a question. *"What was God's original plan for the fathering (and mothering) of humanity?"*

PERSONAL NOTES

FATHERING – THE ORIGINAL PLAN

The fall of man placed a barrier between God and man, which could not be bridged by man alone. Without the fall, parents would have been in full relational fellowship with Father God. They would have a clear understanding of the nature and character of God as their Maker, the source of their life and their Heavenly Father.

When children were conceived and born, they'd be brought up by their parents, under the spiritual covering of their human father, and

PERSONAL NOTES

in the love and nurture of the Lord. As they grew they would gain a perfect understanding of the loving nature and character of God from their own parenting (Ephesians 6:4).

The character and behaviour of their parents would demonstrate to them the character and nature of God Himself. There would be no loss of understanding from one generation to the next and all generations, even to the present day, would still know and understand the loving nature of Creator God (Hosea 11:1, 3 and 4).

There would have been no evil on the earth to cause pain or distress. The children would be totally secure in the love of their parents, because their parents, in turn, were totally secure in Father God's love.

Such security would have given great confidence to every generation of children as they enjoyed using and developing all the creative gifts God had given them. We would all have been utterly amazed at the creative potential demonstrated by every human being – probably to a far greater extent than the amazing things that, nevertheless, have been possible for fallen man.

THE PARENTING PRINCIPLE

The principle I am establishing here is that God, as our Heavenly Father, delegated the job of fathering, one generation after another, to the human parents of every generation (Psalm 127:3-5).

God didn't give babies and very young children the capacity to question and discuss issues with their parents – it's vital for their well-being and growth that they just receive and trust that whatever their parents give them is good. All their energy must be spent on the vital processes of growth. There will be plenty of time later to ask the questions and discuss the issues of life. For now they just need to receive and be content in the loving provision of their parents.

God trusted that each generation would faithfully represent Him, for He'd made children to instinctively believe that whatever they learned from their parents was the truth. So, as children absorbed everything that loving parents gave them, they would, at the same time, be absorbing wonderful truth about the nature and character of God.

Everything a child is given is received and absorbed by them as if it's good – and if it IS good there's no problem. But what happens if what is given to a child isn't good?

FATHERING – THE REALITY

It would be wonderful if the fall hadn't actually happened! But we can't pretend that we're living in a perfect world. We aren't. We can't avoid the stark facts of life on Planet Earth. It's messy. Life's unfair and people suffer in all sorts of ways – especially in the vital growing years that will influence all the years that are to come.

And I'm not just talking here about children who are born into the more obvious traumas of life, such as are experienced in the war-torn or famine-struck places of the world. I'm talking about normal life behind the closed doors of the houses in the street where you live! Maybe even behind your own door!

For example, in some countries as many as 50% of our children are now being brought up by single parent families – mainly families without fathers. Some are in families where the children might not even know which one of the men Mom sees, from time to time, is actually their father! Some of you reading this today will be part of that growing community who were brought up in a fatherless society – a society where the mothers have struggled to be both father and mother to their children. A smaller number have been brought up in a motherless environment.

And many other children, even those who have been brought up in homes with a father present have, nevertheless, been deeply hurt by the mothers or fathers they did have. Parents who may have been so pre-occupied with business, sport, their own interests or, even, church, that they had no real time to nurture their children. Children need active time to receive parental love! Tragically, some mothers and fathers are cruel to their own children and, even, abuse them.

Not only do these children grow up with a belief that fathers and mothers can't be trusted. They are also in danger of growing up with a belief that God can't be trusted. For, as we learned from the God-box illustration, God intended that children should learn about Him from the way their parents behaved. But when the behaviour of the parents is bad it's like telling the children a lie about the nature of God – God,

PERSONAL NOTES

PERSONAL NOTES

Himself, has been betrayed. Sadly, because of the fall, even the very best of human parents still fall a long way short of God's ideal.

Food that is poisoned will kill a child; an inadequate diet that omits essential ingredients will leave a child physically stunted in various ways. But a child who is brought up without love is also deprived and will not know how to either give or receive love. He will eventually grow up with a defensive *'fight for myself'* mentality that shuns the very essence of humanity which he was created to enjoy – relationship.

Without having begun life with the depth of relationship that God intended for each one of us, we would all suffer in the same way. We may not have been deprived of physical food but we are each more than just a body.

We also have a soul and a spirit. If these vital dimensions of our humanity are starved of essential emotional and spiritual nutrients, then we will not develop into a well-rounded adult being, able to cope easily with all the normal ups and downs of life.

We have to face the truth about ourselves and then ask God, *'What can be done about it?'* Looking at realities such as this, can cause some people to be depressed and cry out something like, *"So what hope is there for me?"* If that's you, then be encouraged! God's heart for you is huge and we have been privileged to witness many times God bringing deep restoration and healing to people whose foundations were a long way from what was God's intention.

The whole of this *Journey to Freedom* has been designed to give understanding and hope to all of God's people (Isaiah 49:13b-16a), so that they can receive healing for themselves and know how to minister to others.

A HOPE AND A FUTURE

When we look at the life of Jesus we see Him behaving in the way that many of us would have loved our human father to have behaved: full of love, compassion and concern and interested in others. Scripture tells us that one of the reasons He came was to show us what the Father is like (John 14:9). When we look at Jesus we can truly see the desire of God to be the spiritual Father of His children.

A good father or mother, who sees their child hurting, will always bend down and attend to whatever the problem is. The way a human parent behaves is simply a reflection of the way God longs to 'bend down' and bring His hope and healing into our pain and brokenness (Hosea 11:3-4).

For, as we have already seen, the breath of God is in each one of us, and in spite of the fallen nature of man, apart from those who have completely given themselves over to the ways of darkness, we all still have that divine spark motivating our lives. It's wonderful to know that He longs to heal us of any damage in our lives that has come through our human parenting, so that we can fully connect with Him as our Father! (Isaiah 61:1-3, Jeremiah 29:11).

AND FINALLY

Anne *(not her real name)* had been terribly abused by her human father. The damage was very deep. She had built her own defences around the pain. But she couldn't sustain life under such stress. She was taken into care and had little prospect of ever again being able to live a normal life.

But God intervened. She learnt about the Father's love. Eventually she was able to forgive her human father. And little by little, God put back all that had been stolen from her. Today she is no longer just a lady with a past – she is living in the good of God for today with a hope and a future. ***So be encouraged!***

SUMMARY

God is the very best of fathers. He's really for you and wants you to know Him as He really is, whatever your own personal experience of human fathering has been. He longs to see you restored in Him and fulfilling your personal destiny (Psalm 10:14).

PRAYER

Thank You Lord that You're for me – every step of the way. Please forgive me for ever allowing my own experience of human fathering to colour my understanding of who You are. I choose to receive Your comfort and healing in my heart and trust You as my heavenly Father. In Jesus' name, Amen.

PERSONAL NOTES

Stage 2, Chapter 3

SIN – REBELLION THAT SEPARATES FROM GOD

Each part of this stage of *Journey to Freedom* is a bit like a trailer for a good film! A trailer gives you an insight into what the film's all about and an idea of what's coming later on. Today's 'trailer' is focussing on the subject of sin!

Later on we will need to look more closely at this when we're thinking about the fall of man. For unless we really understand how and why the human race fell from their original place of intimacy with God, we will never fully comprehend what Jesus did for us on the cross.

We are going to begin by getting an overview of what sin is. But don't worry if you are left with some important questions unanswered at this stage. They *will* be answered later.

PERSONAL NOTES

TODAY'S MESS!

We have already reminded ourselves of the Father's love for every human being – including you and me. Now, however, we'll start facing the reality of the mess we see all around us, which has caused such

PERSONAL NOTES

suffering down the ages and has brought a measure of suffering in every one of our lives.

Whilst the practice of sin seems to be very popular with the vast majority of human beings (otherwise we wouldn't all be so experienced at committing it!), the idea of calling our behaviour what it is, sinful, is not at all popular. It's definitely not politically correct!

Sin is also very selfish – in fact sin is all about me and my world and not caring about others. Love cares for others, sin only cares for oneself, but ultimately sin destroys the one we think we are caring for!

As human beings we naturally dislike being told that some of the things we're doing are wrong – not just according to an arbitrary standard put in place by the different governments of the world, but according to an absolute standard which is applied to the whole of the human race.

THE WORD 'SIN'

The word 'sin' is unpopular because it introduces the concept that there is a God in Heaven, who has laid down a line, one side of which is marked 'right' and the other side of which is marked 'wrong'.

People don't like to be reminded of either the existence of God or this fact. And they definitely don't like to think they're being thought of as sinners!

One of the prevailing temptations for all human beings is to be *'wise in your own eyes'* and create your own personal standard of what is right and wrong (Proverbs 3:7). You can then be your own moral judge, determining whether or not you've lived up to your own standards, however high or low they may be. You don't have to submit your behaviour to anyone else, least of all God.

The result of such thinking is that everyone develops their own personal morality, unique to their own way of thinking. There are no longer any *'absolute standards'*. This is even reflected in the varying moral standards of the world's different religions.

While there are some behavioural standards that are common to the different religions, in many cases one religion will say that a certain thing is wrong, while another may say it's OK! The concept of right and wrong can change, therefore, according to one's beliefs. Sometimes people even change religions so they can feel comfortable with a behavioural morality which suits them better!

For example, there are some religions that allow a man to have more than one wife. But in other religions this would be seriously wrong and would warrant excommunication!

This lack of harmony between religions only serves to show how vital it is that we regain an understanding of the true nature of God; what His intentions are for humanity; and what the very idea of right and wrong actually means. For man's ideas about God will always, ultimately, conflict with each other.

THE IDEA OF A MAN-MADE GOD!

Without knowing the true God, we'll only ever have a set of man-originated ideas as a guide for life. And each and every one of us will develop an image of God made according to our own desires. We would manufacture a god to suit our own circumstances.

How can a created being manufacture the God who has created them? How can the creature (you and me) create something that is our spiritual superior (Isaiah 44:9-20)?

We truly need to fear the God who made us and learn to respect His ultimate authority. He doesn't change His character or requirements from one religion to another! He cannot be locked up in the confines of a man-made idol. He's above all those things.

When respect for the ultimate authority of Creator God disappears from the foundation of our own lives (and also from the foundation of government), man is sliding quickly down a very slippery and very destructive slope.

UNDERSTANDING SIN – FREEWILL

To understand sin we first have to understand that we are made, according to Genesis 1:26, in the image and likeness of God, which means we have freewill.

No Christian would dispute that God, as ultimate Creator, exercised His freewill in both the creation of the Universe and in the creation of mankind. That was His choice. He created mankind for the purpose of

PERSONAL NOTES

PERSONAL NOTES

enjoying relationship with us. Whilst we're not equal with God, in order to have relationship with Him we need to have those attributes which enable relationship to exist, the most important being freewill and the ability to give and receive love.

You can't have a real relationship with a robot. You can only programme a robot to do what you want it to do. A robot is incapable of either independent choice or a response motivated by love. It can be programmed to do an extraordinarily wide range of activities. But in every case the robot is only responding to circumstances and instructions, in a pre-planned manner, according to the way it has been made.

My computer is a good example of a sophisticated robot. It does exactly what I tell it to do. It doesn't have freewill to do what it wants. It doesn't write a poem and then ask me what I think of it. I don't have a meaningful relationship with it. I use it and it's a tremendously valuable tool. But that's it. It's a sophisticated tool.

YOU are very different. You have a will of your own and are capable of making independent choices about anything and everything – and this is what you do, thousands of times, every single day of your life. That's how you are made and what you were made to do. You can choose to do whatever you like – both good and bad!

If you choose to do something wrong, a hand from heaven doesn't forcibly correct your behaviour! You are truly free.

CONSCIENCE AND FREE WILL

But deep in the core of your spiritual being you have a conscience. The conscience is part of that eternal dimension , which is in the heart of every human being and comes from the very breath of God when He breathed life into us.

When you're tempted to do something, which is contrary to the will and purposes of God for you, your conscience will remind you of the presence of God and you'll be faced with a choice – either to carry on with your original intentions or to stop and change the direction in which you're going. *Your conscience doesn't over-ride your free will, it simply gives your will the opportunity to come into line with God's best for your life* (Romans 2:14-15).

One of the early saints of God, Brother Lawrence, wrote a book called *The Practice of the Presence of God*. He realised that we can never escape from God's presence, no matter how hard we try! So it is far better to encourage a constant awareness of His presence and to allow our conscience to be a finely-tuned responder to His presence, His will and His loving care.

PERSONAL NOTES

THE ESSENCE OF SIN

The essence of sin is not primarily determined by what we do or do not do when in the presence of other people, but by what we do or do not do when no other human being is present – when it's just us and God and we still choose to rebel against Him!

We're all restrained in our desire to do something wrong – such as stealing money – if we know someone else is watching. That's the only reason road-side cameras are a deterrent to speeding motorists! Someone's watching – it may be through the lens of a camera, but they're watching, nevertheless.

Fear of what might happen if we drive too fast and have an accident can also act as a deterrent. It's interesting that Exodus 20:20 refers to the fear of the Lord as a deterrent from sinning! If we lose the fear of the Lord, then we are, indeed, in great danger. Fear of God is the only ultimate sin deterrent – without it, we have lost our ultimate protection.

Sinful actions are always preceded by sinful thoughts. Every single thing we do begins as a thought in our head. The essence of sin, therefore, is determined by how we think and what we choose to dwell on in our minds. For what we think, we'll then do.

No wonder Paul encouraged his readers to take every thought captive and make it obedient to Christ within! (2 Corinthians 10:5). We may think we are totally alone with our thoughts, but God knows what is going on in our hearts (1 Samuel 16:7).

The origin of sin is always in the core of our being and has its roots in the pride of life, the lust of the eyes and greed. It's controlled by the selfishness of the heart (1 John 2:15-17).

When tempted, we might weigh the supposed benefits of the sinful behaviour against the possible consequences. But in doing this we can then deceive ourselves into wrong courses of action. We might then think that the pleasure of the sin will exceed the cost! In reality that's all

PERSONAL NOTES

that was happening in the Garden when Adam and Eve checked out the fruit on the tree!

In Hebrews 11:24-26 we read how Moses, by faith, chose to be mistreated along with the people of God, rather than enjoy the pleasures of sin for a season! But King David chose the pleasures of sin (with Bathsheba) and the consequences were serious for them both. Psalm 51 expresses what went on in David's heart when his sin was exposed.

Ultimately, therefore, sin is using our free will to make choices which are contrary to the nature and will of God. And in simple terms, sin is rebellion against the God who made us.

EQUAL AND OPPOSITE TRUTHS!

There are many truths we will discover about God which seem to be equal and opposite. For example, because God has given us free will, we have total freedom. But He's also given us boundaries. He wants us to exercise our free will within these boundaries. It's a freedom within limitations.

But those limitations are not hard walls or high fences that can't be crossed, for we can use our freewill to cross them whenever we like. But when we do so, it's like sowing bad seed. The apostle Paul tells us that whatever seed we sow in our lives, the resulting crop will look just like the seed that was sown (Galatians 6:7-9). The greatest blessings are always realised by choosing to sow good seed and live within the boundaries of God.

I'll never forget the man who asked me what hope there was for his son. He had come for help because he had committed adultery, but so had his father and grandfather before him. The crop looked like the seed that had been sown by the generations before him! There *was* hope for him and his son – but he had to choose God's way and receive God's answer. Later we will see how God can set us free from the consequences of bad seed that has been sown in our lives.

THE FORCE OF LAW

When we disobey the voice of God or break His commandments as expressed in the Word of God, we always discover that law comes into force.

It's a bit like being warned not to go near the edge of a cliff because

PERSONAL NOTES

it's dangerous. But then you use your free will to ignore the warning (the commandment) and carry on walking over the edge. When you step over the edge, I can absolutely guarantee that, at that very moment, the law of gravity will come into play – and you will discover the consequences of disobeying the commandment the hard way!

We all know that the physical universe is ruled by physical laws. We can't change such laws, no matter how hard we try. We can't pass a law in the United Nations to adjust the force of gravity. Like God Himself, it's unchangeable. We must live our lives within the confines of those laws. If we don't we'll die – sometimes very quickly.

In a similar way, we are also spiritual beings living in a spiritual universe and there are equally unchangeable spiritual laws that are also in force. If we choose to disobey the commandments of God, we'll discover the spiritual laws that control the spiritual universe.

And that's exactly what mankind has done – disobeyed God's first commandment to Adam and discovered spiritual law the hard way. Man has come under the consequences of law as a result of disobeying God's commandments and committing sin. Death entered into Adam and the whole of the human race as a result (Genesis 3). It's only in Jesus that there is a way of escape from the consequences of man's sinful choices (Isaiah 53:3-6).

THE NATURE OF SIN

The nature of sin, therefore, is much more profound than breaking rules, put in place by one of the many world religions or governments. It is rebelling in one's heart against the fundamental nature and character of God, and choosing not to walk in His ways.

The first commandment tells us not to have any other God than the God who made us (Exodus 20:3). When man listened to the voice of the tempter, Satan, and obeyed him, rather than God, a set of consequences was put in motion, which will continue to affect humanity until the day when God winds up the ages, following the return of Jesus Christ. At the fall, mankind came under Satan's control and Satan became known as the god of this world.

Later on we'll be looking more carefully at who Satan is, and how he gained such a controlling influence on Planet Earth. But for now, all we

PERSONAL NOTES

need to understand is that the rebellion of our first parents has left all the 'sons and daughters of Adam' living in a prison of man's own making, controlled by the guilt and power of sin. Man broke the commandment (not to eat of the fruit of the tree of knowledge of good and evil) and the rest, as they say, is history. Man's history, your history and my history.

THE CONSEQUENCES OF REBELLION

The consequence of man's rebellion (sin) for the human race was to be cut off from the fullness of relationship with God (death). For the rest of time man not only has to contend with the temptations from without, such as were faced by Adam and Eve, but also by the temptations from within.

We've all inherited the rebellious nature of the human heart. Even the Apostle Paul had to wrestle with the temptations of his inner being (Romans 7:14-25).

Physical death did not immediately ensue from what we call the fall of man. But spiritual death, the breaking of relationship with God, *was* immediate and physical death was an eventual consequence. What God had warned Adam about, certainly happened.

NEXT... THE GOOD NEWS

This is very much the bad news – but there is good news to come as we see how God responded to what man had done in choosing to disobey Him. It's good news we can really look forward to!

SUMMARY

Man has really messed up by choosing to resist the loving will of Father God and follow the deceptive lies of Satan. All of humanity is suffering as a result. But it's only by understanding what has happened that we can also understand what God planned to do about it!

PRAYER

I recognise that there's sin in my own heart. I want to make right choices and follow Your ways, Lord. Help me to understand what sin is and then to walk away from it for the rest of my days. In Jesus' name, Amen.

Stage 2, Chapter 4

JESUS – SAVIOUR AND FRIEND OF SINNERS

In the last stage of our journey, we had to face the bad news about what sin has done to the human race. But it's now time for the good news – especially the good news of what the Saviour has done for every member of the human race. For some of you reading this, it may even be the first time that you really understand what Jesus did for you on the cross.

So often I've seen that when people really understand the depth of Jesus' sacrificial love for them, they are themselves able to receive His healing love in their lives, and then they want to walk in His ways.

For me, personally, thinking through and writing this material has been a very profound experience. Looking again at all that Jesus has done for me, has both challenged and inspired me to keep on running the race for the rest of my days!

IN PRISON

A friend of my father's went through the trauma of his son, Simon, committing a crime and having to go to prison. After he'd served his

PERSONAL NOTES

PERSONAL NOTES

time, my father offered to collect him from the prison gates and bring him home.

On the day of Simon's release, I went with my father to the prison and waited outside the gate. At precisely 7.00am a door in the prison wall opened and the young man came out. The prison was no longer his home. He was a free man.

I've never forgotten that dramatic moment when Simon turned his back on the prison walls for the last time. He had paid his debt to society and was now free again to live his life in whatever way he wished.

In days gone by there was another sort of prison in the City of London – a debtor's prison. It was a terrible place, reserved only for those who owed money, but who, for whatever reason, had been unable to pay their bills.

They could not just serve their time and, like Simon, be released. For them, there was only one way out of their stone-walled pit of human misery – someone else had to have compassion on them and pay the debt that was owed.

Charles Dickens, the famous English novelist, tells of how, as a child, he had to work to pay off his father's debts. For his father was in the notorious Marshalsea Debtor's Prison. His father's freedom could only be bought by someone else paying the debt! There was no other way out. Dickens, in his novel *Little Dorrit*, drew on this awful time of his own life and built his personal experience into the story.

MAN'S CONDITION

Mankind is also in a prison. When we look more closely at what happened in the fall of man, we will see how man used his own free will to obey Satan, rather than to obey God. The moment that happened, the special relationship man had with God was broken and the gates of death closed behind the whole of the human race.

Jesus tells us clearly (Matthew 25:41) that Hell had not been prepared for human beings, but for the Devil (Satan) and all his angels. By obeying Satan and coming under his authority, man destined himself to be in the same place and condition as Satan for time and eternity. Mankind, therefore, had placed himself in a prison, controlled by Satan, and there was no way out. So, Satan's destination had also become the destination of man.

PERSONAL NOTES

It was as if man had chosen not only to enter a prison, but to build the walls of his own prison as well – walls that would keep him imprisoned for the rest of time. It was a prison cell of his own making. And every other member of the human race has been conceived and born within those self-same prison walls.

It was like a debtor's jail, for the people inside could only get out if someone else paid the price for their release. There was absolutely nothing they could do from inside the prison, to either organise their escape or pay the price for their release.

Man's authority now belonged to Satan, and Satan used it to draw worship to himself and serve his own purposes. Mankind would have to live and die inside the Debtor's Jail.

Even though man had been created to enjoy eternal fellowship in Heaven with God, mankind was now separated from God and under condemnation. He was in a Debtor's Jail and he had lost his eternal destiny in Heaven.

MOTIVATED BY LOVE

Scripture tells us that God is Love (1 John 4:8). Love is the most powerful force in the world. It was the power of love that created the universe. It was the desire of a loving God to create mankind for fellowship and relationship with Himself.

When a baby's born, most parents adore and love their newborn child. He or she means everything to them. As far as they are concerned their baby is perfect. Their love knows no limits.

But when the child starts to grow bigger, the time comes when their formerly perfect baby starts to misbehave! When that happens, the parents don't stop loving their child. For this is their precious offspring, born of their flesh and even though the child is being naughty, the parents have no desire to try and change their child for a different model! They may be saddened by bad behavior, but this is their child and their love knows no limits.

Throughout life many parents will go to great lengths to show their love for their children – even in very extreme circumstances. I watched pictures of a mother leaving a jail, having visited her son for the last time before his execution for murder. Even though he had done terrible

PERSONAL NOTES

things, deserving of the death sentence, this was her boy and the tears of compassion poured freely down her face as she tried to tell people how much she loved him!

Now, where do parents get that sort of love from? They get it from their Creator. For we are made in the image and likeness of God and even though man messed up big time, that didn't stop God loving His children. We are just like Him! The life of all His children came from the very breath of God (Genesis 2:7), and God longed for the restoration of that fellowship which had been so cruelly stolen from Him, so soon after the creation of man.

The jail, in which man now was, could only be opened by someone with a higher authority than the jailer. While God, ultimately, has all power and all authority, because man had been given authority over the earth by God, it was only a man who had never sinned and never come under Satan's control, who could exercise that authority on Planet Earth and give mankind the opportunity of stepping free from Satan's stronghold.

Death was man's inheritance and the price of death had to be paid (Romans 6:23). But it could only be paid by a man who had never sinned, otherwise his death would be to no avail. All sinners are born inside the jail! Someone from outside the jail had to pay the price.

BORN ON EARTH – BUT OUTSIDE THE JAIL!

And so God's plan of salvation was worked out on the stage of Planet Earth. The babe of Bethlehem was conceived by the Holy Ghost in the womb of a virgin girl.

He wasn't born as a product of normal human relationships. He did not carry, therefore, the stain of sin from His parenting on His being. His inheritance was from God, not from Joseph. He was born outside the jail!

He resisted every temptation of the enemy and never came under Satan's control. When the final act of God's human drama was played out at Calvary, there was only one 'Star' on that most primitive of stages.

The soldiers drove in the nails, but it was love that held the Son of God to the cross. As He hung there, the destiny of every human being, whether born before or after that event, hung in God's balance.

PERSONAL NOTES

Heaven must have held its breath as the Son of God breathed His last as a human being.

At that moment the veil of the temple, which had separated man from the presence of God in that most holy of places, was torn from top to bottom and a way was re-opened for mankind to once again have fellowship with the Father, but this time through Jesus, the Son.

The relationship between Father God and Jesus the Son had never been broken through sin. And on resurrection morning, therefore, there was a Man on earth who had the keys of both Heaven, and Death and Hell in His hand. He had a higher authority than the jailer, Satan, and the price had been paid for the freedom of his prisoners!

Death had been overcome and there was a way that man could once again look forward to Heaven's glory. The invitation to freedom rang out through all the rooms in the Debtors Jail, and down through all the ages of time, as was so simply but profoundly expressed in the old song which said:

There's a way back to God from the dark paths of sin, There's a door that is open and all may go in.It starts at the cross, that's where you begin, When you come as a sinner to Jesus.

Jesus had fulfilled the promise of all those wonderful Old Covenant prophecies. A perfect sacrifice had been made for the sins of the people. The New Covenant had come and as many as chose to receive Him, to them He gave the right to be the children of God (John 1:12). What joy, what release, what freedom! What a Saviour!

NEW BIRTH

Those who receive the good news gladly, who accept the extraordinary gift of salvation that Jesus won for us all on the cross, are given a new life – outside the prison walls! They are literally given a fresh start in life, at whatever age they receive the gift. At that point they are born again.

They are released from the jail of the Kingdom of Darkness and have become citizens of a glorious Kingdom – the Kingdom in which Jesus, the Son of God, reigns as King.

The debt has been paid and Satan is powerless to keep those who

PERSONAL NOTES

choose to believe in Jesus inside the Debtors Jail. They have used their free will to accept God's answer. They are free – for the rest of time and eternity beyond. They are born again to new life! (John 3:16).

THE TRAGEDY OF THE CROSS

The greatest tragedy of the whole history of the human race is that the god of this world (Satan) has so blinded the eyes of humanity that the majority of human beings choose to remain in the familiar surroundings of the Debtors Jail – even though there is now a way out! (2 Corinthians 4:4)

Man still has free will, but, sadly, most people still use their free will to turn away from the joy of salvation, because they prefer the paths of pride and pleasure or choose to stay chained by the demands of wrong religious beliefs. For many it seems too costly in terms of what they have to surrender and they'd rather live life their own way. But the door of hope is still open for all men and women who choose to respond to the love of the Saviour.

It was love that motivated the heart of God to remain faithful to us, even though we'd sinned. Love is still the motivation of those who have received the gift of God for themselves and entered into their salvation, to go into all the world and make disciples – that is the commission that Jesus left with the church (Matthew 28:19).

And it is what *Journey to Freedom* also, is all about – making disciples of Jesus for the Kingdom of God, who will faithfully proclaim the wonderful news of the Gospel throughout their days.

SHEER JOY!

It was the joy of victory, the joy of man's salvation that was set before Him, which gave Jesus the courage to push through the cross – the joy of knowing that He would be able to fellowship in Heaven with you and with me! (Hebrews 12:2) – and the joy of being able to present to His Father, those who'd been redeemed out of the hand of the enemy, Satan.

The Gospel is not just Good News, it's totally undeserved and sensationally good news! What grace, what mercy!

I once had a friend who, throughout the time I knew him, resisted the truth about Jesus. But he said these words that I have never forgotten:

"If I believed what you believe I would be willing to crawl on my hands and knees across broken glass to tell every human being the Gospel of Jesus Christ."

God was merciful to this honest man. He genuinely wanted to know the truth, but had been confused and disturbed by the myriad of different religions that all claimed to have the truth! He had worked hard for me in my business and was a loyal and trusted friend. But he was taken ill and at the last he lay in hospital dying.

I looked into his eyes and shared with him once again the sensational news of the Gospel. I don't know whether the Lord had privileged him at that moment with a distant view of Heaven's glory or the face of the Son of God. But the scales of unbelief suddenly fell from his eyes and I grasped his hand as he invited Jesus to be his Lord and Saviour.

I never saw him again on earth, but I know that one day I will see him again in Heaven. He escaped from the Debtors' Jail at the very last moment, but as the parable of Jesus makes so plain – the reward of salvation is the same for those who come at the end of their lives as those who find Him at the beginning! (Matthew 20:1-16)

The love of Jesus surpasses everything. Jesus truly is both wonderful Saviour and friend of sinners. He's my friend – and I trust He's yours. Put your hand in His and He will be your companion through every day of the rest of your life. This good news has transformed my life. I pray it has transformed yours and you will want to keep on serving the Lord Jesus for the rest of your days.

SUMMARY

Jesus came from Heaven's glory to show us how much the Father loved us. Jesus is the friend of sinners and gave His life to pay the price of Freedom for all of humanity. But only those who accept the gift can claim their.

PRAYER

Thank you Jesus for being such a wonderful Saviour. Thank You for Your amazing sacrifice on the cross. Thank You for forgiveness for my own sin. Thank You for being my Friend – in time and eternity. In Jesus' Name, Amen

PERSONAL NOTES

Stage 2, Chapter 5

HOLY SPIRIT – EMPOWERMENT FOR GOD'S PEOPLE

Have you ever wondered how Jesus did such extraordinary things and then, how the Church has not only survived for two thousand years, but has defied every attempt by the enemy to eliminate believers and destroy it! It is an incredible story! I wish we'd more time to look together at the testimony of some of the amazing saints down the ages, who have kept the flame of truth burning so brightly, even when the darkness has tried to extinguish the light. People like:

- Stephen, the first Christian martyr, who was stoned to death (Acts 7:54-60);
- Bishop Polycarp, who was burned at the stake for his extraordinary faith and trust in God;
- The Bishops of the Church of England, who died in Oxford in the same way because they were committed to putting the truths of God into the language of the common people;
- The Huguenots, who endured extraordinary persecution in France, because of their faithfulness to the God of the Bible;

PERSONAL NOTES

PERSONAL NOTES

- Young believers in Uganda, who suffered a terrible fate in the early days of the East African Church;
- And, in more recent days, the countless believers in China who paid the ultimate price for their faith and whose names are written in Heaven.

I have reason to be personally thankful to God for the Huguenots, because my own direct ancestor, Jacob de Villiers, was one of those determined believers who would not renounce his faith. He fled France on the good ship Zion to South Africa, in 1680, with his brothers Abraham and Pierre, and many generations later I am still being blessed by the fruit of his faithfulness.

Where did all these people, and countless millions more throughout human history, get the courage to remain faithful to their Saviour? Was it just the prospect of Heaven for those who were born again? Or was there something more? Let's look at the Word of God together.

POWER FROM ON HIGH!

Scripture tells us that Jesus was conceived by the Holy Spirit. And He was clearly led by the Holy Spirit all His life. But there was a critical moment in the earthly story of the Son of God, when He went to be baptised by John the Baptist.

John's baptism was a baptism of repentance. But Jesus had never sinned. John knew that Jesus was the perfect Lamb of God who would take away the sin of the world. No wonder John couldn't understand why sinless Jesus was in the line, awaiting baptism in the River Jordan (Matthew 3:1-17). John argued that Jesus should have been baptising him, not the other way round!

But Jesus was adamant. It was necessary for Jesus to be baptised. For this was the moment when Jesus associated himself with sin – yours as well as mine – by allowing Himself to be baptised in a baptism of repentance.

Three years later, He was to die for the sins of the world. But at this critical moment, He stood in an act of repentance, on behalf of all those who would believe in Him for the forgiveness of their sins. This was the moment above any other, when Jesus publicly accepted His commission from Father God – the whole reason for Him coming to Earth.

So when He came up out of the water, the joy in Heaven could be contained no longer! The Father was thrilled at what He was seeing, for the great salvation plan was being fulfilled.

From Heaven's glory, the Holy Spirit of God was poured out in full measure upon Jesus. The people saw the Spirit descend upon Jesus in the form of a dove. And they heard the Father's voice saying, *"This is my beloved Son. I am pleased with Him"* (Luke 3:22).

Heaven approved – the first step was being taken towards the eventual completion of the plan of salvation. Jesus was now full of the Spirit in a new way.

As a result He was then led by the Spirit into the wilderness, to face the most severe temptations Satan could throw at Him. In a later study we will see how Jesus resisted them all and came back from the wilderness not just full of the Spirit, but now operating in the power of the Spirit! (Luke 4:1-14).

PERSONAL NOTES

SEEKING THE KEY

Many years ago, when I was sensing God's call on my life for the healing ministry, I was looking for God's direction. I didn't know how to respond to the call, so day by day I continued to pray into the vision, but for many years there was no apparent response.

There then came a certain day, when I was crying out to God in Church. I was desperate. And all I heard the Lord say to me by way of response was, 'Go home and read the Bible!'

The problem for me was that I did read the Bible most days, and had done so since being a young child. So what did the Lord mean? As I walked home that night, I began to understand that He wanted me to read it more like any other book – straight through, not just a few verses here or a few verses there!

I started that night at the beginning of the New Testament and read all the way through Matthew and Mark's Gospels. It was all very familiar. But when I got to the last chapter of Mark's Gospel, and read those words *'Believers will lay their hands on sick people, who will get well'* (Mark 16:18), I was suddenly electrified in my spirit. God was speaking to me!

I looked at my hands and they looked very ordinary hands, and I wondered what this verse really meant. I read on, right through Luke's

PERSONAL NOTES

Gospel and then John's Gospel and, finally, into the beginning of the Acts of the Apostles. Then, once again, I was arrested by God!

There in chapter 1 and verse 8 was the key I was looking for: *'When the Holy Spirit comes upon you, you will be filled with power!'* My hands without the Holy Spirit were just hands.

But through this scripture, God was speaking to my heart and was saying that the hands of any believer, who is filled with the Spirit, and who is doing what God has asked them to do, will be filled with power.

BAPTISED IN THE SPIRIT

From that moment on I began to seek the baptism of the Holy Spirit for myself. I'd read various books about the work of the Spirit, but till I began to respond positively to the call of God upon my life, the experience of the Spirit in this New Testament, Pentecostal fashion, was foreign to me.

A few nights later I was suddenly wide awake, at about 1.00am in the morning. I was glowing from head to foot. I had no idea what was happening, till I heard the Lord's gentle voice saying, *"It's OK, it's only me!"* These were words that my parents used to say when they returned to the house, after I had been left alone for a time as a child. They were words of comfort and security. God was assuring me, by using these very familiar words, that the owner of the house (God) was in residence (in me), for, as Scripture says, our body is the temple of the Holy Spirit. (1 Corinthians 3:16 and 6:19).

From that moment on I was alert to the Spirit of God in a way that was totally new to me. I knew that without the Holy Spirit having drawn me to God in the first place, I could never have been born again. I knew, also, that it was the Holy Spirit that on many occasions had brought the Scriptures to life for me. There was no doubt that I had experienced the Spirit of God guiding me, directing me and even protecting me. But this was different.

I knew that God had heard and answered my prayer and within a short time I received the gift of tongues and was able to worship God in a new language. It may or may not have sounded like the tongues spoken by the disciples on the Day of Pentecost, but I was so aware of the presence of God. I had a new and determined desire to live out the vision God

PERSONAL NOTES

had given me for the healing ministry. In some ways it felt as though my Christian life had begun afresh, all over again!

Not everyone's experience of being baptised in the Spirit is the same. God deals with each one of us in a unique way. Some may have a very dramatic experience, while others may simply just become aware of the reality of God's indwelling presence. Like conversion – everyone's experience is different! But it's important that you do know that you have been filled and are continuing to be filled with the Holy Spirit day by day. If you're not sure how to pray, seeking God for this, then you will find help below, at the end of this stage of the journey.

THE FRUIT AND THE GIFTS OF THE SPIRIT

Later we will look more closely at the gifts of the Holy Spirit – the supernatural abilities that come to every believer who is baptised in the Holy Spirit of God. But it's important to remember at this stage that the gifts and the fruit are not the same.

The fruit of the Spirit is the very nature of the God who is love. While the gifts of the Spirit are received in a moment, it can take a significant period of time walking with the Lord, for the characteristics of His loving presence to become evident in our lives and to change us from the inside out.

It is the fruit that flows from love – joy, peace, kindness, etc (Galatians 5:22-23) – that is the true hallmark of a life that is being lived in fellowship with God. Of course we need the gifts to do the works of the Kingdom, but the fruit is the vital qualifying factor for the exercise of the gifts, and without the fruit, any manifestation of gifts is out of order and is meaningless (1 Corinthians 13:1-3).

MY PRAYER FOR YOU

It is my prayer for you that your heart's desire will not only be to grow in the character of Jesus, but also to receive the Spirit of God and the gifts of the Holy Spirit to help you live your Christian life. When Peter preached to the people at Pentecost he said, *"Repent and be baptised, every one of you, in the name of Jesus Christ for the forgiveness of your sins. And you will receive the gift of the Holy Spirit. The promise is for you and your children*

PERSONAL NOTES

and for all who are far off – for all whom the Lord our God will call." (Acts 2:38-39).

As we reach the end of Part 2 of our journey together, I would like to invite you to say a prayer with me. It's a simple prayer – I know you may have prayed a prayer like this before – but, whether you have or you haven't, may I invite you to make Jesus Lord of every area of your life?

Within the work of Ellel Ministries we meet many Christians who are well aware of their need for salvation and are looking forward to Heaven when they die, but who really struggle with making Jesus Lord of their lives here on Earth! Often this is the reason – they remain unhealed and are not able to be baptised in the Holy Spirit.

In reality, Jesus is the key to everything, and making Him Lord is the most important thing you can ever do as you seek to live for Jesus here on earth. For thousands of people who have come for help at one of our Ellel Centres, it has been the master key that has unlocked their healing and transformed their life.

SUMMARY

The Holy Spirit was God's gift to Jesus and is also His gift to the Church. Without the Spirit we cannot fulfil our destiny. With the Spirit we can not only grow more like Jesus day by day as we trust Him to change us from the inside out, but we can also be empowered with the gifts of the Spirit to do the works of the Kingdom of God.

PRAYER

If you want Jesus to be Lord of every area of your life, say this prayer slowly, phrase by phrase, meaning it from the heart:

Thank You, Jesus, for dying on the cross for me. I confess that I am a sinner in need of a Saviour. I choose to repent and turn from my sins. I invite You now to be Lord of every area of my life – Lord of my mind and all my thinking, my beliefs and my imagination; Lord of my emotions and all my reactions; Lord of my will and all my decisions; Lord of my body and all my behaviour; Lord of my sexuality and its expression; Lord of my family and all my relationships; Lord of my work, my finances, my needs and my possessions; Lord of my spirit and my relationship with God. Thank You that Your blood was shed that I might be set free from the punishment due for my sin and that my name is written in the Book of Life. Come, Lord Jesus, and reign in my life for all of my days. Amen.

Then you can pray like this for God to fill you with His Spirit:
Thank You, Lord, for the promise of Your Holy Spirit. Come Lord Jesus and fill me to overflowing, that Your Spirit will empower me day by day to live for You. In Jesus' Name, Amen.

PERSONAL NOTES

STAGE 3

The Bible – My Guide for Life

Without a map, I get lost. Without the
Bible I am lost before I even
begin the journey!

Stage 3, Chapter 1

GOD'S AMAZING LETTER TO THE HUMAN RACE

PERSONAL NOTES

We are now going to focus our attention on the importance of reading the Bible as our daily guide for Christian living and take a fresh look at how it can be a source of great blessing every day of our lives. We will be seeing how God chose to reveal His plans and purposes in the Bible, and how critical this amazing book is for each one of us.

We've already covered a significant amount of ground in our journey of discovery – a journey which will take us deep into the things of God and equip us to live a godly life.

The most important decision any of us can ever make is to invite Jesus to be the Lord of every area of our lives. We will return to this subject on numerous occasions as we experience the personal transformation that only He can bring.

It's only the presence of God that can ultimately change everything for us in our lives. In His presence, we're motivated by who He is, to become the people that only He can make us to be! It's His presence that equips and empowers us to fulfil our destiny. The Bible talks about our steps being ordered by the Lord (Proverbs 16:9). When He

PERSONAL NOTES

orders our daily steps through life, we can certainly trust the outcome.

There are many occasions when I've sensed the Lord ordering my steps by taking me in a particular direction or encouraging me to do a certain thing at a certain time. Time and time again I've been amazed at the outcome – what a faithful God we serve! There have also been times when I have ignored the leading of the Lord, but always at a personal cost.

His leading may sometimes take you in directions which might seem surprising at the time but which, in retrospect, will prove to be a source of great blessing or, on some occasions, help you to avoid unforeseen pitfalls. For me, the Lord's direction has often been through a particular word of Scripture.

THE BIBLE IS A LOVE LETTER FROM GOD!

I well remember striking up a friendship with a girl in my teenage years. Then we started writing letters to each other! The daily delivery of post became very exciting as I wondered if there would be a letter for me! And then, when one did come, I read it through time and time again – I didn't want to put it down!

That is how we need to approach the Word of God. It's a love letter from God Himself. It's a letter to the human race from the most loving Father there has ever been. If we can learn to treasure what God has said in His Word and store it up in our heart, then it will be the source of Truth and guidance for all the days of our life, and also be the very best defence we can ever have against deception and the inroads of the enemy.

If you can learn to take in from the Word of God every day and then live it out in your daily life, I guarantee that the truth of God's Word will bring that promised personal transformation, which so many people are longing for, and which is at the heart of our *Journey to Freedom*.

It has been exciting to look again at the wonderful gift of Salvation that Jesus brought to us through His death and resurrection. And then discover together how the Holy Spirit is such a vital key to living the Christian life. This same Holy Spirit was the inspiration behind the most important book in the world – The Bible – a book that doesn't just contain the Word of God, as some people say, but which actually ***is the Word of God*** to the human race.

Paul expressed it this way in 2 Timothy 3:16-17, *"All Scripture is God-breathed and is useful for teaching, rebuking, correcting and training in righteousness, so that the man of God may be thoroughly equipped for every good work."* Our *Journey to Freedom* is all about getting thoroughly equipped for every good work that God wants each one of us to do.

PERSONAL NOTES

THE WORLD'S MOST VALUABLE POSSESSION!

The Queen of England has been on the throne for a very long time – well over half a century. Her father, King George VI, died when she was still quite young. I'm old enough to remember that day in 1952 very well. The whole nation went into mourning with the death of the king who had brought us safely through the war.

The Queen's coronation, as Her Majesty Queen Elizabeth II, took place on the 2nd June 1953. Television was still in its infancy. Only a very small number of relatively wealthy people could possibly afford such an amazing machine! To watch the Coronation on his TV, our family were guests of our local Doctor in the north of England.

At least twenty people were crammed into a small room as we focused our attention on a tiny black and white screen and watched the proceedings in Westminster Abbey, so far away in London. Even though I was only nine years of age, I was enthralled by everything that was happening.

It was a holy moment in the nation's history when, right in the middle of the Coronation service, the Queen promised to maintain the laws of God and the true profession of the Gospel, upon which the Archbishop of Canterbury presented her with a Bible, and said these words:

"We present you with this Book, the most valuable thing this world affords. Here is wisdom. This is the Royal Law. These are the lively oracles of God."

What an incredible statement – *the most valuable thing in the world! Of more value than all the world's riches*! More important than any other book – a book that doesn't just contain wisdom, but *IS wisdom*! The *Royal Law* – which even Kings and Queens acknowledge as having an authority greater and higher than theirs. *The lively oracles of God* – this is an old usage of the word "lively", simply meaning "living" and the oracles of God are simply God's revelations to humanity.

PERSONAL NOTES

What a statement describing this most amazing of books – it's the ultimate source of Truth (John 17:17), because it's the source of knowledge about the One who described Himself as The Truth (John 14:6). Without the Bible we would today have no knowledge of God's extraordinary revelation of Himself to mankind.

Richard Wurmbrand, who survived fourteen years in a communist jail for his faith, put it this way: *"The Bible is the only book capable of satisfying the spiritual needs of the world."*

Everything you will learn about on our *Journey to Freedom* has its origin in the Bible. It is the most important book you will ever possess.

THE STORY OF THE BIBLE

Some people are excited by history – others find it boring! But whether you like it or not, history is important! Much of the Bible is, itself, a history book – not a 'dry as dust' and very boring catalogue of events, but a living record of the people who made history, and of the lessons we can learn from their experiences.

The Bible itself has a remarkable history as well, starting from the way the Jewish Rabbis first gathered together the ancient books and put them together in the Tanakh. The Tanakh contains the same books as our Old Testament but in a different order.

Then, in the early days of the Christian Church it took nearly 400 years for the Church Fathers to be totally agreed before God on which books should form the New Testament Scriptures.

Our Bible today contains 66 books in total and has been written by over 40 different authors over about 1500 years! *There may have been 40 writers, but there was only one ultimate Author, the Holy Spirit, who inspired all the writers.*

Because the Bible is God's Word to the human race, the god of this world has done everything he can, down the centuries, to oppose those who would want to make Bibles available to people in a language they can understand. It is hard to believe today that hundreds of people were even burned at the stake because of what they were doing. People like John Huss, William Tyndale and Archbishop Cranmer all paid this ultimate price, so that people could have the Bible in their own language.

It wasn't until 1604 that the most famous Bible translation of all time was authorised by King James of England and published in 1611. With over a billion copies in print, it's the most printed book in the history of the world! And even though the language of the King James Bible is that of the early seventeenth century, it's still the preferred translation of many people today.

THE BIBLE TODAY

Even though the Bible is freely available in most countries of the world today, opposition to the Bible is not just a thing of the ancient past. Even in our own lifetimes a huge price was paid by those who tried to get Bibles to persecuted believers behind the iron curtain or in China. Many spent years in jail as a result and many more, especially in China, lost their lives. Even today there are many millions of people without easy access to a Bible.

The only reason the Bible is so opposed by the enemy of souls is because it contains the Word of Life! (Psalm 119:50). How tragic it is that so many people, even church-going Christians, in countries where there is no shortage of Bibles, do not even know what it contains and rarely, if ever, read it! Little do they realise what enormous treasure they are ignoring.

Perhaps the biggest battle of all over the Bible is yet to be fought – getting all those people who are able to read it, to actually do so!

Mahatma Gandhi, that great leader of the Indian people, had opportunity to be strongly influenced by Christianity in his younger days in South Africa. His brother actually became a Christian and went to the same church as my mother in her youth.

But Gandhi could not stand hypocrisy, in any form and his tragic summation of the attitude of the Christians he had known, towards the Bible, is found in these words;

"You Christians look after a document containing enough dynamite to blow all civilisation to pieces, turn the world upside down, and bring peace to a battle-torn planet. But you treat it is as though it is nothing more than a piece of literature."

It is true, the Bible is great literature, but it is far more than that – it is

PERSONAL NOTES

PERSONAL NOTES

the very bread of life without which man cannot truly live. As we dig into the Bible together we are going to unearth extraordinary and life-changing treasure. As the Psalmist wrote, in Psalm 119:105, *"Your word is a lamp to my feet and a light for my path."*

LIVING BREAD

Today there are many English translations available – the most common of which is the New International Version (NIV). Alongside these are many others such as the New Revised Standard Version, the New King James Version, the New American Standard Bible, the Good News Bible and, more recently, the English Standard Version.

All these versions have their followings and I have no intention of telling you which one to use. Most of the quotes in this book are from the New International Version (NIV), for the simple reason that this is the Bible that most readers will be using.

In many ways it doesn't matter which version you read – as long as you read it, take it in, digest it and live it. I personally find it helpful to read the Bible in several different versions. I've found it specially helpful to use a traditional translation as my main Bible and then to read one of the modern paraphrases such as The Good News Bible (Today's English Version) or The Living Bible to help me further understand what different passages are saying.

SUMMARY

The Bible is a miracle, compiled over hundreds of years and inspired by the Holy Spirit of God. It has been constantly opposed by the enemy of souls because it is God's Word to a fallen world. It's the most precious thing anyone can possess and is God's timeless message to mankind.

PRAYER

Thank you, Lord, for those people who gave their lives in years gone by, so that the Bible could be made available for everyone to read. Help me to treasure this book – the most precious and valuable thing that there has ever been and ever will be – and allow You to speak to me through it, all my days. In Jesus' Name, Amen.

Stage 3, Chapter 2

FEEDING ON THE LIVING BREAD

When I was young, I was encouraged to read a little bit of the Bible – every day. It was a habit that became an important anchor point in my life. I honestly don't know where I would be today, if it were not for the Word of God that has been hidden in my heart over many years.

I can remember times of temptation when Scriptures, that I had learnt years earlier, would come suddenly into my mind. The Psalmist understood this principle very well. In Psalm 119:11, he said, *"I have hidden your word in my heart, that I might not sin against you."* What precious protection the Word of God is. It is living bread for the hungry soul!

I thank God that my parents cared enough to give me *Junior Notes*, the Scripture Union Bible-reading notes for children. I learnt to enjoy looking up the verse for the day and reading the little bit of teaching and saying the prayer. Sometimes, it seemed like just one too many things to do in the rush and tumble of school life, but I have never regretted the discipline and understanding that was built into my life in this way – one step at a time, one day at a time.

PERSONAL NOTES

PERSONAL NOTES

SCRIPTURE IN SONG

I also learnt Scripture through singing Christian songs at Sunday School and Bible Class. Many had catchy tunes, easy to remember words and I absorbed a huge amount of Christian truth through them. They really helped to put the Bible into my heart.

Even today those songs come easily to memory and remind me of the simple truths which, over sixty years later, I can confirm have been totally reliable all of my life. Simple truth, firmly believed, has a profound impact on the life of any man or woman. Few of those particular songs were great poetry or were set to great music, but they put the Word of God into my heart in an unforgettable way. I was *"feeding on the living bread"* as the words of one of those choruses said.

In the eighteenth century, Charles Wesley put the preaching of his brother John into song, and came up with some of the most amazing hymns that have ever been written – hymns such as, *"And can it be"* and *"Jesus, lover of my soul"*, which I am sure people will still be singing when Jesus comes again! They put the truths of Scripture into the hearts of the people, who learnt the songs, sang the words and understood the truths described in the verses.

Hymns and songs have always been a great way of getting God's Word into the heart of man. So much so that many songs of worship made their way into the Bible itself. The songs of King David (the Psalms) are just that and I have found that reading something from the Psalms, as part of my regular reading of the Word of God, has always been a great blessing to me – as well as a significant challenge!

THE NEED FOR FEEDING

When we are young we need food for two primary purposes – firstly for growth and, secondly, for the energy we need to live each day. A mal-nourished child will never reach its physical potential. A regular supply of food in a well-balanced diet is essential – both for growth and daily energy. But when we are older, we still need food for daily living. We never grow out of the need for the right form of sustenance to keep us going.

God created us with spirit, soul and body, and in exactly the same way as our body needs feeding, so do our spirit and soul. Good parents

PERSONAL NOTES

are constantly talking to and playing with their children and doing things with them, teaching and training them as the years go by. They are feeding the soul. Little by little a baby becomes a toddler, a toddler becomes a child, a child becomes a young person and a young person becomes an adult – not just in body but in knowledge, understanding, attitudes and responsibilities.

A child who is only fed physical food, and is given no stimulus to the mind and the emotions, or training in how to use their will to make good choices or discipline, will always grow up to be a very inadequate and deprived adult. This is obvious to all and sundry, and even governments do everything they can to provide the necessary educational support services for parents, so that when children grow up they will be able to take their place in society.

However, what is necessary for the body and soul is also essential for the spirit. In fact, I would go as far as to say that, if the spirit is not nurtured with the right sort of spiritual food, the effect will not just be on the spirit, but on the soul and the body as well. A spirit that's nurtured in the things of God will protect the soul from making the ungodly choices that can have such devastating effects on every area of life.

There are all sorts of things that I could have got involved in as a young person, but I thank God that my early spiritual training meant that I had the courage to say *'No'*, when attractive temptations presented themselves to my soul! It is only by the grace of God that I can now give testimony to His keeping power.

Not everyone is so fortunate. Every day, for example, we read of young people who are suffering because of drug overdoses, teenage pregnancy, binge drinking, sexually transmitted disease or street violence. If their spirit had been rightly nurtured, their conscience would have clicked into operation and there would have been an inner strength to draw on to resist temptation.

In making decisions they would have avoided the situations and relationships which led to the partying where, for example, the drugs were available. Every day our newspapers are full of stories of what can happen to people in whose lives the Word of God has no influence.

We can have the most well-developed adult bodies and souls, but without the parallel development of our spirits, we can never be powerful, mature and dynamic Kingdom people. We will always be vulnerable to

PERSONAL NOTES

the inroads of the enemy into the heart, and to the wrong choices which can so often lead to disaster.

The Psalmist expressed this so powerfully when he said: *"How can a young man keep his way pure? By living according to your word"* (Psalm 119:9).

TAKING IN THE TRUTH

The spirit needs spiritual food both for spiritual growth and also for daily sustenance so we'll have the necessary spiritual energy to meet today's needs. This isn't just true when we are young, or young in the faith, but throughout our lives. Just as we cannot depend on yesterday's food for today's bodily energy, we cannot depend on yesterday's experiences of God to be sufficient for today's relationship with Him. We need to keep in touch with Him.

When people become Christians, at whatever age that might be, as children or adults, unless they are fed the right sort of spiritual food, they will remain as spiritual babes with a lot of growing to do. As such they are very vulnerable. They are in danger. Many former believers have fallen away from the faith, because they never had the opportunity to grow in their knowledge of God. In this life we all have more to learn – we will never exhaust the knowledge of the things of God!

One of the fallacies, exploited by the enemy, is that if people become Christians when they are adults, they don't need as much training as young children. The fact is they need more! For during all their growing and pre-Christian adult days, they have absorbed so much of the world's culture and standards that there can be a lot of 'un-growing' to do before real Christian growth becomes evident.

Paul's encouragement to grow to maturity in Ephesians 4, is an urgent call to the Body of Christ not to be tossed about on the uncertain waves of false doctrine and even deception, but *"through speaking the truth in love... to grow up into Him, who is the Head, that is Christ."* (Ephesians 4:14-15).

The sad fact is that in today's church we have a lot of believers, who may be mature adults in every other way, but who are babies when it comes to the things of the Spirit and the ways of God. I believe that the largest single reason that many have remained as spiritual babes, and never entered into their true destiny in God, is because ***they have never learnt to feed their spirits with a daily diet of the Word of God***. Many, also, have not been in churches where there is regular, systematic, Spirit-filled teaching from the Word of God, to help people grow in the things of God.

In Nehemiah Chapter 8 we read of Ezra, the priest, bringing the people of God back to an understanding of the Law of God after a time of being away from Him. A special wooden platform (pulpit!) was erected for the purpose (v.4). The people listened attentively and as the Law was spoken out, Ezra also taught the people *"making it clear and giving the meaning so that the people could understand what was being read"* (v.8). A good teacher will not only tell people what they're going to learn, but he'll carefully explain its significance so people can really understand the importance of the teaching.

Let me give you an example. Most people know that one of the Ten Commandments says, *"Do not commit adultery"*. But all that does, for many people, is make the idea of sexual temptation much more attractive! Many of the people who come on Healing Retreats at Ellel centres have had ungodly sexual relationships in their past, even though they knew, at the time, what the Word of God said.

A number of years ago the Lord showed us how to teach what the consequences of sexual sin actually are. When people see the results of having permanent ungodly soul-ties that are established through sexual sin, they are quick to repent and seek God's forgiveness and healing. We will look at this more closely in Parts 19 and 20 of our journey. I have lost count of the number of people who have said to me, *"if only I had known these things when I was young – I wouldn't now be living with the consequences of my mistakes."*

In Nehemiah's day, the systematic teaching of the Law, and its explanation, had an immediate effect. The people were joyful at what they heard, but then the Word of God brought conviction of sin, which led to repentance, forgiveness and worship and personal transformation. Lives were being changed and people were growing up into maturity because they were now absorbing the Law of God. (Nehemiah 9:3). The Word of God was having an effect.

You will find it worthwhile to take some time out and read the whole of Nehemiah chapters 8 and 9. It is a remarkable record of how people

PERSONAL NOTES

PERSONAL NOTES

were transformed by the presence of God through taking in of the Word of God.

GETTING STARTED

I am praying that these lessons will be a tremendous help to you on your journey, but, believe me, they're not a substitute for reading the Word of God itself. Whenever particular Scriptures are mentioned, get your Bible out, look up the references and read them for yourself.

And may I make a plea to you?! Never read the Bible without a pen, pencil or coloured marker in your hand. Whenever you read something that particularly impacts you, underline it – or make a note in the margin. You will never regret being able to turn the pages of your Bible in later years and be reminded of the things that God said to you in the past. This Bible will become your own personal tutorial book with God!

If your own Bible is a precious memento, and you don't want to mark it, then get another one that you don't mind writing on. It is essential that you keep a note of what God says to you personally through His living Word.

Some of my most precious possessions now are my father's Bibles – they are covered with his own markings, detailing God's working in his life. His markings are different from mine, but they are a precious reminder to me of my heritage. Making a record of important things God says to you is a key part of anyone's spiritual journey.

For many years I kept a personal spiritual diary, recording some of God's dealings with me. When I look back now on those notes, I can see the hand of God being traced through my own ups and downs in my own journey of life. Sometimes my diary was like an occasional letter to God, in which I shared my heart with Him. At other times I would record things that I knew God had said to me, as well as the questions I had for Him and various experiences of spiritual significance. And then there were the days when there was nothing. And that's OK too!

You may like to go over what we've already shared together on our journey, and make a note of the things that have impacted you already.

Next we will look at ways of reading the Bible so we can make sure that we take it all in! Every chapter matters to God and it must, therefore, matter to us! I trust that from this day on you will want to take in something of the Word of God every day.

PERSONAL NOTES

SUMMARY

God wants us to grow into mature Christian believers. If we don't feed our spirit, however, we will remain spiritual babes and will not grow in our faith. Reading the Bible, written by the Holy Spirit, is the best way to learn about the ways of God and how to live a godly life.

PRAYER

Help me, Lord, never to forget that your Word is a love letter to your people. Help me to read it with the enthusiasm and excitement of knowing that you want to speak into my life and help me walk in your ways. Help me also, Lord, never to forget the lessons I learn on this personal pilgrimage with You. In Jesus' Name, Amen.

Stage 3, Chapter 3

TAKING IT ALL IN!

We have seen how important it is to feed daily on the living bread of the Word of God (Deuteronomy 8:3 & Matthew 4:4). The physical food we eat becomes part of our physical being. And what we feed on spiritually becomes part of our spiritual being. So, just as we're concerned to eat good food, and avoid those things that would make us physically ill, we need also to take in good spiritual food, and avoid the bad stuff which, sadly, can also have a major impact on our lives – but not a good one.

Many of the people who come to our centres for prayer are suffering the long-term consequences of "bad spiritual stuff" (everything from occult practices to wrong beliefs about God and the consequences of wrong choices). These things can become part of them, and they need help, healing and sometimes deliverance.

So, how do we take in the good and avoid the bad? In Philippians 4:8, Paul urged his readers to think about *"whatever is true, whatever is noble, whatever is right, whatever is pure, whatever is lovely, whatever is admirable – if anything is excellent or praiseworthy – think about such things… and the God of peace will be with you."*

PERSONAL NOTES

PERSONAL NOTES

This is wonderful advice and a wonderful promise, and obviously everything in Scripture comes into the category of being excellent and praiseworthy. But what about all the other things in life? How do we know the difference between the good and the bad, for sometimes they can look very much the same. We have to have a way of measuring the difference and sorting out the bad from the good.

Experts are people who have a lot of experience and are able to give good advice, based on their years of training and practical experience. Their field of expertise can be anything from financial affairs to tasting tea or refining gold! Experts are paid a lot of money for their advice, often just because they have learnt to know the difference between the good and the bad. They are advisers to those who need to benefit from what the experts know.

OUR RESIDENT ADVISER!

So how do we get such expert advice about spiritual things and the affairs of life? The key is having constant access to our own personal Adviser, which is a wonderfully accurate name for the Holy Spirit.

Once we have recognised that the ultimate Author of the Bible is the Holy Spirit, and that the Bible really is the Word of God to us, then it doesn't make a lot of sense not to be diligent in reading it. And not just bits of it, all of it!

As we take it in, it's as if God puts a straight edge of understanding into our spirit, against which we can instinctively measure things and discern the difference between the good and the bad. The Holy Spirit becomes our resident Adviser, with the Bible as our reference book! (Hebrews 4:12).

Many, many times people have asked me for advice on all sorts of things to do with living the Christian life. In perhaps ninety per cent of these cases, all I have had to do was give them the advice which they could have read for themselves in the Word of God! The problem for many was very simple. Because they weren't reading God's Word, they didn't know what was in it. They were not giving God the opportunity to give them His advice through reading His Word.

Max Reich, a Jew and a Messianic Believer in Yeshua (Jesus) summed it up this way, *"The Christian who is careless in Bible reading will be careless in Christian living."* I can vouch a thousand times and more for the truth of this statement. So very often we have sought to help those who have been careless in Christian living, because they were ignorant of what the Word of God actually said.

C.S.Lewis, famous for his Narnia stories, but also a great theologian in his own right once said, *"Either the Bible will keep you away from sin, or sin will keep you away from the Bible!"*

The fact is, the more we take hold of the Truth, the more that Truth takes hold of us. It simply becomes part of our spiritual understanding. And if our lives are in godly order, with our spirit being led by the Holy Spirit and our soul and our body taking their rightful place under the headship of the spirit, then the understanding we have in our spirit will be like a permanent reference point of truth, against which we can test all things (as Paul tells us to do in 1 Thessalonians 5:21).

Andrew Murray, that extraordinary missionary saint who founded the South Africa General Mission, and whose writings on prayer and many other topics from a hundred years ago are still best sellers today, put it this way, *"Some read the Bible to learn and some read the Bible to hear from heaven... The Spirit will teach us to love the Word, to meditate on it and to keep it."*

When we are able to *"hear from Heaven"* through God's Word, the Scriptures become a spiritual compass, against which we can test the direction we are travelling at all times. Without a compass an explorer would quickly get lost. It is absolutely vital to know which direction you are travelling and compare it with the direction you want to go. If there's a difference between what the compass says and the direction you are heading, then you have problems. God gave us His Word so that we would have a permanent reference point to help us keep on course during life's journey.

Another way of looking at it is to consider that the Bible is the map and the Holy Spirit is the compass who shows you which way on the map to go. One without the other is relatively ineffective!

PROMISE BOX CHRISTIANS!

Promise Boxes are not as common now as they used to be. My Aunty Gladys had one. On every one of the hundreds of thin cards in the box

PERSONAL NOTES

PERSONAL NOTES

was a promise from the Bible. I used to enjoy picking one of the cards out of the box and seeing what scripture I had selected. If I didn't like it, or didn't understand it, I would put it back and try again!

Sadly, it's not only children who treat the Bible like that. If what people are reading confronts their behaviour in any way, they will often turn to something else, instead of allowing the Holy Spirit to bring conviction and change (James 1:22-25).

Each one of the promises in Aunty Gladys's box contained wonderful truths, but with the benefit of hindsight I can see that if people depend on a Promise Box, or whatever its modern day equivalent may be, for their daily intake of the Word of God, then life is going to be like living off a box of cherries and not eating any real food!

For the promises of God are a bit like the cherries on a cake. Wonderfully tasty, but if they are disconnected from the cake of the rest of the Word of God, they will create an illusion of unreality. Even cherry cakes are not all cherry! The promises only have relevance when read in the context of when and how they were given, and can only be claimed when we fulfil the conditions for the fulfilment of the promise.

A popular, and valuable, equivalent of the Promise Box today, are daily readings made up of a book of devotional commentaries on a particular verse of Scripture. And there are some very good ones. One of the best is one that my wife and I read from time to time. It's called Morning and Evening and is based on the writings of that great Victorian preacher, C.H.Spurgeon. We really enjoy reading it and there are occasions when the daily reading has been a particular blessing in our lives.

But Spurgeon would have been horrified if his book of daily readings had become a substitute for reading the Word of God itself. This is what he said about his own books of sermons, from which the devotional volumes were compiled, *"If my sermons kept people from reading the Bible for themselves, I would like to see the whole stock in a blaze and burned to ashes!"*

Spurgeon's Morning and Evening has 730 devotionals , based on 730 verses from the Bible – one for the morning and one for the evening for each day of the year. But there are 1189 Chapters in the Bible and 31,273 Verses. So, if you used Spurgeon's book every day (or any similar devotional volume), you would only ever read 2.33% of the Word of God! You would hardly be scratching the surface of the treasure that God has laid up for you in His Word.

PERSONAL NOTES

While devotionals are excellent – and Ellel Ministries has its own daily devotional called *Seeds of the Kingdom* at www.seedsofthekingdom.com – they should never become a substitute for reading the Word of God for yourself.

I meet lots of Christians who can quickly tell me some of their favourite Scriptures, such as Psalm 23, John 3:16, Romans 8:28 and Revelation 3:20. But whilst these and other similar favourite Scriptures are precious and important, if that's all you know, then there are huge holes in your spiritual understanding. Promise Box Christians will know some of the truths of the Word of God, but their spirit will not contain the straight edge of God's Truth which comes from regularly feeding on the living bread.

Here are some more things that Spurgeon said about Bible reading: *"Hear the true word of God: lay hold on it and spend your days not in raising hard questions, but in feasting on precious truth… The more you read the Bible and the more you meditate upon it, the more you will be astonished with it… The Bible sanctifies and moulds the mind into the image of Christ."*

READING IT ALL!

I hope by now you are understanding the message I am trying to get across. In essence it is this. While there are wonderful texts in the Bible, many of which you may know by heart, you cannot live effectively as a disciple of Jesus with a Promise Box mentality towards the Word of God. Unless you correctly handle the Word of truth (2 Timothy 2:15), making the time to take in the whole of the Bible you will miss out on so much and you will not be *"thoroughly equipped for every good work"* (2 Timothy 3:17). It is the God-breathed Word of God that actually equips us for life.

Many years ago, when I was taking my degree examinations, I learnt up on every subject that I knew might come up in the exam paper. In reality, only about 10% of the knowledge I had gained was necessary to pass the examination. But I had no idea which 10% would be required of me. So I couldn't take a chance and only learn up on 10% of the material – that would have been a recipe for disaster – I had to learn it all, so that whatever came up, I was properly prepared. The result was that I passed the exam.

PERSONAL NOTES

But when it comes to the Bible, so many Christians think that by knowing a few good texts, they are sufficiently equipped for the trials and temptations of life. They are not! They need to take it all in, so that whatever comes up in the 'examination of life', they will be fully equipped for every situation and every good work that the Lord puts before them.

John Newton, the former slave ship captain, who became an Anglican clergyman and wrote many wonderful hymns, including *Amazing Grace*, turned to God in a terrible storm in which his ship nearly sank. He was close to meeting his maker. But God spared him and during the rest of the voyage he began to read the Bible – an experience which marked the beginning of his pilgrimage to faith.

Many years later he said, *"I know not a better rule of reading the Scripture, than to read it through from beginning to end and, when we have finished it once, to begin again. We shall meet with many passages which we can make little sense of, but not so many in the second reading as in the first, and fewer in the third than in the second: provided we pray to Him who has the keys to open our understandings, and to anoint our eyes with his spiritual ointment."*

There are two principles here that John Newton is drawing to our attention – one, read it all, whether you understand it or not and two, always pray to God that the Holy Spirit will give us understanding of what is written. One of the earliest prayers I can remember learning, is one my Dad taught me to pray as a child, which is found in the Bible itself in Psalm 119:18. *"O Lord, open my eyes that I may see wonderful things in your law."*

Christians are uniquely privileged among all the peoples of the world. They are the only people on the planet who can read their favourite book and talk to the Author at the same time, asking Him to explain its meaning!

SO HOW DO I READ IT ALL?

If some of you are thinking that reading right through the Bible is too hard for you, let me tell you about Hannah. She first came to Ellel Grange in her early twenties. She had been terribly damaged by years of abuse.

God brought her a lot of healing, but when she went home she had to take her life into her own hands with God's help. She found that reading the Bible every day was the best thing she could ever have done. She didn't always understand what she was reading, but day by day she felt herself getting stronger as she made the Word of God her own – this is what she said:

Because of what happened to me the Doctors said I was a psychotic depressive. But Jesus said, 'I am the way the truth and the life'; He's also the Alpha and Omega, the first and the last. So I knew He had something better for me.
One morning I decided that I was going to read the whole Bible in a year. It wasn't very easy to read it every day, but it was the best thing I ever did! As I read the Bible, I learnt a lot – and I struggled a lot, but I knew Jesus was always there for me. It says, 'knock and the door will be opened'. It was for me! So, GO ON, KNOCK, and see how close Jesus comes to you. I hope your experience is as good as mine. JESUS NEVER LETS US DOWN.

SUMMARY

It's clear from Scripture that Jesus accepted the Old Testament Scriptures as being the inspired Word of God. And the same is true for the New Testament Scriptures – they are God-breathed. Making a plan to read the whole Bible, one step at a time, is a vital part of our Christian pilgrimage.

PRAYER

Lord, I want to take in from your Word day by day. Forgive me for times when I have chosen not to read the Bible and have missed out on so much of what you had wanted me to understand. Help me, Lord, to read the most precious book in the world, as your gift to me and the whole of mankind. In Jesus' Name, Amen.

PERSONAL NOTES

Stage 3, Chapter 4

GUIDANCE FOR DAILY LIVING

I probably get more questions asked about guidance than on almost any other topic! It's great that so many people are genuinely concerned to know what God's will is for their lives, but it's alarming that such a high proportion of these people have been Christians for a long time, and yet they have never learnt, or been taught, how to listen to God's voice for themselves!

Everyone wants to know about guidance, but they don't necessarily want to persevere and do the work of developing a relationship with the Guide, which is what it all comes down to. If we don't know the Guide, how can we receive His guidance?

It seems that many people have decided that they would prefer to *'get a word'* for their life from someone else, rather than hear the voice of God for themselves. This is really dangerous, for if we don't know how to let God speak to us directly through His Word, how can we ever test, before God, what other people might be saying to us?

Sadly, there are many people today who are waiting for God to fulfil a 'word', that might not have been from Him in the first place. No

PERSONAL NOTES

PERSONAL NOTES

wonder the Scripture commands us to test all things (1 Thessalonians 5:21). Testing isn't necessary when something is obviously ungodly and bad – we can just reject those things. Testing is for the things that look, sound and, even, feel good!

Satan will not initially try and deceive us through things that are obviously bad and wrong – he's far too subtle for that. He will try and deceive us, and then lead us astray, through things that seem, on the face of it, acceptable and good. Satan's 'good' is always the enemy of God's 'best'. It's not for nothing that Scripture warns us that Satan sometimes masquerades as an angel of light (2 Corinthians 11:14).

GUIDANCE FOR LIFE

There are dozens of Scriptures which talk about the way God speaks to us and shows us the way to go. One of my favourites is Isaiah 30:21 where it says, *'Whether you turn to the right or to the left, your ears will hear a voice behind you saying, "This is the way, walk in it".'*

Perhaps the most well known 'guidance scripture' is Proverbs 3:6; *"In all your ways acknowledge Him and He will direct your paths."* And when Jesus was teaching the disciples about the work of the Holy Spirit in John 16:13, He said, *"When He, the Spirit of Truth, comes, He will guide you into all truth."*

In each of these well-known Scriptures the emphasis is on God speaking directly to us about the conduct of our own life, leading us into what is true and right. While there may be times when God clearly speaks through others (and there have been some important occasions like this in my own life), we must learn to know and follow the voice of God for ourselves, and not depend solely on what others might say. At times when we are on our own, and out of contact with Christian friends, unless we have learnt to recognise and follow the voice of the Lord we could be in deep trouble.

AVOIDING DECEPTION

It's absolutely essential for us, in these very testing days, to be able to differentiate between what is true and what is false, and to recognise deception for what it is. Learning to know the voice of God, in the midst

PERSONAL NOTES

of so many competing voices, and then to obey it, is one of the most important foundational keys to living the Christian life.

It's well worth repeating the story of the Eastern shepherds, who brought their sheep to a watering hole and sat and talked while their flocks drank. After the flocks had drunk their fill, the shepherds prepared to go on their way to find fresh grazing for their sheep. But how would they manage to separate out their flocks again which, by now, were so mingled together it was impossible to identify which sheep belonged to which flock?

When the shepherds got up and left the watering hole, travelling in four different directions, they simply spoke to their sheep. As if by some magical pre-arranged signal, the flocks separated themselves out and each one followed their own shepherd. No human sorting was necessary!

The event was not as miraculous as it looked. It was simply that the sheep had all grown accustomed to the voice of their own shepherd, when there were no other competing voices to distract them. So, all the shepherd had to do was talk to his sheep. Guidance for the sheep was simply a matter of recognising their own shepherd's voice and following him.

In a very similar way, it's vital that we learn to recognise the voice of our own Shepherd (John 10:27) and understand His ways. The more we read the Word of God, the more we will understand the ways of God. Knowing that God won't lead us on a pathway that's contrary to His ways, gives us confidence to be able to trust Him, when we sense Him leading us in a particular direction.

But if we don't know what's in the Word of God, then we won't have any means of testing what we think God is saying to us. This is what God said to Joshua, when he was taking on responsibility for leading God's people, following the death of Moses: *"Do not let this Book of the Law depart from your mouth; meditate on it day and night, so that you may be careful to do everything written in it. Then you will be prosperous and successful"* (Joshua 1:8).

MEDITATING ON THE WORD

God's instruction to Joshua was to meditate on the Law of God. Meditation is a spiritual equivalent of carefully chewing some favourite food! We take our time to enjoy it and savour it.

PERSONAL NOTES

In exactly the same way, God asks us to carefully digest His Word, so that we can understand what it means and learn how to apply it in our lives. This is what I do when trying to understand something fresh from God's Word.

First, I pray a simple prayer, based on those words from Psalm 119:18, "Lord, open my eyes, so that I can really see and understand what you are saying to me through this passage from your Word." Then I read the passage two, or sometimes, three, times. Each time I am trying to read it from a different perspective.

If you take a picture of a building from one angle, you may be surprised at how different it looks from a different angle. When the perspective changes, the picture changes. In a similar way, I would first look, for example, at a passage and ask myself how it seems from my own perspective. But then I would read it again and put myself in God's shoes and try and see it afresh, this time from His perspective. I would then read around the passage – what came before and what came after, and look up any cross-references to other scriptures that my Bible provides.

Finally, if what I'm reading is about people, and there are different characters in the passage, I might read the story again, putting myself in their shoes, trying to see things from their perspective. For example, when you read the stories of Jesus' encounters with either Nicodemus or Zaccheus, you get a whole new insight into what was happening when you see it from their perspective!

All the time I am looking to see what is relevant to me, and then, having taken in everything I can, I pray about any particular things that I sensed God was saying to me.

Sometimes God is clearly speaking to me for today through the passage I am reading, but most times, I am simply storing up understanding in my personal library of faith, so that at some future time of need, I can draw on the treasure that I have now made my own.

TESTING A WORD FROM THE LORD

The entire Bible contains the Word of God because it IS the Word of God. But there are times when a specific Scripture jumps out of the page in such a powerfully relevant way, that we recognise it is as being more than just part of the biblical record. At that moment, something from the written Word, becomes a specific word from God into our lives for now.

Such a word can come to us in many different ways. In my own experience it has sometimes been spoken out by a preacher when quoting a scripture in a sermon. At other times it has suddenly impacted my spirit as I read the Bible for myself. And then again, a scripture I may have read many years ago has suddenly come into my memory, for no other reason than that God was using it to speak to me in my present situation.

The first time God spoke to me about what he wanted me to do with my life, was when I was starting to restore a broken car and found that the chassis was bent. As I looked at the chassis, I sensed God saying to me that I could restore the broken car, even with a bent chassis, but that ***He could*** restore broken lives. Then He asked me the question, *"Which is more important?"*

Of course, broken lives are more important than broken cars and, yes, the Bible does talk about God restoring broken ***lives***. So what I sensed God was saying to me was consistent with what I already knew was in Scripture – and that's the first stage in testing a word from God. Is it consistent with the general message of Scripture?

Jesus' personal mission statement was taken from Isaiah 61:1, which He quoted to the congregation in His own synagogue in Nazareth. He said that He had come to heal the broken-hearted and set the captives free. Then in Luke 9:1-2, Jesus sent out His disciples to preach the Kingdom, heal the sick and cast out demons.

The word that I sensed God had spoken to me was, therefore, not only consistent with the life and ministry of Jesus, but also with what Jesus asked His disciples to do. A number of years later, when I was sensing the time was coming, when God would open up the ministry I had seen in vision, Ruth Hawkey, a visiting preacher at my local Methodist Church, spoke about Abraham going out in faith, but not knowing where he was going. As she preached, the vision God had given me for a healing ministry was burning within me.

It was like a dormant seed that was suddenly bursting into life at that moment. I knew God was telling me to start moving forward in faith, even though I didn't know where that would lead! Through what Ruth was saying, God was speaking right into my spirit.

PERSONAL NOTES

PERSONAL NOTES

Then, on the way out of the church, I spoke to Ruth about what God had said to me through her sermon, and thanked her for it. She then shared with me the other side of the story. She knew that God had given her that specific word for someone at that service, but she didn't know who. Then she gave me the other part of the word and quoted to me, from John 2:5, these very specific words, *"Whatever He tells you to do, do it."*

As Ruth spoke out those words, it was as if a starting pistol went off in my head. The time had come. The vision, which I had been nurturing and believing in for years, really must have been from God, and the time for its fulfilment was coming soon. God was giving me clear direction, through His Word, to go and do what Jesus had spoken into my heart.

The preacher that day was simply being obedient to what God had given her, and her obedience was a very significant moment in my own pilgrimage. I still know Ruth today, over thirty years after that event, and she remembers it well. She and her husband Joe have, for many years, been much loved visiting teachers on our schools!

FILLING IN THE DETAILS – LUKE 9:11

God can not only use Scripture to point us in the general direction for our lives, but also to help us with some of the details as well! Let me illustrate from my own experience how God used specific scriptures to speak into my own life.

As the vision for the work of Ellel Ministries grew, I began to seek the Lord more specifically and ask the necessary questions. For example, what would this work actually look like? At that time I knew very little about the healing ministry, but the desire to see people healed by God burned deeply in my heart.

I began to read the Scriptures with a greater sense of purpose, looking for God's answers to my questions. My Bible was liberally marked with everything that God was teaching me about healing. And as I read the Word of God, the vision for *'Healing Retreats'* was born in my spirit. I *'saw'* that people would not just come for prayer, but would also receive teaching to help put a solid foundation into their lives. But what would I teach on these retreats?

I then started looking specifically for all the teaching Jesus gave about how to get healed. To my shock and amazement, there wasn't any! At least, I couldn't find any. So I now had a problem – how do you run a Healing Retreat?

I searched the Scriptures again and systematically scoured the Gospels for clues. It was as I read Luke 9 that I came to the story of the feeding of the five thousand and was impacted by some words I had never noticed before. All my previous focus in this passage had been on what Jesus did to feed the five thousand, not on what He was doing with them before He fed them!

God was opening my eyes, for Luke 9:11 tells you what He had previously been doing: *'Jesus welcomed the people, spoke to them about the Kingdom of God and healed those in need of healing.'*

As I read these words, it seemed as though they were standing out from the page. God had got my attention. I meditated on this simple statement and as I did so, it was as if I was hearing the voice of the Lord speaking clearly into my heart about how He wanted the ministry to be run.

First, people needed to be really welcomed, because a sincere welcome speaks to the stranger of love. And when people feel loved, they are much more likely to listen to what is being taught. When I thought about it, it seemed so obvious and simple. Yet although it is one of those simple understandings, it is also very profound.

Then, after the people had been welcomed and loved, they needed to be taught. And the teaching we needed to give them wasn't teaching about how to get healed, but about the Kingdom of God. The Lord was showing me something very significant: ***if the foundational principles of living a godly life under the Lordship of Jesus are not in a person's life, then it will be very hard for people to either receive or keep the healing they need.***

And finally, we should pray for the people, who now know they are welcomed and loved and, hopefully, have also understood some key principles of Kingdom living, to be healed.

And so, the foundational principles for the whole of the ministry, since 1986, were established through a specific word from God from the scripture: Luke 9:11. As the Ellel teams have ministered around the world, on literally thousands of three day Healing Retreats, we have seen God do extraordinary things in people's lives, and seen them make huge strides forward in their Christian pilgrimage.

PERSONAL NOTES

PERSONAL NOTES

THE LIVING WORD

The writer of the book of Hebrews truly summed up how the Word of God can operate in our lives in chapter 4:12, *'For the Word of God is living and active. Sharper than any double-edged sword, it penetrates even to dividing of soul and spirit, joints and marrow; it judges the thoughts and attitudes of the heart.'*

In our journey we will be constantly referring to the Scriptures. We will experience, first-hand, how God uses His Word to speak directly into our lives and lead us into the plans and purposes He has laid out for each one of us.

SUMMARY

God's Word is the most powerful means through which He guides and directs His people. As we get it in, then the Holy Spirit can get it out. As the days of our life move forward, we can listen to what God is saying to us through His Word and apply it in our lives. But we also have to persevere in our relationship with God and exercise faith as we wait on Him. We can then watch God work miracles of His grace within and through us.

PRAYER

Help me, Lord, to have my eyes open to see the wonderful truths that are in the Word of God. Help me to have spiritual ears that are alert to hear what it is that You're saying to me as I read your Word, day by day. In Jesus name, Amen.

Stage 3, Chapter 5

INSPIRATION AND ENCOURAGEMENT AT ALL TIMES

I am trusting that, by now, you will have understood something of my heart for each one of you. My deepest concern is that no-one should miss out on developing a personal and life-transforming relationship with the living God – a relationship in which you can totally trust Him, every step of the way, whatever the circumstances of life and whatever He asks you to do for Him.

I have been writing this during a very difficult season in my own life, a season in which I have had to put what I have been teaching to the test. I have had to say an earthly goodbye to someone with whom I have walked as a brother in the ministry for many years. Whilst he may be no longer with us in an earthly sense, he is still very much with us in a spiritual sense. He's now joined to Christ in eternity, and we're joined to Christ in time. Jesus is the bridge between one side of the curtain of death and the other, between time and eternity.

None of us knew that his home-call would be so sudden, but in all the circumstances surrounding his passing, it has been abundantly clear to everyone that God has been in charge. Shortly before he died, this is

PERSONAL NOTES

PERSONAL NOTES

what he wrote, *"I have experienced for myself, deep in my spirit, the reality of Jesus' love and peacefulness. My life is so safe and secure – I have known it all my life in my thoughts – but now I know it like a solid foundational rock, securely placed in my spirit. A rock of experience – not just knowledge, strong enough to build my life on."*

How can someone be so safe and secure in Jesus at a time of such personal crisis? The answer, in his case, was that over a long period of time he had developed a close relationship with God and had fed on the Word of God and made it his own. His writings were impregnated with the truths of Scripture, and for many, many years they had been a constant source of encouragement and inspiration to him. He had taken in of the spiritual food and the food had become part of him.

His life was founded on the Rock of Jesus Christ. My aim is that through this *Journey to Freedom* everyone should become more firmly established on that solid and totally dependable Rock.

ENCOURAGEMENT

The word 'encouragement' is a friendly word! We like it, because it gives us a sense of security and well-being. When we are encouraged we immediately feel better and strengthened for whatever we're doing. And when things are difficult, a person who encourages us is always a welcome friend. A person with the opposite message can soon depress and undermine us and then we are vulnerable to the temptation of giving up.

But what does the word 'encouragement' really mean? We need to know! Whilst we understand the blessing of words of encouragement, sometimes the real meaning of words gets lost in changing circumstances or understandings. If you have come to associate the word 'encouragement' with just a 'pat on the back' to comfort you and make you feel better, you have not understood its real meaning, and you have missed the point of how the word is used in the Scriptures! The real meaning is much deeper than this.

This is what the dictionary says: *To encourage: to give **courage** to, put **courage** in, or to inspire with spirit and hope.*

The real meaning of the word 'encouragement' is associated with the words 'courage' and 'bravery', not a comforting pat on the back. The very word 'bravery' implies a successful completion of a task in the face of danger, even great danger. A brave person is someone who doesn't turn back when things get tough.

The word 'encouragement' is much more associated with giving strength for battle than making someone feel better with a few kind words. Indeed, initially words of real encouragement (giving courage to) may not make you feel any better at all, but they will give you the strength to push through with something you may even be frightened of.

One of the greatest encouragers of all time was Winston Churchill. He was voted *'the man of the century'* by the British people. He was the Prime Minister during the Second World War and largely through his remarkable leadership, the British people were able to lead the Allied Forces to a great, but terribly costly, victory in this most awful of conflicts.

When he was appointed as Prime Minister he did not try and soften the situation with supposedly comforting words! He did not give either Parliament or the people a gentle pat on the back to give them false encouragement, but he did set before them the reality of what the nation was facing. He did not cover up the horrors of war, but spoke about the situation as it was. One might have thought that such blunt talk would have had a negative effect, but in reality it did the very opposite. People were given courage to fight.

Here is something of what Churchill said in two of his most famous speeches:

13 May 1940: I have nothing to offer but ***blood, toil, tears and sweat****. We have before us an ordeal of the most grievous kind. We have before us many, many long months of struggle and of suffering. You ask, what is our policy? I can say: It is to wage war, by sea, land and air, with all our might and with all the strength that God can give us; to wage war against a monstrous tyranny, never surpassed in the dark, lamentable catalogue of human crime. That is our policy. You ask, what is our aim? I can answer in one word: It is victory, victory at all costs, victory in spite of all terror, victory, however long and hard the road may be; for without victory, there is no survival.*

4 June 1940: We shall go on to the end, ***we shall fight*** *in France,* ***we shall fight*** *on the seas and oceans, we shall fight with growing confidence and growing strength in the air, we shall defend our Island, whatever the cost may*

PERSONAL NOTES

PERSONAL NOTES

be, ***we shall fight on the beaches, we shall fight*** *on the landing grounds,* ***we shall fight*** *in the fields and in the streets,* ***we shall fight*** *in the hills;* ***we shall never surrender****.*

These speeches set the tone for the years of conflict ahead. They prepared the people for battle. They gave courage to the people, because they now knew there was a man in charge of the nation who knew what he was doing. It gave them confidence that even though the fight may be long and hard, that they would win through. In short, the people were given courage – they were encouraged!

It was about three thousand years earlier that a relatively young man was commissioned to take up the reins of leadership from Moses. Moses would not be able to enter the Promised Land himself – this assignment was given to Joshua.

Moses was told to *'commission Joshua, and encourage and strengthen him, for he will lead this people across, and will cause them to inherit the land that you will see'* (Deuteronomy 3:28). This assignment from the living God, to take God's people across the River Jordan and to occupy the land, was not an easy one. To achieve this huge objective, battles would have to be fought – battles against fearsome peoples, in a land where even giants lived (Numbers 13:32).

God knew that Joshua would need all the courage he could muster. So, in Joshua 1:6 after Moses had died, God further said to Joshua, *'Be strong and courageous'*. He reinforced this message in verse 7 by adding the word *'very'*: *'Be strong and very courageous'*. And then again in verse 9, in the strongest words of encouragement of all, *'Be strong and courageous. Do not be terrified; do not be discouraged, for the Lord your God will be with you wherever you go.'*

This was God's way of encouraging Joshua – telling him the reality of the situation, but at the same time assuring Joshua of His presence wherever he went. It's the presence of God that we all so desperately need to have. And what a massive difference it makes to know that God is with us! That's the ultimate seal of encouragement for every situation in life we might have to face.

When David faced a terrible situation, having discovered that the Amalekites had carried off all the women from his village, as captives, and even his own men were turning against him, what did he do?

PERSONAL NOTES

1 Samuel 30:6 tells us that *'David encouraged himself in the Lord.'* He went to the God who had promised to be with him and drew down courage from on high. David's relationship with God was such that he knew exactly what to do, he went to God for encouragement – he took courage on board and was then able to press on, and in a remarkable victory recovered everyone and everything that had been taken.

So, encouragement can be defined as being strengthened by God for the battles of life. In Ephesians 6 Paul painted a dramatic picture of the Christian life being warfare, in which we're under constant threat from the enemy of souls. In other places he referred to the Christian life as an endurance race.

Whatever picture fits best with you, without courage you will neither be able fight spiritual battles nor endure in the marathon race of life. And the Scriptures are your best possible source of courage. They are the vitamin pills, the spiritual glucose and the solid food that will equip you for the journey ahead.

In Churchill's speeches of encouragement during the Second World War, he left no room whatsoever for the possibility of defeat. He knew that, no matter how long the battle would rage, victory would come. In just the same way we can be encouraged to know that because Jesus personally overcame Satan at the cross, we too, can be certain of victory over all the powers of darkness. The Word of God encourages us to be steadfast and immoveable and, by faith, hold the ground. Jesus is our Rock, the sure foundation that we can put our trust in (Hebrews 6:18-19).

INSPIRATION

Medically, when you breathe, you inspire – meaning you expand your lungs and take in breath. Spiritually, when you are inspired, you take on board the breath of God and allow Him to be the source of hope and strength for the challenges of life.

The dictionary defines 'inspire' as: *to infuse with an encouraging or exalting divine influence, to bring about a change in the heart and will of one's hearers; to energise the soul with the influence of God.*

I love those last few words – energise the soul with the influence of God – for that's exactly what the Holy Spirit does for us. He equips us with strength and courage and He energises our soul.

PERSONAL NOTES

It's hard to separate out these two important words – encouragement and inspiration. They are like two sides of the same coin. When we are inspired by the Holy Spirit, then we are energised by God. And when we are encouraged by God, it's always to do those things that He has inspired us to do.

Problems arise in our Christian walk when we try and do things in our own strength – things that God hasn't asked us to do and which, therefore, God can't give us the courage for. This is what happens when people falsely believe that something has been inspired by God, when it hasn't! They use up all their energy and resources in trying to be obedient to a false vision, and often finish up very disillusioned and discouraged, even angry with God, blaming Him for not doing what they wanted Him to do.

This is why it's so important to test even those things that seem to come from God, and to learn how to recognise and avoid the deceptions of the enemy.

When Jesus faced Satan during His wilderness experience, He countered the temptation to turn stones into bread by saying, *'Man does not live on bread alone, but on every word that comes from the mouth of God.'* (Matthew 4:4) And again, in John 6:63, Jesus said, *'The Spirit gives life; the flesh counts for nothing. The words I have spoken to you are spirit and they are life.'* In these Scriptures, Jesus was underlining how critical it is that we live by inspiration – as we breathe in the Word of God from the heart of God, it gives us life. What a privilege, what a blessing!

COMFORT

I don't want to leave our look at the Bible, without mentioning the word 'comfort'. Whilst encouragement is giving courage, comfort is showing care, compassion and understanding, which are all outworkings of the fact that God IS love. They are expressions of the heart of God towards His children.

In the Bible we read about *'the God of ALL comfort'* (2 Corinthians 1:3). And we also read of the compassion of God when He says, *'Blessed are those who mourn, they shall be comforted'* (Matthew 5:4), and of His wishes for the people who love Him, *'Comfort, comfort my people'* (Isaiah 40:1).

God really does want us to know the precious comfort of His loving

PERSONAL NOTES

presence in the deepest recesses of our souls. And one of the very best ways of knowing that comfort, is simply to make meditation on the Word of God a lifelong habit. Something that comes as naturally as breathing, as you think about the things God has said to us in His precious Word.

I have known some very difficult times in my own life, and I have been utterly amazed how God draws living water for me out of the deep well of His Word – living water that has truly comforted me in my innermost being. God has come to me at my most vulnerable and hurting, and wrapped me in spiritual cotton wool as He has brought healing balm to my soul. The Psalms especially are full of His comforting words, but throughout the Scriptures the comfort of God is abundantly evident.

Every day, as you read God's Word, more gems are added to your spiritual understanding. You don't have to worry about remembering them all, just don't forget that if you get them in, the Holy Spirit will get them out – exactly when you need them!

AT ALL TIMES!

The Scriptures are a constant source of encouragement, inspiration and comfort. When we're facing challenges and temptation, the Word from God comes to us fresh from the Word of God. And as the Psalmist reminds us (Psalm 121:4), the God of Israel doesn't fall asleep. He's always ready and willing to hear our cry and answer our prayer.

To be in a relationship means we also need to know how to communicate with those we're in relationship with. So in the next part of our journey we will go to the very centre of how we relate to God – how we can both speak to Him and hear His voice also. Prayer is not just something we do when we decide to pray – it needs to become a 24 hour, 7 day a week experience.

I pray that as you think over all the things we have shared about the Bible, that you'll be able to look at God's Word in a very different way. The saying at the head of this stage of the journey is really true: *'Without a map, I get lost. Without the Bible I am lost before I even begin the journey!'*

But with the Bible, you have the map in your hand and with the Holy Spirit in your heart you have the key to understanding it. Take it all in,

PERSONAL NOTES

store it up and then live it out for the rest of your days. The Bible really is the most precious thing that exists on the planet! It contains the keys to life.

SUMMARY

The Bible is a constant source of courage for life's journey. Through its pages God encourages us and inspires us to live for Him. Without the Bible we are lost, because we would have no true knowledge of the living God and be ill-equipped to do the works of the Kingdom of God.

PRAYER

Lord, I don't want to have the false comfort of being patted on the back, when what I really need is your courage to really live the Christian life. I pray that starting from today you will give me fresh inspiration from Your heart to mine and encourage me in all that I seek to do for You. In Jesus' Name, Amen.

STAGE 4

The Vital Breath of Prayer

Prayer is the blood which flows
in the artery which connects
God's heart to mine!

Stage 4, Chapter 1

PRAYER – THE CHRISTIAN'S VITAL BREATH

If you own a car it's absolutely essential that you know how to fill it up with fuel. A car without fuel is a useless museum piece going nowhere! And a Christian who doesn't know how to pray, is like a car without fuel – in danger of becoming a museum piece in the church, occupying space but out of touch with God and going nowhere!

Many hymn-writers have tried to express the nature of prayer in their poetry, but none has done so more effectively than James Montgomery. He was a Scottish contemporary of John Wesley. His parents were Moravian missionaries in the West Indies, but they died when James was very young.

He was a brave man, who went through many difficult times, including two spells in prison for having the courage to speak out and publish poems and articles in support of the great causes of his day, including abolition of slavery. He certainly needed to know how to pray! Some of the greatest English hymns are from his pen.

PERSONAL NOTES

PERSONAL NOTES

THE AIR WE BREATHE!

It was James Montgomery who coined the phrase, *'the Christian's vital breath'*. In his hymn *'Prayer is the soul's sincere desire'*, he includes these remarkable words:

Prayer is the Christian's vital breath, The Christian's native air.

In describing prayer as *'vital breath'* and *'the Christian's native air'*, he was expressing a profound truth about prayer – that praying in the life of the believer should be as natural and as essential as breathing. If we cease to breathe we begin to die, and if we cease to pray our relationship with God can also begin to die.

The Apostle Paul expressed a similar thought when he said in 1 Thessalonians 5:17 that we should *'pray continually'*, or in an older version of the Bible, *'pray without ceasing'*. Now, words like these immediately invite a challenge! How can we possibly be constantly in prayer and also fulfil the normal routines of life? Surely, we must also concentrate on the business of living, working, family and leisure. How can we possibly be praying at all times?

But, if I were to say to you, *"How can I possibly be constantly breathing and also fulfil the normal routines of life? I can't possibly do all these other things and breathe at the same time"* – you would simply laugh at my stupidity! For everyone knows that if you don't breathe you can't live, move or do anything.

Breathing is of greater importance than all the other physical things in the world that you might like to do. Without breath you will have no oxygen, without oxygen your body can't function and you will quickly die. So, of course, breathing has to be of higher priority than every other function of life. But we don't actually have to think about it, we just take breathing in our stride, as we go about our daily routines, whatever they may be. It is an automatic process.

This is the message that James Montgomery and the Apostle Paul are both trying to get across in respect of prayer – *that prayer is the oxygen of the spirit and the soul.* It is the channel of access to the heart of God and the channel of blessing from the throne of God. It is of greater importance than anything else we do. And if we don't pray, we're cutting ourselves off from the supply line of grace, leaving ourselves as helpless as a fish out of water, flapping on the river bank and waiting to die!

PERSONAL NOTES

A 24/7 PRAYER MEETING!

Clearly, if prayer is to be considered as important as breathing, we have to quickly dispense with the idea that we can only pray at prayer meetings, or at the beginning and end of the day, or when we say Amen to what the minister says in church on a Sunday morning, or through any other discipline which inevitably limits prayer to a time and a place.

No, I'm not saying that corporate prayer at prayer meetings isn't important, it is. Nor am I saying that the prayers at church services don't matter, they do. But what I am saying, is that if we haven't learnt how to live and breathe the air of prayer, then much of our other praying will be as lifeless as a set of lungs without oxygen, no matter where or when we do our praying.

If it's true, which it is, that we can never escape from the presence of God (even if we wanted to!) (Psalm 139:7-12), it's also true that God is always there to fellowship with us in prayer – He can never escape from our presence either! Brother Lawrence put it this way, *'You need not cry very loud; He is nearer to us than we are aware of!'* A relationship with God is like a 24/7 prayer meeting, twenty four hours a day, seven days a week – forever! He's always there, and He's never absent from the meeting! He loves to enjoy your company and He loves you to enjoy His company.

So the key foundation stone of a life of prayer is simply a constant awareness of the presence of God. He's interested in what we are doing, and wants us to participate in what He's doing.

There are many great men and women of God whom I would love to have met and learned from. High on my list of such people would be that great Indian saint of God, Sadhu Sundar Singh. He said that prayer *'is the desire for God Himself…'* and that *'the true spirit of prayer does not consist in asking God for blessings, but in receiving Him who is the giver of all blessings, and in living a life of fellowship with Him… in perpetual communion.'* He was absolutely right.

As you read the Scriptures you quickly realise that for Jesus this constant fellowship with the Father was the most important thing in His life. He only did what the Father told Him to do (John 5:19). He only went where the Father told Him to go. He only said what the Father told Him to say. How did He know how to do all these things? Because He lived in that precious 24/7 relationship with God, which is the essence of prayer.

PERSONAL NOTES

Now, in any close relationship, such as marriage, for example, you don't have to be constantly talking to remain in the marriage. You're married whether you're speaking or whether you're silent. But either of you can open up a conversation at any time – because you're in permanent relationship with each other. You don't have to request permission to speak, or go to a special place for a meeting before you can start a conversation. And you can start a conversation at anytime, anywhere. Your marital status gives you that privilege – and of all the people on earth, it's only your spouse, who can enjoy that unique privilege with you.

It's interesting that Paul uses the marriage relationship to paint a picture of the relationship between Jesus and the people who together form the Church (Ephesians 5:22-33). Jesus is described as the Bridegroom and the Church as His bride. So it's clearly God's intention that the relationship between Himself and His people was meant to be an intimate one in which both parties participate constantly in the relationship.

A relationship with God is also a bit like a telephone call that goes on forever. Neither of you puts the receiver down – the line is held open for time and eternity. And the calls are free!

It's through prayer that we keep in touch with our Heavenly Father. It's through prayer that He shares with us His vision for our lives. It's through prayer that we bring before Him our needs and circumstances. It's through prayer that we can express our love to Him. It's through prayer that we can hear His gentle voice bringing encouragement, correction or direction into our lives. It's through prayer that we talk to Him about things we don't understand – such as passages in the Bible or the circumstances and events of life.

I could go on and on and on about all the things that are achieved through prayer – that intimate spiritual fellowship between God and His children. But now we are going to look at some important aspects of prayer, which were highlighted by Jesus in what we call *'the Lord's Prayer'*.

GETTING A RIGHT PERCEPTION OF GOD AS A LOVING FATHER

Before we can proceed further with our study of prayer, it's vital that we understand something very significant about the nature and character of God. For, unless we have a right understanding of what He's like, we won't feel comfortable about the sort of intimate relationship with God that I'm encouraging you to have.

I once said to a lady, who had had a very difficult upbringing that she really needed to know the loving care of God, her Heavenly Father. The moment I said this, she turned on me sharply and literally spat the words out of her lips, *"Don't ever talk to me about God being a Father – if He's anything like my father, I just don't want to know Him!"*

It took me a while to understand why her reaction was so violent against me, but when she told me her story I began to understand. Her father had been violent and abusive and would regularly beat her and her brothers and sisters – just for being there. He would go out drinking most nights and when he came home drunk he would beat all the children.

To escape this tyranny, one of them would sit up and wait till Dad was seen coming down the road outside. The child 'on guard' would then wake the others and they would all rush out into the back yard and lock themselves in a coal shed, hiding there until Dad had come home and would be fast asleep. *"That's what fathers are like,"* the woman said.

She clearly had a major problem. For in her mind, she had assumed that the image of what fathers are like, that she had learned from her Dad, was representative of what all fathers are like – even God the Father. She had, understandably, grown up with this belief in her heart, and there was no way she was ever going to respond to any prayer which addressed God as Father.

My own experience of parenting was the very opposite of this, and as a result I grew up knowing that talking to God as Father was really safe. I learnt about prayer from a Mum and Dad who prayed and included their children in their praying.

But many, many people have a major problem with prayer, not because they disagree with the idea of prayer, but because their image of what God is like has been so badly distorted by their own human fathering, that it's impossible for them to relate to God in a loving way.

As we have already seen, it was God's intention that human parenting would be the means of giving one generation after another a true picture of the nature and character of God. In this way all generations would understand how much Father God loves His children, because

PERSONAL NOTES

PERSONAL NOTES

they would have learned about what good fathers are like from their own parents.

But man fell into sin. Satan became the god of this world and became known as the father of lies.

In John 8:42-47, Jesus addressed some of the wicked, religious leaders of His day by saying that they were behaving like their father the devil and were carrying out his desires! So, when people do bad things, it's important to realise that they're not doing these things because they are behaving like their Heavenly Father, but that they are behaving like Satan, who's a false god and a false father.

But because God designed children to learn about Him from their parents, children instinctively believe that the way they were treated is the way God would treat them. So we meet people who don't believe God is interested in them, because they had a father who was only interested in himself and not in them.

Some believe that God must be far too busy to be interested in them, because that's exactly how their human father behaved. And this can even be the case in Christian ministry, where fathers are too busy with the 'things of God' to spend time with the 'gifts of God' (their children).

Yet others look on God as a sort of Father Christmas, who is just there to give them presents from an eternal Christmas tree! This is sometimes because their own human father was always giving presents to his children – but often this was a substitute for the real relationship the child craved and needed with Dad. For some fathers, giving presents was cheaper and more convenient than spending time with the children.

So some people have an image of God in their heart as someone who's not really interested in them as people, but who can be depended on for an endless stream of presents, as a substitute for a real relationship. It's no wonder that such people look on prayer as bringing to God their shopping list of current needs and have no interest in a relationship with God Himself.

And when children are abused and violated by cruel parenting, it's very hard for them, as adults, to believe that God isn't going to treat them in the same cruel and off-hand way or, at the very least, that He simply wants to *use* them for His own purposes.

So it's very important when trying to understand the importance of prayer, and the need for it to be central in our Christian life, to begin by

PERSONAL NOTES

asking God to help us get a right perception of who He is and what He's like. Jesus was obviously very much aware of the problem, for on several occasions He told people that He and the Father were one, and that if people had got to know what He was like, they would also know what the Father was like. In John 14:7 Jesus said, *'If you really knew me, you would know my Father as well.'*

Many times, when praying for people to be healed we have realised that they had no problem in relating to Jesus, as God. But when it came to praying to God as Father, they had a real problem. So Jesus made it very clear that one of the reasons He had come, was to show us just what the Father is really like. Fallen man was not giving people a good impression of the nature and character of God. The image of God people had received needed to be changed.

PUTTING THINGS RIGHT WITH FATHER GOD

Before we move on I would like to ask you to spend some time thinking about how you really see Father God. What does He seem like to you? And then think about how you saw your own human father. Ask yourself if there's any way in which you have believed that God the Father has some characteristics and habits which aren't true to who He is. Are they a reflection of the distortion you may have experienced through the parenting you received?

It's easy to deal with it, if we really want to know God the Father – as He really is:

First, simply speak out forgiveness to your Dad (and maybe also your Mum) for everything they did that has given you a wrong impression of what Father God is really like.

Next, tell God you're sorry for believing things about Him that are wrong, and ask Him to forgive you.

Then, thank Jesus for coming to show you what Father God is really like – loving, kind, gentle, caring, compassionate, understanding and selfless.

Finally, ask God to set you free from all the false things that the father of lies (Satan) has sown into your mind and understanding ever since you were conceived and born.

PERSONAL NOTES

Now, drawing on the enabling power of the Holy Spirit within you, start putting into practice what we have been talking about – living with a constant awareness of the presence of God. Start talking to Him as a friend – as the very best Dad there has ever been and you could ever have. Tell Him how much you love Him, share your thoughts, your visions, your dreams, your concerns, your feelings, your temptations. Tell Him about the bad or difficult things as well as the good and exciting things. He's interested in them all. This is prayer!

We take our dog for a walk every day. I enjoy these times with Barney, but for me personally, they're also a very precious time of fellowship with Daddy God – that's what the Hebrew word *'Abba'* often used to address Father God, really means.

As I walk down the lanes and along the edge of a canal, I tell God about all the things that are happening in my life. If you were to listen to my thoughts, or even hear my spoken words, you wouldn't recognise them as prayers in the traditional sense – by that I mean the sort of prayers after which you would say an Amen in church. But they're just as much prayer, and possibly more so, than the most formal and carefully worded prayer you have ever heard.

It's simply me chatting to Father God. Some people would think that was irreverent – but I don't think so. At the heart of all these 'prayers' is the simple recognition that Father God is the most important 'person' in my life and I want to be involved with Him and I want Him to be involved with me.

It's not surprising that on these walks, I enjoy some of my most creative thinking. Often I come back, having had a real time of fellowship with Father God and having heard Father speaking to me as well. In fact some of the best ideas I have ever had have suddenly popped into my mind at times like this! No guessing as to Who they came from! God is also Creator and He loves us to be creative with Him.

READY FOR MORE?

Now we're ready to move on in our understanding of prayer, and to look at what Jesus taught His disciples about prayer. This is important for us, for what mattered for the disciples of Jesus also matters to us!

SUMMARY

Prayer is much, much more than just spending occasional times talking to God, or repeating prayers. Prayer is the means of communication in the very special relationship that God longs to have with us. It's vital that we get a right understanding of what God is like, otherwise we won't be able to trust Him when we talk with Him.

PRAYER

Thank you Father God that You're really interested in all Your children, including me. Help me to always remember that no matter how I may feel, You do really care for me, and that You want to have a relationship with me. In Jesus' Name, Amen.

PERSONAL NOTES

Stage 4, Chapter 2

THE LORD'S PRAYER – WORSHIP AND ADORATION

We have now realized that prayer without relationship is definitely not what God intended! Indeed, we saw that the very essence of prayer is the expression of an intimate relationship between Father God (Abba) and us (His children).

Children, who love their Daddy and have no fear of him, have that glorious habit of breaking into the most serious of conversations with the most simple and seemingly unimportant comments, questions or requests. For the child, at that particular moment, their question is the whole of their world. They are completely oblivious to whatever other issues may be occupying Daddy's mind.

And that's how it should be! Daddy might be wrestling with major family or financial problems, struggling with his work or trying to work through some deep theological issues, but all his son or daughter wants to know is 'Why are dandelions yellow?' or 'Where's my teddy bear?'

In a similar way, God may be watching in anguish as the nations rebel against Him and wars are about to break out across the world, but one of His children is praying for someone who's sick. Or another may be

PERSONAL NOTES

PERSONAL NOTES

quietly seeking the Lord for understanding of His Word. Does God say He's too busy for such things? Of course not. He loves to hear and answer our prayers, and relate to us as if we're the only person on the planet. I learnt to talk with God in this sort of way as a child because I was used to hearing my own Dad talk to God like that, and my grand-father before him.

But that level of intimacy with God is not something that all people desire or feel comfortable with. To them it can seem rather threatening to be letting God so deep into their inner being in such an informal way. If they want to pray at all, they seem happier with the security of more formal prayers. These prayers don't require any personal accountability, or involvement with the God they are praying to, and people who are only able to pray in this way are missing something vital to a living relationship with God.

Please hear me carefully – I'm not saying that formal, written prayers, are unnecessary or wrong. I personally love some of the great prayers of the Church, prayers that Christians have been saying for hundreds of years, and which are full of profound truth. But if such prayers are not set in the framework of an intimate relationship with God, they can become the sort of dead routine for which Jesus so strongly criticised the Pharisees and religious leaders of His day.

Many of the Psalms are based on the intimate relationship David had with his God. He freely interspersed his expressions of adoration and worship with the intimacy of his own spiritual experiences. The most well-known Psalm of all, Psalm 23, is a wonderful example of how a man of God could talk so naturally and personally about the Lord being his Shepherd. There was nothing dead and formal about these words. They expressed David's personal experience of the God he knew and trusted so well! He was testifying to the reality and the nature of his relationship with God.

Take a few moments to read through those beautiful words of Psalm 23 and see how closely and intimately David had learned to walk with God. I'm sure that David also used more formal words that had become part of prayer and the worship of God in his day, but, if those prayers were outside of a personal relationship with God, would they have had any meaning or be effective?

In Isaiah chapter 1 God expressed His personal pain, because His

PERSONAL NOTES

people did all the right things as prescribed in the Law of God, but their hearts were far from Him. He even went so far as to say that He wouldn't hear their prayers (verse 15)! It's obvious that an intimate relationship with His people really matters to God.

There was an occasion when Jesus was in the streets with His disciples and there were people making a show of their public praying. They would often do this, either in the synagogues, or on street corners – places where everyone could see them. They made a show of their repetitive praying. Jesus pointed them out to the disciples and called them hypocrites (Matthew 6:5).

He said they already had their reward in full (probably the pride – the feeling of how good they thought they were). This means that the prayers themselves were of no value whatsoever! They were of no benefit to them or to others! Then Jesus told the disciples that this wasn't the sort of praying He wanted them to indulge in – He very firmly said, *'don't be like them!'* (Matthew 6:8).

But Jesus didn't just tell His disciples what they shouldn't do. As a wise teacher He also gave them a pattern, a guideline to follow, as they developed their own prayer relationship with God. We call it 'the Lord's Prayer'.

HOW JESUS TAUGHT HIS DISCIPLES TO PRAY

This pattern for praying has been enshrined in the service books of almost every Christian denomination for the past two thousand years. But more often than not, the Church has constantly made use of it in a way which is exactly the opposite of what Jesus intended!

Jesus was trying to move the disciples away from just repeating prayers as the hypocrites were doing. He wanted them to learn something entirely new – a pattern for guiding their prayer life. It was to be an outline for praying which they could use in all the circumstances of life.

In calling this prayer *'the Lord's Prayer'*, we have got it slightly wrong! It wasn't a prayer that the Lord could pray in its entirety – for part of it shows us how to deal with sinfulness and Jesus had never sinned! So it would be more accurate to call this wonderful prayer – *'the Disciples' Prayer'*, for it's a prayer that Jesus intended His disciples throughout

PERSONAL NOTES

history to make their own. But we will continue to use the more familiar *'Lord's Prayer'*, now we have understood just who this prayer was intended for.

If we use the prayer wisely, it will become a life-changing daily experience, helping us to walk forward confidently in God, knowing the reality of His presence and power in our lives. We will be looking at how to apply this prayer in our lives in the following four sections: Adoration and Worship, Kingdom Authority and Trust, Forgiveness and Deliverance and Protection.

ADORATION AND WORSHIP

'Our Father in Heaven, hallowed be Your name.' (Matthew 6:9 NIV)
'Our Father, who art in heaven, hallowed be thy name' (Traditional)

The first part of this pattern for prayer, that Jesus wanted us all to use, is all about worship. It's about recognising God as our Father and that He's holy and that He's the source of everything we are.

In many ways, our services and fellowship meetings have given us a wrong impression of what worship is all about. People talk about having some worship, or ask who's leading the worship, or, say 'we'll have twenty minutes worship'. What people are talking about is singing Christian songs, which of course can be a very blessed and powerful part of our worship relationship with God. But to think that singing Christian songs is the sum total of worship is to miss the heart of what worship really is.

It's sometimes helpful to get a Hebraic insight into the things that we read about in the Bible. In Hebraic tradition everything we do is seen as worship, and every breath we take contributes to a life of worship, because in living the very life God breathed into us, we are giving glory back to Him, our Creator. Therefore, we are always worshipping!

This gives us a huge insight into how to live a godly life. For if we look on everything we do as an expression of worship either of the God who gave us life, and without whom we could do nothing (Acts 17:28, Colossians 1:17), 'or of His enemy, Satan, then that immediately acts as a challenge to our way of life. It should act as a brake on our temptation to sin. For it's impossible to sin against God at the same time as truly worshipping Him!

If we recognise that every breath is a gift from God and, therefore, an act of worship, why would we want to waste our breath on doing something that causes us suffering, and God grief and pain?As we learn to love and adore God as the ultimate source of everything that is good, it changes our attitude to every area of life and opens our eyes to see the whole of creation from a very different perspective.

Every day I consciously look at something God has made and marvel at the creative genius that lies behind this amazing world! That's a form of worship. Today I looked intently at the amazing camouflage pattern on the wings of a moth that strayed into our house. Tomorrow it might be the petals of a rose. And the day after it could be a painting created by an artist using their God-ordained creative gifts.

OUR FATHER...

The first word of *'the Lord's Prayer'* is *OUR* – and that's a plural word. We can't pray this prayer and begin it with the words *'My Father'*! God has created us for relationship, and while God is the ultimate Father of every single one of us, He has also created us to be in relationship with each other. Jesus was drawing our attention to something very important – none of us is an island, separated from the rest of humanity. God is Father to the whole of the human race. We are brothers and sisters with the whole of humanity.

In a family brothers and sisters are defined as being the children of the same parents. And while there's always some friendly rivalry between brothers and sisters, they are, nevertheless, united as siblings by a common and inseparable bond.

Even though my own brother and I were four years apart we were very close to each other. We each knew that whatever happened to us, and wherever in the world we were, if we were in need, then our brotherly relationship and bonding would supersede every other situation. We were brothers, we loved each other and we mattered to each other.

By introducing this prayer with the word, our, Jesus was saying that all of us in this human race are brothers and sisters – for we all have the same Father. Even our enemies have the same Heavenly Father as we do!

PERSONAL NOTES

PERSONAL NOTES

And God wants us to look on every other member of the human race as our brothers and sisters – people who matter to us!

...IN HEAVEN

There are many concepts in Scripture that are hard for us to understand. We read, for example, that we can never escape from God's presence (Psalm 139:7-12), which means that there's nowhere I could go in all of creation where God is not present – even in this fallen, sinful world. At the same time Jesus tells us that Our Father is in Heaven, where there can never be any stain of sinfulness. There can't be any overlap between the fallen sinfulness of the physical realms (over which man was given dominion) and the holiness of the heavenly realms in which God resides. Yet God is always there for us, wherever we are – in Heaven or on Earth.

As a true Father, God is always there for His children. He is close enough to hear the faintest cry of the human heart that cries out to Him, at the same time as residing in the holiness of Heaven's eternal realm. There, Father God and Jesus the Son await the end of the ages, when Jesus shall come again to reign on earth and then take His Church home to be with Him in Heaven for eternity.

For now, I'm content to appreciate the mystery from a distance, knowing that at the present time we're looking at these things as a poor reflection in a darkened mirror. But one day all will be made clear (1 Corinthians 13:12).

HALLOWED BE YOUR NAME

The very name of God is holy. In Jewish tradition the name is so holy that it would be an offence to even print it on paper, and so the name is never fully written down. We don't worship the name of God, but we do worship the God whose name is holy and we do honour and respect His name. We worship Him by honouring His name – not just by saying that we honour it, but by the way we live our lives.

Christians, as the people of God, are the representatives of the living God in this fallen world. We serve Jesus as the King of our lives. What we do, therefore, really matters, for as the King's representatives, His name is written on our hearts. We belong to Him (Jeremiah 31:33).

PERSONAL NOTES

We are identifiable as citizens of the Kingdom of Heaven. We may not be wearing a uniform, like members of the Salvation Army do, but Scripture does urge us to be clothed in righteousness (Romans 3:22, Isaiah 61:10 & Ephesians 6:14) – that should be the uniform of the disciples of Jesus. Charles Wesley expressed this thought perfectly in the final verse of his great hymn *'And Can it Be'*, perhaps the most well-known of all Wesley's hymns:

No condemnation now I dread; Jesus, and all in Him, is mine! Alive in Him, my living Head, and ***clothed in righteousness divine****, Bold I approach the eternal throne, and claim the crown, through Christ my own.*

If someone is wearing a uniform, identifying himself as a member of a particular organisation, and then commits some crime or does something morally indefensible, the individual will not only carry personal responsibility for what he does, but also be responsible for damaging the name and reputation of the organisation he belongs to.

In just the same way, when Jesus' representatives fall into sin, they not only have personal accountability for what they have done, but they are responsible for the shame that has been brought to the Name of God and the Body of Christ as a result. His Name has been dishonoured by our behaviour.

Conversely, we honour and hallow the name of God when we choose to walk in holiness. Scripture puts it this way, *'Just as He who called you is holy, so be holy in all you do'* (1 Peter 1:15). We hallow His name by walking in holiness, not by saying the words *'hallowed be your name'*. Hallowing the name of God is a way of life, not just a group of words that are part of *'the Lord's Prayer'*. So, as we use the prayer we ought to be thinking about whether or not our life is honouring to God.

OTHER NAMES OF GOD

There are many other names used to describe the nature and character of God in Scripture. Names such as Jehovah-Jireh (God my Provider), Jehovah-Rapha (God my Healer), Jehova-Rohi (God my Shepherd), Jehova-Tsidkenu (God my Righteousness) and El-Shaddai (God Almighty). All of these, and many more, are like different facets of a

PERSONAL NOTES

diamond. Each one gives a different insight into God Himself. Each one sheds more light on the glory of God.

The more we learn about the nature and character of God, the more we will love Him, and the more we will want to honour His name. We won't want to allow our behaviour to discredit the organisation which we belong to – the Church.

The Church is the family of God, the Body of Christ here on earth (1 Corinthians 12:27), the people of God who are called out of darkness into His glorious light (1 Peter 2:9).

AND FINALLY

Journey to Freedom is not designed to give people more information. It's designed to be a series of practical steps helping each one of us to walk in the ways of God for the rest of our lives. So, as a practical step forward, may I encourage you to ask the Holy Spirit to shine the light of truth into any areas of your life which could be seen as dishonouring to the name of God. When we're aware of a problem we can do something about it!

SUMMARY

The prayer Jesus taught His disciples to pray was not meant to be just repeated without understanding, but to be lived as a day to day experience of intimate relationship with the living God. We truly worship God and honour His name by choosing to walk in His ways because we love Him.

PRAYER

Lord, I thank You that I'm a member of the most wonderful family in the world – the Body of Christ. I acknowledge You as my Lord and choose to honour Your name and to worship You through walking in obedience to Your call on my life for the rest of my days. In Jesus' name, Amen.

Stage 4, Chapter 3

THE LORD'S PRAYER – KINGDOM AUTHORITY AND TRUST

'Your Kingdom come, Your will be done, on earth as it is in heaven' (Matthew 6:10)

PERSONAL NOTES

I first learnt *'the Lord's Prayer'* as a child. On my bedroom wall was a wonderful picture of Jesus looking out over Jerusalem. I would often look at that picture and somehow I knew, in a childlike but certain way, that I could really trust Jesus. He wasn't just a picture on a wall, He was real, alive and He loved me!

At night I would kneel and say my prayers with my mother or my father. Always, my simple prayers were concluded by us saying together *'Our Father'*. I knew that this was what Jesus taught us to pray. And the main prayers, at almost every church service I ever went to, were neatly rounded up by everyone saying *'the prayer that Jesus taught us'*. It didn't matter whether the service was in an Anglican Church, a Presbyterian Church, a Baptist, a Methodist or a Brethren one! *'The Lord's Prayer'* has truly entered into the spiritual culture of all the traditional churches.

It was only in my teenage years, however, that I stopped to think about what the words of *'the Lord's Prayer'* might actually mean. I read a wonderful

PERSONAL NOTES

book by G.A.Studdert Kennedy, an amazing army chaplain from the First World War. He had learned how precious and important this prayer was while caring for soldiers in extreme life and death battle situations! In his book, *The Wicket Gate*, he took people through his understanding of the various phrases of the prayer – it opened a window on Heaven for me.

Until then, I just knew the prayer as *'the Lord's Prayer'*, without having any deeper understanding of how Jesus wanted the disciples to pray. But since then, each time I have been prompted to study the prayer again, it's as if there has been endless treasure to dig out from a rich mine of truth!

YOUR KINGDOM COME

Albert Schweitzer, a missionary Doctor who founded the world famous Lambarene Hospital in Gabon (formerly French Equatorial Africa), said *"There can be no Kingdom of God in the world, without the Kingdom of God being in our hearts"*.

Schweitzer had truly grasped a vital, foundational truth. It determined how he spent his most remarkable life. Because man had originally been given authority by God over the world, it's only through man that God's Kingdom authority can be exercised on the Earth.

The world, however, had become full of evil, because man's earthly authority had been given over to the evil one and the Kingdom of darkness reigned. As a result, the only way the Kingdom of God could now be established in the world was through the higher authority of the Kingdom of Heaven being established in the hearts of the followers of the King while they lived on planet Earth.

That way, wherever God's people **ARE**, the Kingdom of God **IS**! This is exactly what Jesus meant when He said to some of His disciples, *'Tell the people that the Kingdom of God has come near you'* (Luke 10:9).

But what, in practical terms, does this actually mean? When we look carefully at the four Gospels we discover that each one has a different emphasis. John's Gospel, for example, is clearly the ***Gospel of the Evangelist***. But Matthew's Gospel has always been known as the ***Gospel of the Kingdom***. For it is full of references to the Kingdom of God or the Kingdom of Heaven.

Jesus tells us in *'the Lord's Prayer'* that Father God lives in Heaven, so it doesn't really matter whether we talk about the Kingdom of God or the

Kingdom of Heaven – it means the same thing. **It is the Kingdom established by the living God which is administered from His home in Heaven.**

A Kingdom is only a Kingdom if it has a King. The King of the Kingdom of Heaven is Jesus. The Bible refers to Him as *'King of Kings'* (Revelation 17:14). Just before Jesus began His work, John the Baptist, the last of the Old Testament prophets, told the people to *'repent, for the Kingdom of Heaven is near'* (Matthew 3:2) – meaning that the King of Heaven was about to begin His ministry on Earth. And when Jesus began His teaching ministry, He used exactly the same words (Matthew 4:17).

Throughout Matthew's Gospel, Jesus tells many different parables – most of which begin with words such as, *'The Kingdom of Heaven is like...'* In these parables Jesus used many different pictures to help His hearers discover the truth about God's Kingdom. Parables which began with *'the Kingdom of Heaven is like a man who sowed good seed in his field' (Matthew 13:24)*, or *'like a grain of mustard seed' (Matthew 13:31)*, or *'like treasure hidden in a field' (Matthew 13:44)*, or *'like a merchant looking for fine pearls' (Matthew 13:45)*, or *'like a net let down into the lake' (Matthew 13:47)*, or a number of other equally graphic illustrations.

It's clear from all these parables that the concept of the Kingdom of God was very important to Jesus – and that He wanted His followers to understand it also. For, in Luke 9:1-2, when Jesus sent His own disciples out to do the same sort of work that He had been doing, He said to them, *'preach the Kingdom of God'*.

At the same time He gave them His power and His authority to *'drive out all demons and to cure diseases'*. There is obviously, therefore, a strong link between the disciples needing to have Jesus' power and authority and His instruction to them to preach about the Kingdom of God.

KINGDOM PRAYING

So when the followers of Jesus pray the words *'Your Kingdom come, on earth, as it is in Heaven'*. What are they actually praying for?

Some people think this is a prayer that's looking forward to the second coming of Jesus, when Jesus will reign on planet Earth for a thousand years (Revelation 20:4), a period of time known as the Millennial Reign. Such a prayer might sound something like this, *'O Lord, things are so bad here on earth, that we can't survive much longer without you, We'd love to see*

PERSONAL NOTES

PERSONAL NOTES

life on earth be like it is in Heaven. So please, Lord, come again soon and set up your Kingdom here on earth!'

The problem with such an interpretation of the prayer is that at the time Jesus gave *'the Lord's Prayer'* to His disciples, they hadn't even understood that Jesus was going to die on the cross and be raised again from the dead. They hadn't received any teaching about how Jesus would ascend to Heaven and afterwards would come again to Earth! They were only at the beginning of their learning experience about eternal truths!

No, this is not a prayer about the second coming. Above all Jesus intended it to be a prayer of immediate relevance and importance to His disciples. Jesus was also giving the whole of Church, for the whole of time, an important pattern for their regular daily praying and living.

But Jesus himself DID know that one day soon He would be returning to Heaven. He also knew that God had originally given authority (dominionship) on planet Earth to mankind (Genesis 1:26-28). So He knew, also, that the only way the Kingdom of Heaven could come on earth would be through men and women, as Albert Schweitzer had so rightfully concluded. The authority of the King of Kings would first of all have to be established in their lives through relationship with Him.

Because Jesus delegated His power and authority to the disciples, they were able to do the works of Jesus, including giving commands to the demons. Whenever mankind exercises the authority of Jesus over the works of darkness in this way today, then he can also establish Kingdom authority here on earth in the name of Jesus, wherever he goes *(Matthew 16:19)*.

When Jesus told the disciples to tell people that the Kingdom of God had come near them, He was simply saying that whenever Kingdom authority is established, the Kingdom of God exists there and then. So if we have invited Jesus to be Lord and King in our lives, then that is where the Kingdom of God is – right there! Wherever the reign of the King is established, the Kingdom of God is established also.

When Jesus is Lord of our family, our home, our church, our place of work, our business and even our nation, the Kingdom of God is established in these places here on Earth. Within this Kingdom, the disciples of the King will be at peace with God and with each other. Others will then have the opportunity of being introduced to the King and of entering the Kingdom of God for themselves.

PERSONAL NOTES

However, this can't be regarded as a permanent state of affairs. The position of authority is only maintained when God's Kingdom people maintain their stand as disciples of Jesus. The god of this world will continually try to undermine them and win back the ground.

As a result of the fall we have to contend with the weeds that grow up in the ground and pose a threat to the plants we want to nurture (Genesis 3:17 and 18). No-one has to plant those weeds! And unless we make an effort to remove them from our garden, they will very quickly claim back the territory as their own!

In just the same way, the enemy will claim back territory that mankind allows him to take. This happens if God's people move away from a place where they formerly lived and worked, give up the struggle for holiness and godly order in their lives, or cease to exercise Kingdom authority in the places they are responsible for. That's why there's so much in Paul's epistles about the need for perseverance and endurance! And that's why we need to keep on praying throughout our lives *'Your Kingdom come'*!

Just over a hundred years ago the valleys of Wales were alive with the songs of believers as revival swept through the nation. Thousands of people were born again, hundreds of Chapels were built and the glory of God came down. But there was little perseverance in discipling the believers and holding the ground that had been won for the Kingdom of God. And a movement which nevertheless bore amazing fruit in many other parts of the world, including Korea, as quickly died back to virtually nothing in the very place which gave it birth. The enemy had claimed back the ground.

SO, WHAT DOES THIS PRAYER MEAN FOR ME?

When we pray *'Your Kingdom come, your will be done, on earth, as it is in heaven'* what we're really praying is this: *"Lord, help me to live day by day, having the strength of will and purpose to choose to do your will in every area of my life. That way, I know your Kingdom will be established in my life, and in everything I'm responsible for."*

This is not a passive prayer. After praying it we can't just sit back and wait for God to act! It's a very active prayer, requiring our full participation in the ongoing will and purposes of God. No wonder Paul encouraged his readers to take every thought captive and make it obedient to Christ! (2 Corinthians 10:5).

PERSONAL NOTES

Paul knew that if our thought life could be brought under the Lordship of Jesus, then our actions would also be godly and God's Kingdom purposes would become the norm for our lives. There's no doubt that if we choose to walk in godliness, even though it may be hard, we may encounter the roaring lion that Peter describes the devil to be (1 Peter 5:8), but God will strengthen us by the power of His Spirit to do His will and to be overcomers.

Earlier I mentioned Albert Schweitzer. He was a great man – a great theologian, a great musician and a great physician. He could have had the world's adulation in any one of those career disciplines. Instead he chose to be obedient to the will of God for his life, and sacrificed all his time in building and running a mission hospital for the desperately poor and needy in West Africa (Isaiah 58:6-12).

There's no doubt that he knew the joy of seeing the Kingdom of God established on earth, and in his place of service he lived a very full life for more than 90 years! This is what he said to others who visited him, *"I don't know what your destiny will be, but one thing I do know: the only ones among you who will be really happy are those who have sought and found how to serve."*

It's only in finding and doing the will of God for our lives that we enter into our destiny and build God's Kingdom. So let's pray, with renewed endeavour, *'Your Kingdom come – in all of my life and in everything I do.'*

You may find it helpful to make a list of all the different things that your life consists of – such as personal dreams and ambitions, home, family, relationships, private thoughts, hobbies and recreation, church life, work, finances, public life etc – and then spend time bringing each of these areas before the Lord, asking yourself if you have established His Kingdom authority in those places. This will give you clear guidelines for using *'the Lord's Prayer'* to initiate a life-transforming effect on everything you are and everything you do. And isn't that what our journey is all about? Letting God transform our lives from the inside out!

TRUSTING GOD FOR 'OUR DAILY BREAD'

'Give us today our daily bread' (Matthew 6:11)

In many of the things Jesus said there's both a natural and a spiritual meaning. To understand this we often need to look at different scriptures, so that one scripture can provide understanding about another. When the children of Israel were wandering in the desert and unable to farm the land, God continually fed them supernaturally – every day (except on the Sabbath) He gave them manna, the bread of Heaven, fresh on the ground, daily (Exodus 16:35). For forty years God never forgot the daily physical needs of His children.

In a similar way, Jesus provided bread and fish for the five thousand, as He blessed the boy's five loaves and two fish. As the disciples distributed the little in their hands, they found that it multiplied as they gave it away – so much so that there were twelve baskets full of leftovers! (Luke 9:10-17).

Everyone knows that physical bread is a basic food and is essential for physical life. But on other occasions Jesus used the image of bread as a picture of the spiritual food which is also essential for daily life.

In John 6:35 He referred to Himself as the Bread of Life, and said, *'He who comes to me will never go hungry, and He who believes in me will never go thirsty.'* When He was talking to the woman at the well (John 4:1-26) He said that *'whoever drinks the water I give him will never thirst… it will become in him a spring of water welling up to eternal life.'*

In these passages, Jesus is referring to the lifelong spiritual sustenance of our inner being. Without this we would never be able to be part of the answer to the previous part of the prayer – *'May your Kingdom come'*.

It's clear, therefore, that Jesus is concerned for both our physical and our spiritual needs and that when He encourages His disciples to pray for their daily bread in *'the Lord's Prayer'*. He's referring to the supply of the essential basics of life – both physical and spiritual.

He's not referring to all the things that we might want or might like to have. Not that it's wrong to want things beyond our basic needs. God gave us the whole world and everything in it to enjoy! But when it comes down to the essential basics of life Jesus is encouraging us to cry out to trust Him and cry out to Father God to show us how He can meet those needs.

PERSONAL NOTES

THE DIVINE LAW OF GOD'S PROVISION

I believe that when we choose to walk in relationship with God in loving obedience, with Jesus as our Lord, we will discover that there's a divine

PERSONAL NOTES

law in place. Whenever we draw on Jesus for the living bread and the water of life to meet our spiritual needs, then the blessings that flow from our relationship with Him will overflow into the physical realm. Then we will start seeing God meeting our physical needs in ways that may surprise us.

This principle is at the heart of the blessings promised in Deuteronomy 28 to those who walk in obedience to the Covenant provisions of a loving God. When we walk forward with clean hearts we're in the best place for God to bless the works of our hands. Then, as a result, we'll know His extraordinary provision for doing the Kingdom works that we were made for!

I can testify to the truth of this principle through personal experience. When I was in the business environment, as a publisher and bookseller, before the work of Ellel Ministries began, the most profitable projects were always those that developed from ideas which arose supernaturally. Things would just *'happen'*, which were beyond the obvious. Ideas or dreams would seemingly come from nowhere. When I followed up those *'supernatural'* ideas, it was as if God had gone before me and prepared the way. He truly is the best businessman!

The Apostle Paul summed up his life of service of God, with a statement of faith based on his extraordinary experiences of God's provision, *'My God will meet all your needs, according to His glorious riches in Christ Jesus'* (Philippians 4:19). Amen!

SUMMARY

Giving Jesus His rightful place as Lord of our lives, is the most important step we can take towards ensuring that the Kingdom of God will be firmly established in and through everything we are and everything we do. God rejoices to meet our physical and spiritual needs for 'daily bread' as we choose to love and serve Him.

PRAYER

Lord, I want to walk in Your ways and do Your will in my life. Thank You for showing me that as I choose to make You Lord of each area of my life, that this releases Your power, authority and provision into everything I do. That's how I want to live for You. In Jesus' Name, Amen.

Stage 4, Chapter 4

THE LORD'S PRAYER – FORGIVENESS

'Forgive us our debts, as we also have forgiven our debtors' (Matt 6:12 NIV)

'Forgive us our trespasses, as we forgive those who trespass against us' (traditional ancient version of the prayer used in churches throughout history)

'Forgive us our sins, for we also forgive everyone who sins against us' (Luke 11:4 NIV*)*

PERSONAL NOTES

TAKING THAT DEEP BREATH!

You may like to take a deep breath before considering the next part of *'the Lord's Prayer'*. The reason I said that should be obvious! We all desperately need to know that our sins have been forgiven by God. But in this prayer Jesus links the forgiveness of our own sins, to whether we have also forgiven those who have sinned against us! And, for some people, this is a huge difficulty.

PERSONAL NOTES

For, in praying with thousands of people over many, many years of ministry, the largest single obstacle I have found to people knowing the healing and restoring power of God is their un-forgiveness of others who have hurt them! Don't worry that Luke's version of the Lord's Prayer refers to *'Forgive us our sins'*, whereas Matthew's version says, *'Forgive us our debts'*. The meaning is just the same. Matthew makes it abundantly clear that Jesus emphasised the need to forgive others for their sins by saying: *'For if you forgive men when they sin against you, your Heavenly Father will also forgive you. But if you do not forgive men their sins, your father will not forgive your sins'* (Matthew 6;14-15).

So there you have it, straight from the mouth of Jesus – if you don't forgive others, then God won't forgive you! If we're honest, those are words that none of us really want to hear. For when other people have hurt us, we instinctively rise up in self-defence and justify our reactions with thoughts such as *'they don't deserve to be forgiven'*! And that's true – they don't deserve to be forgiven.

But, my friend, neither do you or I deserve to be forgiven. Forgiveness is not a matter of whether we deserve it or not – it's a matter of grace and mercy, motivated by love.

BUT JESUS... YOU DON'T UNDERSTAND... IT'S SO HARD!

It's so easy to start arguing with Jesus about having to forgive others! And the arguments can seem so sensible.

Just look at what they've done to me – why should they get off? Why should I suffer for what they've done and then forgive them as if it doesn't matter? They've ruined my life. It's not fair! Surely, Lord, my situation is much worse than anyone else's?

But then our mind turns to that scene at Calvary. Jesus, the totally sinless Son of God, is being nailed to a wooden cross for something He's never done, and from His lips come these words, *'Father, forgive them, they don't know what they are doing'* (Luke 23:34). Our arguments melt away into insignificance when we think about what He did for us.

Recently I visited Rwanda, in Central Africa. In 1994 there was a terrible genocide in Rwanda, when about a million Tutsi people were massacred by the Hutus. On this trip it was wonderful to spend time with people from both sides of that terrible conflict, and see how God is rebuilding the nation through forgiveness and reconciliation.

One of the people who suffered greatly in the genocide was a fourteen year old girl called Frida. All of her family were killed on the same day and she was buried with them all. But, miraculously, the heavy blow to her head hadn't actually killed her and she was still alive fourteen hours later, when she was dug out of the grave. Her suffering was terrible.

A few years later she became a Christian and her life was totally transformed. It was then, as she read her Bible, that she understood Jesus was asking her to forgive the people who had done these terrible things. The man who killed her father was now in prison, so she went to the jail to speak forgiveness to him.

It was this act of obedience to Jesus that opened the door to her healing. Twelve years after her terrible ordeal, at Ellel Grange on a nine week training school, she was physically healed of the constant head pains and nightmares that had been a result of her terrible experience. Forgiveness opened the door to both healing and restoration.

Forgiveness didn't change Frida's history, but it did change her future. It meant that Frida would be able to live the rest of her life, without being in the chains of bondage that un-forgiveness ties round so many hearts.

It isn't true to say that Jesus doesn't understand our own situations. He not only understands, but He has walked through the ultimate forgiveness test himself – forgiving those who were taking His life, for something He hadn't done. Jesus helped Frida walk a similar pathway – a journey that she will never regret.

I once prayed with a lady who had been bitter for thirty years, because of what cruel people had done to her. She had vowed never to forgive them. But the consequence in her life was a steadily deteriorating physical condition that was slowly eating her life away. In just the same way bitterness was eating her heart away.

She wanted prayer for her physical condition, but forgiving those who had hurt her was not on her original agenda with God! She was quite angry when I taught about the need to forgive on the first session of her Healing Retreat. But it was only when she chose to forgive that the power of God was released into her life. She then received major physical healing for the condition that had formerly crippled her.

PERSONAL NOTES

PERSONAL NOTES

SO WHY MUST I FORGIVE OTHERS?

It's clear from *'the Lord's Prayer'* that for disciples of Jesus forgiveness has to be a way of life. But it's not easy and even Simon Peter struggled with the teaching and challenged Jesus with a question we could all have asked. *'How often do I need to forgive my brother, Lord? Seven times?'* (Read the whole story in Matthew 18:21-35).

Jesus' reply must have shaken Simon, for what he heard coming from Jesus' lips was, *'Not seven times, Simon, but seventy times seven!'* That's a Jewish phrase which means *'don't even start counting, there's no limit.'*

Jesus knew that if He set a certain number of times that we would have to forgive, we would simply store up all our venom and hatred and let it all out on, say, the eighth time. The fallen heart of man can't be trusted!

Also, if there was a limit to the number of times that we have to forgive other people for what they do to us, then there could also be a limit on the number of times that God would forgive us. And that's something none of us would want to contemplate.

While the people who are forgiven will certainly be blessed by our actions, the primary reason Jesus wanted us to forgive others was that our own hearts would be free of the bondage that un-forgiveness locks us into. We need to release people from the hook tying them to us and place them firmly into the Lord's hands for Him to deal with.

There is no doubt that un-forgiveness and bitterness is a primary source of stress, pain and, on occasions, physical sickness. Even the medical profession recognises this fact. For example, some doctors say that those who are bitter and unforgiving are more likely to suffer from conditions such as arthritis.

FORGIVENESS AND TRUST

I am sometimes asked whether forgiveness of others means I have to trust the people I've forgiven. The answer is a clear 'No'. Once trust has been broken it takes time for it to be restored again. The person who has harmed me needs to prove that it's safe for me to trust them again in the future. I need to know that I will be respected and not taken advantage of.

However, there are some areas of sin, such as sexual abuse, which mean that an offender should *never* be trusted again with the lives of vulnerable people. This is for their own sake as well as for everybody else's. It is not right that through misplaced trust, they should ever be released back into a similar area of responsibility and temptation.

PERSONAL NOTES

FORGIVENESS AND JUSTICE

Some people don't want to forgive because they see it as excusing the person from any responsibility and accountability for what they have done. But forgiveness is nothing whatsoever to do with escaping justice!

If a burglar broke into my house and stole things that were precious to me, I would, of course, be upset and angry. But I would forgive the person who did it, because I wouldn't want to remain in bondage to un-forgiveness. Despite forgiving the person who had done it, I would still want the burglar brought to justice. He broke the law of the land and should pay the price for what he has done.

Forgiveness releases me from the consequences of bitterness. It doesn't release the burglar from the requirements of justice. I know some people have found it too hard to forgive, especially those who have suffered the kind of terrible things that went on in places like Rwanda. They thought that if they forgave someone, it also meant they had to allow that person to escape all the consequences for what they had done. That is not the case.

The sin of mankind separated the human race from a holy God. We inherited the death sentence. The death of Jesus on the cross was an outworking of justice. The price of death was paid – but by a sinless man who couldn't be held beneath the waters of death. Justice was required and justice was carried out. God's desire for us was to be forgiven and restored to a right relationship with Him, but this didn't mean that the requirements of justice could be avoided. God's Son, Jesus, made a way back to God for each one of us who chooses to receive Him as our Saviour.

SO, BACK TO 'THE LORD'S PRAYER'!

So why did Jesus include a commitment for us to forgive others in a prayer for God to forgive us? He was simply applying what is often

PERSONAL NOTES

referred to as the golden rule – *'do to others as you would have them do to you'* (Luke 6:31).

We all want God to forgive us for the things we have done wrong, the things that are contrary to the Law of God. Jesus is simply saying, if that is how you want God to treat you, then the attitude of your own heart towards those who have sinned against you determines whether or not God is able to answer that prayer.

The greatest blessing that any of us can ever experience, is having our sins forgiven – both in time and eternity. Nothing releases the power of God more immediately or more effectively into our lives, than receiving His forgiveness. The cleansing flow of forgiveness from the heart of God truly washes away our sin and makes healing possible in our lives. And the flow of blessing starts when we forgive others.

When we forgive others we are releasing them from our concern solely into the hands of God, to whom we will all have to give an account – and He is the only truly righteous and merciful judge!

UNFORGIVENESS AND THE NEED FOR HEALING

Few of us stop to think, when we are being bitter and unforgiving, how deep and dangerous are the consequences of ongoing un-forgiveness – especially when tied to bitterness, anger and a desire for revenge.

These are Satan's weapons and when we use them against others, they rebound upon us. It has the effect of opening the door of our lives to the work of the enemy. No wonder Paul warned us about not giving a foothold to the enemy (Ephesians 4:27).

When the door of un-forgiveness is left open, the consequences can spread much further than our feelings. For it sometimes happens (quite often, in fact) that our body begins to reflect the bitterness in our soul and there are physical consequences. How do I know that? Because of the large number of people I have seen get physically healed when they have chosen to forgive, and they've asked Jesus to set them free from all the consequences of their un-forgiveness.

I've met many people who have been abused, injured in accidents, unjustly accused, betrayed, taken into ungodly relationships or suffered the pain of rejection – some people were disabled, either physically or psychologically, some were victims of accidents and other people's carelessness.

PERSONAL NOTES

Most came for prayer because of the symptoms they were experiencing – everything from depression through to major physical conditions, but there was one pathway on their road to healing that none could avoid treading – the pathway of forgiveness. Whatever the root of their problem, as they forgave those who had hurt them, the power of God to heal and deliver was released into their life. Each personal story is a miracle of God's amazing grace.

I will never forget teaching on forgiveness at our first major conference in Hungary in June 1991. During that very week, the last of the Russian occupying forces were leaving the country. The people were so crushed by the loss of freedom and direct oppression from the occupying forces, that many of them showed the signs of that crushing in their bodies, and in the way that they walked. As I looked at the hundreds of people present, my heart went out to them and I longed to see them released from their bondage and begin to walk tall again as a free people

There was only one way forward, and I knew I would be walking on sensitive ground when I talked to the people about choosing to forgive their Russian oppressors. They had all been brought up in the control of the communist system. Many had been treated very cruelly, much of their property had been stolen and even their very identity as human beings had been taken from them. Forgiveness of the Russians was not something they really wanted to think about.

But as I taught from the Word of God, it was clear that the people were understanding the message of *'the Lord's Prayer'*. If they really wanted to know the release of God's love and power into their lives, they desperately needed to express their forgiveness to their Russian oppressors. Very tentatively, I took them through a prayer of forgiveness, inviting them all to say the prayer with me in their own language. As I did so, I was praying that the Holy Spirit would begin to touch their lives. He did!

After they had all prayed the prayer, I then prayed for them. I asked that God would release them from the spiritual chains of oppression, and set them free from the control of their spiritual enemy. I had no idea what would happen next. None of us could have anticipated how the power of God would come down on all those wonderful people.

Many were being delivered from the evil one (the next phrase we will look at *in 'the Lord's Prayer'*) and then I prayed for physical healing as our

PERSONAL NOTES

large ministry team mingled with the people, praying for them one by one and anointing them with oil for healing.

It was a totally unforgettable sight. The Shepherd of the sheep was moving amongst His flock healing, delivering and restoring them. About 75% of those present confirmed later in the conference that they had been healed of back problems as a result. It was totally extraordinary! God really was setting the captives free. Before our very eyes we were seeing the fruit of what Jesus was teaching in *'the Lord's Prayer'*. What happened that day was truly miraculous.

Since then there have been many such days – either when teaching a crowd or when ministering to the needs of an individual. I now know from experience that Jesus knew exactly what He was doing when He included the need to forgive others within the framework of the Lord's Prayer.

WHAT SHOULD I DO?

We are now seeing in a very practical way why Jesus didn't want us to repeat prayers without living them! We cannot truly pray the Lord's prayer without being challenged about the need to forgive others. But it is only as we do it that we fulfil the conditions for our own forgiveness.

And I know it's hard! To forgive others goes against all the natural desires of the flesh. We certainly discover the carnal nature when we choose to follow Jesus – it opposes everything godly in our lives, just like the weeds in our garden oppose the growth of the plants and vegetables we are trying to nurture. The enemy does not want us to forgive, as that releases us from his control. Sometimes we feel able to make a choice to forgive in our mind and with our will, but our emotions take a long time to catch up with our choice.

My strong recommendation would be that you spend a quiet moment thinking back through your life and really praying this section of *'the Lord's Prayer'*. Have a piece of paper handy and ask God to show you the names of all the people who have hurt you in the past. Go back in your memory as far as you are able – even to early childhood.

Write down the names of everyone who has hurt you on your piece of paper. Some of you may finish up with quite a list! Then take those names, one by one, think about what was done and then *ask God to help you by the enabling power of His Holy Spirit to* speak out your forgiveness. Finally, *again by the enabling power of the Holy Spirit,* release each person on your list into the freedom of your forgiveness and ask Jesus to set you free from all the consequences of un-forgiveness there have been in your life. You will be amazed at what God begins to do in your life as He lifts the burden that the enemy has put upon you.

And once you have brought your forgiveness up to date – dealt with everything you know of from the past – then, perhaps, at the end of each day in the future, you could think back over the previous twenty four hours and speak out your forgiveness to anyone who, on that day, has offended you in any way.

Keeping our hearts clean like this on a daily basis is a precious discipline which will always equip us for living the life of a disciple of Jesus Christ.

PERSONAL NOTES

MORE READING

You can read much more about the importance of forgiveness in my book ***Forgiveness – God's Master Key*** available on the Sovereign World website at www.sovereignworld.com.

SUMMARY

Jesus linked the forgiveness of our own sins to our willingness to forgive others. If we don't forgive those who have hurt us, then we lock ourselves in a prison of our own making. Turning the key of forgiveness is the only way out of the jail.

PRAYER

Thank You, Jesus, for dying on the cross for me, so that I might be forgiven. Help me to forgive all those in my past who have hurt me and then to keep my forgiveness of others up to date on a daily basis, so that I may never again be in bondage to the enemy through un-forgiveness. In Jesus' Name, Amen.

Stage 4, Chapter 5

THE LORD'S PRAYER – CRYING OUT TO GOD

'And lead us not into temptation, but deliver us from evil. For Thine is the Kingdom, the power and the glory, forever. Amen' Matthew 6:13 (KJV and *traditional version of 'the Lord's Prayer')*

'And lead us not into temptation, but deliver us from the evil one' Matthew 6:13 (NIV)

The traditional version of this amazing prayer ends with a glorious statement of truth which simply underlines everything that has gone before about Kingdom authority, and the fact that every single thing we know of on this planet has its source in the presence and the glory of God.

We mustn't let the absence of this statement from some modern translations of the Bible rob us of the joy of affirming the glorious truth of the Gospel in this way, as it has been done by the church since the very earliest times.

PERSONAL NOTES

PERSONAL NOTES

A CRY FROM THE DEPTHS

But before we reach that glorious climax to the traditional prayer, there is an extremely important petition, which cries out to God from the very depths of fallen humanity. It's a cry that keeps us in touch with the spiritual reality of living in a fallen world – a world that has Satan as its god till Jesus comes again *(2 Corinthians 4:4)*.

For, as we have now well-established together, there is an unending war on for the souls of men. And temptation is the primary weapon Satan uses to seduce us from the highway of holiness (Isaiah 35:8).

It must be obvious to all that for God to be true to Himself, He can't encourage us to walk in righteousness without also wanting to protect us from wrong choices that would lead us into unrighteousness. But therein lies God's dilemma! He has given us free will. And for us to enjoy His protection we must want to have it and ask Him for it. Otherwise God would have to go *against* our free will in providing us with His protection. To do that would be contrary to His creative order for the human race.

If we didn't have free will, we couldn't have a relationship of love with our Creator. But having free will puts us in constant danger of succumbing to temptation and grieving the God who loves us so much. This is the reason that we need to constantly desire the Lord's protection from the wiles of the evil one, for ourselves and also for those whom God has placed under our direct covering for spiritual protection. This would especially apply to our children and our children's children.

Psalm 91 speaks of the shelter and protection that God wants His children to enjoy – but the fulfilment of those wonderful promises is incumbent on us choosing *'to dwell in the shelter of the Most High'* (Psalm 91:1). The promises don't apply to those who would want to live outside the covering of God. This clearly indicates that we have to take an active role in securing God's protection for our lives. If we do our part then God is able to do His part!

DOES GOD TEMPT US TO SIN?

The phrase *'lead us not into temptation'* might be interpreted to mean that God could be the source of temptation. This is clearly one of those statements from scripture, where we need clarification from another scripture. We find the answer in James 1:13:

PERSONAL NOTES

'When tempted, no-one should say, "God is tempting me." For God cannot be tempted by evil, nor does He tempt anyone.'

Nothing could be clearer than this statement, which might even have been written by James to clear up questions people were asking about the meaning of *'the Lord's Prayer'*! God can never be the source of temptation. So what does this phrase from *'the Lord's Prayer'* about temptation actually mean?

Let's read the next verse from James chapter 1 as well:

'But each one is tempted when, by his own evil desire, he is dragged away and enticed.'

So temptation is enticement from the enemy to do those things which arise from the evil desires which are inherent in our fallen, carnal nature. That is not God's heart desire, so God Himself can never be the source of either the evil desire for sin (from a carnal nature) or the enticement (the temptation which comes from the evil one).

SO, WHAT DOES THE PRAYER MEAN?

Let me answer this question with a story from my own experience. When I was nineteen I sailed alone round Africa. I wanted to explore my own heritage and roots in that most amazing of continents. So, with some money left to me by *Ouma*, my South African grandmother, I bought a ticket on a ship of the Union Castle Line. I was also an innocent young man, growing up with all the normal desires of the flesh and could have been quite vulnerable to a variety of temptations.

I know my parents were praying for me – probably harder than I realised at the time and every day! And saying *'the Lord's Prayer'* was part of my own daily devotions. While the desires of my flesh might have been saying one thing, I had no desire in my spirit to succumb to ungodly temptations, which I knew I would regret for the rest of my days.

I boarded my ship, the *Stirling Castle*, at Southampton, fully aware that life on board an ocean liner was potentially full of temptations. I was to share a cabin with two other men, but I had no idea who they would be. I was first in the cabin and took the top bunk. The next guy came shortly

PERSONAL NOTES

after that and just before sailing time, the door of the cabin was slowly pushed open by our third companion, a very elderly man.

I looked down from my top bunk and was both shocked and pleased when he looked up at me and revealed the clerical collar around his neck! I was shocked, because I instantly knew that the very presence of this man would be a godly check on all that I might have wanted to do on the ship; and I was pleased because in my spirit I was rejoicing that I was to share the cabin with a fellow believer and God was answering my prayer.

His name was Rev.Dr.Ennals. He was ninety five years old and even though seventy-six years divided us, we had a unity that transcended age. The following Sunday morning, just south of the Bay of Biscay, Dr.Ennals led an evangelistic service on the deck of the ship and I played the piano! God had ensured that my personal colours were now carefully nailed to the mast of the Gospel throughout that thirteen day voyage!

There were several hundred passengers on board. The Rev.Dr.Ennals was, to my knowledge, the only clergyman on the ship. I am certain that whoever was responsible for making the cabin allocations was guided by the hand of God. The prayer *'lead us not into temptation'* had been remarkably answered (whether in answer to my parent's or my own prayers I'll never know). But I did know that there was no way during that voyage that I could let the temptations of the flesh overcome the choices of the spirit. God was in charge of my life!

So, for me, the meaning of this vital phrase from *'the Lord's Prayer'* is two-fold:

Firstly, *'Lord, please do not lead me along pathways where the temptations will be so strong that I won't be able to resist them'* and

Secondly, *'Lord, will you please go ahead of me as my shield and protector, so that when I do face temptation I will be strong enough to resist the devil in whatever form his temptations may take.'*

Of course, for these prayers to be an effective expansion of the prayer *'Lead us not into temptation'*, they have to be the desire of our heart. There's no point in praying the prayer with our lips and having a completely different intent in our heart.

The essence of God's answer to these prayers is summed up in a wonderful promise from the book of Proverbs:

"He holds victory in store for the upright, He is a shield to those whose walk is blameless, for He guards the course of the just and protects the way of his faithful ones." Proverbs 2:7-8.

PERSONAL NOTES

BUT WHAT ABOUT TESTING?

Just after Jesus was baptised by John the Baptist and filled afresh from on high with the Holy Spirit, Scripture tells us that He *'was led by the Spirit into the desert to be tempted by the devil'* (Matthew 4:1). Couldn't that mean that when people are tempted by the devil it has actually been organised for us by the Holy Spirit?! And if that's so, how could Jesus encourage us to pray *'lead us not into temptation'* when, seemingly, behind our backs, the Holy Spirit and the devil are laying traps for us?!

In some ways every single temptation we face is a test – the enemy tests us to the limit, always looking for a gap in our defences that he can exploit. But the testing Jesus experienced, when the Spirit of God led Him into the wilderness specifically to be tested by the devil, is testing of a different nature and of a different magnitude.

As is clear in the story of Job, this sort of testing is specifically allowed and even encouraged by the Holy Spirit. It takes place when men or women know that God has called them and their resolve to follow that calling is being tested.

This kind of testing isn't just a trap of the enemy to tempt you to sin. It's a specific onslaught on your calling, which God allows for your own good and your own strengthening. You may not like it, but it's vital that we are tested to the limit before a work of God begins.

Having read the personal stories of many Christian pioneers and shared hearts with leaders across the world, it seems that this sort of experience is far more common than is generally appreciated. The following is an account of my own personal experience in this respect.

Shortly after God gave me the vision for the work of Ellel Ministries, I experienced a night of spiritual terror. The vision was burning in my heart and I knew that this was what God had made me for. I was joyfully pressing on with thinking and dreaming about the work, when on this particular night it seemed as though God had left me. I discovered something of what it was like to be in the spiritual realms,

PERSONAL NOTES

but without the Spirit of God. It was a lonely and very frightening night-time experience.

It was my own *'long dark night of the soul'*, which culminated in what felt like a personal visitation from Satan. Whether or not it was Satan himself I will probably never know, but it certainly felt like it! I was wrestling with an evil being and I knew that of myself I didn't have the resources to win the fight.

I knew also that there was only one issue at stake in this spiritual battle – the vision that burned within me. I knew that if I agreed to give up the vision, the devil would leave me and the battle would be over. But I knew also that if I gave up the vision I would spend the rest of my days heartbroken that I had not done what God had called me to do. I could never give up the vision and I was constantly reiterating this to the enemy as the battle raged.

Throughout this terrible experience every part of my being was involved. My whole body was covered in the sweat of battle. I don't know how long the battle had been going on, but there suddenly came a moment when I was aware once again of the presence of God and I was able to call out to Him again. Immediately, the devil left me. He was unable to hold any ground in the presence of God. That night I believe the Lord allowed the devil to test my calling under God to the limit.

I have often thought about that moment, especially in times of great hardship and pressure, and it has given me great encouragement to know that there's nothing the enemy can do that can stand in the presence of the Lord. He IS sufficient for every crisis and every need. I can even thank God now for that time of testing, for since then, over the years, it has often been a comfort to my soul to realise that He really was with me in my extremity.

We need to be constantly on our guard against the many other temptations (testings) of the enemy, when he will target all our 'soulish' desires and seek to divert us from the path of holiness. But when we set out to be obedient to God with our lives, let's not flee from those times of testing which the Spirit of God prepares for us – they're to strengthen us and encourage us for the future.

And it's really great to know and have proved the truth of 1 Corinthians 10:13, *'No temptation has seized you except what is common to man. And God is*

PERSONAL NOTES

faithful; he will not let you be tempted beyond what you can bear. But when you are tempted, he will also provide a way out so that you can stand up under it.'

DELIVER US FROM THE EVIL ONE

Sometimes people say to me that believers should never need deliverance – no born again believer can ever be affected by the presence of an unclean spirit, a demon! Then why did Jesus encourage us to pray for deliverance from the evil one? (The traditional version, does simply say 'deliver us from evil', though 'the evil one' is definitely the implication of the Greek text).

We need deliverance from the evil one in two ways. We need the deliverance which is the protection of God. It comes from Him and keeps us safe from attacks of the enemy, as we walk in obedience to Him. But we may also need the deliverance ministry that Jesus constantly did throughout His ministry, as He fulfilled the prophecy of Isaiah 61:1 and proceeded to set the captives free by casting out demons.

We will learn much more about this later on when we look specifically at the work of deliverance as part of God's healing provision for His church.

AND SO TO GOD BE THE GLORY!

'Yours, Lord, IS the Kingdom, and the power and the glory, forever!' (Matthew 6:13 KJV)

What fantastic truth brings this wonderful prayer to a close. If this was the only sentence of *'the Lord's Prayer'* that we really got hold of and lived its meaning all our days, it would totally transform our lives forever!

MORE ABOUT PRAYER

In these sections about prayer and praying it has only been possible to look at the vital foundations for a godly prayer life that Jesus stressed as being of primary importance for His disciples.

Of course, there are many other aspects to prayer which are also

PERSONAL NOTES

important such as waiting on God, listening to God, intercession for others, spiritual warfare, thanksgiving and praising God in all circumstances.

But if we haven't got the foundations in place then these other aspects of prayer would be in danger of just being words, instead of a real expression of a prayer relationship between the heart of man and the heart of God.

SUMMARY

We have seen how God wants each one of us to live in such close fellowship with Him that prayer, as conversation with God, just becomes a way of life, embracing every part of our being. Prayer was never intended by God to be something that was just an activity of the human spirit, isolated from the rest of our humanity. The whole of our being needs to be involved in our relationship with Him. We should never lose sight of the fact that God is everywhere and that wherever we are, we are in God and that's where the Kingdom of God is. 'The Lord's Prayer' or 'the Disciples Prayer', as I called it, provides us with a wonderful pattern to use as the basis for all our praying, embracing as it does, worship, submission to God's Kingdom authority, confession and repentance of sin, forgiveness, intercession for our needs and prayers for protection from all the attacks of the enemy. Adapting this pattern into a daily discipline for prayer is a dynamic and life-changing experience – a brilliant foundation for the daily transformation that God will bring to you on our Journey to Freedom.

PRAYER

Lord, teach me to pray! Show me how to use 'the Disciples Prayer' as a foundation for my daily praying and keep me, Lord, from all the traps that the evil one may lay for my life. I not only want to begin my life of discipleship well, I want to finish it well too. Thank You for the promises of protection in Your Word for those who choose to walk the highway of holiness. In Jesus' Name, Amen.

STAGE 5

Healed for a Purpose!

God's purpose for my life is more important to me than anything else on the planet!

Stage 5, Chapter 1

WHAT DOES HEALING MEAN?

Now that we have completed the first four stages of our *Journey to Freedom*, we are starting to look at some of the practical consequences of the things we have already been sharing and learning. We will also need to go back over some of the topics that we have already looked at very briefly, and take them to a greater depth than was possible during the introductory stages of our journey.

Way back in 1970, when I looked at the bent and broken chassis of my old car, God used the wreck of this *Alvis Speed 20* to point me in the direction He had for my life. When God told me that I could restore this broken car, but that He could restore broken lives, He certainly got my attention and through this experience began to show me His purposes for the rest of my days.

So it was no surprise to me that from that moment on I would keep on having further learning experiences along life's journey, all of which would contribute to what God was trying to teach me about healing in those far off days. I discovered that healing was definitely on God's agenda for His Church today!

PERSONAL NOTES

PERSONAL NOTES

But I was also discovering how much work God had to do in me, so that I could be ready and equipped for the work He had for me to do. I had much to learn, and not all the lessons were easy ones. I made mistakes as well, and sometimes I learnt more through the mistakes than I did through anything else! I learnt also that God doesn't reject us because we make mistakes, but I realised that if I didn't learn from the mistakes, I would have to keep on taking the same test – time and time again!!

MY OWN JOURNEY

When I wrote *"My relationship with God is the most important thing in the world. After that, His purpose for my life is more important than anything else on the planet"*, I was expressing something of my own personal conviction on the journey towards the ministry, that eventually opened up for me with Ellel Ministries.

Ever since I was personally born again at the age of nine, I have been conscious that calling and destiny are important to every single believer, and it's our responsibility to seek to walk in the ways of the Lord with all our heart. We all have a purpose to live for. Nobody is without value or purpose in the Kingdom of God.

In the churches of my youth and young adulthood, however, healing did not seem to be either on the agenda or taught from the pulpit. Reaching out to people outside the church with the Good News of the Gospel was encouraged, but healing ministry to people inside the church was unknown.

It seemed to me that once people were 'saved', what was expected of them as believers was that they should play their part as a member of the various organisations in the fellowship, contribute to the offerings and get ready for taking their place in the congregation of Heaven, after a good send-off (funeral)!

The whole concept of seeing *'Your Kingdom come on earth'* as a realistic expectation of praying the Lord's Prayer seemed very far indeed from the expectations of the leadership – even though this prayer was said at every single service!

Healing ministry to people in the church was not on the agenda of the leadership. If someone was sick, in whatever way, whether physically or, even, psychiatrically, then the appropriate solution was always to send people to the doctor and then pray for them to get better from a distance. While I thank God for doctors, doctors cannot give pills that will treat the human spirit or heal the root causes of the conditions of the soul. Some medication can definitely help people cope with the symptoms while they are struggling for survival. But there is a huge difference between treating the symptoms and healing the root of the problem.

In common with many churches, sometimes the only time when people were the subject of personal prayer was when they were ill. Their names would be read out at the Communion service and a prayer said for their healing. But the idea that there could ever be a link between a person's illness and their spiritual condition was, seemingly, an unknown truth.

Deep down I was unhappy with this and during college days I was trying to break out of this theological mould without even realising I was in it! Somehow, I *'knew'* that God had answers that no-one was giving me! I started going with a team of young ministers in training at Wycliffe Hall Theological College, Oxford, to conduct ward services at local hospitals. On other occasions I would go with them to an institution for young offenders. I learnt to play the piano-accordion to provide some musical accompaniment, so that I could relate to these obviously very damaged young people. I was groping in the dark!

At college, several times a day I would pass between the portraits of that great evangelist, John Wesley and that great children's author, Lewis Carroll (pseudonym of Rev. Charles Lutwidge Dodgson). John Wesley had been instrumental in changing the face of England in the eighteenth century, as the evangelical revival swept the country under his leadership. Lewis Carroll had changed the face of children's writing in the nineteenth century with his amazingly imaginative writings about Alice in Wonderland.

Both Wesley and Carroll had been students of my college, Christ Church, and both, in their different ways were an inspiration to me. Like John Wesley, I have never lost the love of seeing someone come to faith in Christ and I still love reading the creative writing of people like Lewis Carroll! But Wesley and Carroll did not provide the answers I was looking for, though I now understand from many of Wesley's writings

PERSONAL NOTES

that he really did understand the need for healing in many of the people who came to faith through his preaching.

While at Oxford, I cast my eyes up and down the theological spectrum, went to all sorts of meetings and tried to help many people in different ways – largely without success. I eventually left Oxford with a degree in chemistry, but with more questions than answers about the issues of life that really mattered, and what my own personal calling before God would eventually be.

BROKEN LIVES AND BROKEN HEARTS

I was twenty-six years of age when God spoke to me about broken lives and broken hearts as I looked at the wreck of that Alvis Speed 20. It was as if I suddenly knew what I had been looking for. I couldn't articulate it theologically, with chapter and verse from the Word of God, but I knew that what I was sensing wasn't from me, and that it exactly fitted all the things I had been looking for in my life during those years of searching.

As I looked at that car, with its bent and broken chassis, I knew that unless someone took the time to lovingly and carefully dismantle every single part of the vehicle, find out what, if anything, was wrong with each one and then carefully re-assemble the parts in accordance with the maker's instructions, that this whole vehicle would be destined for the scrap heap and never run again.

In earlier years I had spent many hours in scrap yards looking for precious bits of motor car, that would help me keep another vehicle running. There wasn't much wrong with many of those cars in the scrap yard – most had just run out of people who loved them enough to care! Their owners had been attracted by the latest model in the showrooms and no-one wanted the old models any more.

It didn't take a great deal of imagination for my mind to wander from the picture of a field full of broken down, unwanted motor cars, to seeing some of the people in a full congregation of Christians. I saw in my mind that many were going through the motions of going to church, singing hymns, putting money in the offering plate, listening to sermons and going home again, but that for them it was much like sitting in a field of broken down cars, wondering when the wrecker would come and crush them to bits!

These people, just like the car in my garage, needed someone to love and rescue them. No amount of praying for my old Alvis would change anything – I had to get my hands dirty on the job. And in much the same way, no amount of praying from a distance for the people, whose lives had been damaged by a thousand and one possible experiences, would do anything more than prop them up, so that they could remain unhealed in their broken down state.

When I heard the voice of God say to me, *"I can restore broken lives"*, my heart leapt within me. I still loved the wreck of that old Alvis, and saw its potential in the hands of the restorer, but a greater love of seeing God restore broken lives took its place. Nearly forty years have passed and there is still a lot of work left to do on the car – one day it might be finished, but of much greater importance and value are the thousands of lives that God has touched between then and now.

PERSONAL NOTES

ACCORDING TO THE MAKER'S INSTRUCTIONS

The only way I could restore the bent chassis of the car was to obtain a blue print (the engineer's original drawing) of exactly how the steel frame of the car should be. I wrote off to the manufacturers and, amazingly, a few weeks later I was sent a copy of the chassis design blueprint. Immediately I could see exactly what had happened in the accident, but more importantly, I could now see what work had to be done in order to restore the chassis to its original dimensions.

Everything was distorted and had to be put back in order, before it would be possible to start the work of restoring all the mechanical parts of the vehicle, putting them back on the chassis and preparing for the rebuilding of the body. Many years of work were to lie ahead of me, **but the most important key was *'the maker's instructions'***.

It became very obvious to me that the reason why so many people in churches across the world were ineffective as members of the Kingdom of God, and could only go through the motions of living a religious life, was that the foundations of their life (their spiritual chassis!) had been distorted and they were trying to live their life in a state of disorder. No amount of prayer for healing the external symptoms and problems could ever be properly effective, because the very foundations of their lives were out of line with God's best for them.

PERSONAL NOTES

The original maker's instructions were absolutely critical to the restoration of the chassis of the Alvis. And in exactly the same way our Maker's instructions, according to His Word, are equally critical to the restoration of broken lives.

Jesus constantly used parables to teach the people eternal truths. In my own life, God has also used many parables, often about things such as old cars, in which I am naturally interested, to teach me many things. It's exciting to be constantly looking out for those pictorial lessons from life that Jesus will use to teach us about how to walk in His ways.

A DEFINITION OF HEALING

I am often asked about what Christian healing actually is. Sometimes people look at you talking about healing and then expect you to come down off the platform and start performing miracles! For the miracles of Jesus are their only framework of reference for the healing ministry.

While there are times when I have seen God do extraordinary things in people's lives – things that others may well describe as a miracle – in almost every single case where I have seen God move in power to bring healing and restoration it has been in response to the person choosing to get their spiritual foundations into Godly order – or, to use the above illustration one more time, to get their chassis straightened!

So, the definition of healing that I am most comfortable with, and which fits most accurately with the teaching of Scripture from Genesis to Revelation, is this:

The restoration of God's order in a person's life.

This simply covers everything! It covers those who are struggling with a physical illness. Their body is out of order. It covers those who are wrestling with the pain of forgiving others for what they have done. It covers those who have been traumatised through abuse or accidents. It covers those who don't want to face up to the reality of unconfessed and unforgiven sin in their lives. It covers those who have entered into wrong relationships and are struggling with the consequences of sexual sin. It covers these and many more things. It covers everything.

PERSONAL NOTES

THE STORY OF KING DAVID

King David was an amazing man of God, who had learnt to trust and obey his God from a very early age. This was the man who killed Goliath and became the hero of the people. But David also had a weakness and at one stage of King David's life (2 Samuel 11 and 12), everything got very much out of order!

As King, he should have been away with his army at war. But, he stayed at home and fell into the temptation of lust, when he saw a beautiful woman bathing. He summoned her to his palace and committed adultery with her. She became pregnant.

Now he had to cover up the consequences of his sin. So he summoned Bathsheba's husband, Uriah, back from the battle and tried to persuade him to go home and sleep with his wife, so that the baby would appear to be his. But Uriah could not be bought in this way. He was too loyal to his King and country. So David then arranged for Uriah to be at the centre of an unwise and dangerous military operation and he was killed.

This left the way clear for King David to marry Bathsheba, so that people would just think, when the baby was born, that she had had an early delivery. Everything David did was designed to get himself out of trouble, but in reality every step took him deeper and deeper into the consequences of his original sin. Sin can only be hidden from view by further deception and more sin!

Finally, God broke this cycle of sin and deception by sending the prophet Nathan to confront David with what he had been doing. David confessed and everything he had done was brought out into the floodlight of exposure. There was critical disorder in David's life.

Yes, what David had done was outright sin, breaking the seventh commandment (Exodus 20:14), but his sin was not David's only problem! When David described something of how he had been feeling in Psalm 51, his Psalm of contrition, he described himself as being sick – his bones ached (v.8), he'd lost his joy (v.8), he couldn't stop thinking about what he'd done and was probably losing sleep (v.3), he felt dirty and in need of cleansing (v.2), he was aware of the inner lies which he'd used to try and defend his integrity with falsehood (v.6), he felt impure in his heart (v.10), he'd lost his steadfast determination to be God's man (v.10), and, perhaps, worst of all, he was living in fear – the fear that the Holy Spirit (who had been on him since his anointing

PERSONAL NOTES

for Kingship) would be withdrawn from him (1 Samuel 16:13). What a mess David had got himself into.

It's blindingly obvious that David was now very sick and in need of healing. And it's equally obvious that if Nathan had not come with the convicting word of the Lord, that David's life would have gone downhill pretty fast. In today's age, he might have started looking for counselling for his damaged emotions, medication for undiagnosed aches and pains, sleeping pills to cover the night hours and probably a referral to a psychologist or a psychiatrist for treatment of his depression!

There are many situations, especially for victims of violence and abuse, when the services of a psychologist or a psychiatrist have helped a person through to a place of stability, from which they have then been able to face their real healing need.

But in King David's case, he did not need ANY of these treatments for the manifold conditions he was now suffering from. What he needed was the restoration of God's order in his life, which in his case could only come through confession of his sin and repentance, followed by forgiveness and restoration.

I am using David's story as an illustration of how people can be in need of healing. They aren't sick in the traditional medical sense, but they're still desperately ill. There are many people today, even in our churches, who have wrestled with un-confessed sin for years and years. For some, the battle to keep it all in has become too great and they have collapsed under the strain, succumbing to a range of possible sicknesses and conditions.

Others are not like David, but they may be struggling, even, thirty or forty years after the event, with the consequences of things like sexual abuse which devastated their early life and which is still devastating their lives today. I will never forget praying with an eighty-one year old lady who shared for the very first time about sexual abuse that had happened to her when she was fourteen.

She had never revealed the secret, because she felt under a mistaken moral obligation to respect the reputation of the uncle who had done the damage. Because of fear of men she had never dared risk developing a relationship that might have led to marriage. What devastation she had been forced to endure.

The joy she entered into when she was finally able to talk it all out,

PERSONAL NOTES

forgive her uncle and then receive deep inner healing and deliverance was amazing. I knew that the joy of the Lord, and His great love for her, would be her strength in her latter days, in a way that could never have been possible previously.

RESTORING GOD'S ORDER

As we work through these things together, we will see how the restoration of God's order in the foundations of our lives is critical to seeing God's power to heal and restore, being released in the rest of our lives.

Satan uses an unhealed past to control our lives in the present and to rob us of our future destiny (John 10:10a). God doesn't just want you to be healed so that you will feel better – wonderful though that is. He wants you to know the blessing of a life fulfilled, living in the security of His Kingdom and rejoicing in His love (John 10:10b). Little by little, as you apply the lessons of *Journey to Freedom* into your own life, you will see God changing you from the inside out. The couple who went through our Modular School, doing one course a month over a two year period, began the School with a catalogue of issues in their lives. But as the school progressed, they dealt with their issues one by one. The transformation in their lives was amazing as step by step they gave God first place in every area of their lives, and He brought His order out of their chaos. It's easy to love such a miracle working God!

SUMMARY

In order to establish God's healing in our lives we need to give God permission to rebuild the foundations of our lives according to the Maker's instructions. Then we can believe Him to not only heal us, but restore our destiny and give us His purpose to live for.

PRAYER

Lord, thank You that You want to rebuild my life. Help me to walk with You through every area so that little by little You can put things right. I want to walk in Your ways and enjoy Your presence forever. In Jesus' Name, Amen.

Stage 5, Chapter 2

WHY DO I NEED HEALING?

SO WHY DO I NEED HEALING...?

And you might want to add to this question ***'...especially when I don't think I'm sick'***! Surely, all we need is the Gospel and to know that we're born again? Isn't that sufficient? When we get to Heaven we won't have any problems, there will be no more crying or tears there (Revelation 21:4?).

Yes, that is the wonderful truth of the Gospel, but it doesn't deal with the time between when we were born again and when we will finally go to be with God at the end of our lives. We're living in that period of time. We can't live in either the past or the future. It's only possible for us to live in the present, one moment at a time. We're always in the present moment and that's the only moment that matters throughout our life.

The whole of the Bible was written by the Holy Spirit to be a constant source of inspiration and encouragement for the people who are still living in time – and that means you and me, right now. There's absolutely nothing in the Bible to indicate that God wants us to remain in the state that we were in when we were first born again.

Even the Apostle Paul was still pushing forward towards the end of

PERSONAL NOTES

PERSONAL NOTES

his life! *'But one thing I do, forgetting what is behind and straining toward what is ahead, I press on toward the goal to win the prize for which God has called me heavenward in Christ Jesus'* (Philippians 3:13-14). The Christian life is a pilgrimage with a purpose, in which we build our lives on God's Kingdom principles, seek to avoid all the traps of the enemy, reach out to others who are not yet part of the family of God and minister the healing love of God to the hurting members of His family.

But if we're going to minister His love to others, we must first choose to receive His love for ourselves, and allow Him to have His way in our lives. ***And it's that process which I'm now referring to as healing.***

I recently read a news report about a famous painting that had been vandalised. The person who daubed this priceless work of art with meaningless splodges of paint had been caught. He now has plenty of time in jail to think about what he did. He's paying his debt to society.

Putting the man in prison, however, was not going to solve the problem for the art gallery. The damaged painting was still hanging on the wall. The answer for the painting was to bring in specialist restorers. It would take months of painstaking work to remove every trace of the modern paint and restore the surface of the original painting so that no evidence would remain of the damage done.

You might say that the prison sentence was dealing with the man's sin, while the art restorers were bringing healing to the classic painting. Dealing with one, without the other, would not be satisfactory.

Remember that our primary definition of healing is simply ***'the restoration of God's order in a person's life'***. Well, applying this principle to the painting, the restoration of order required the detailed attention of the restorer to the area that had been damaged. God, as our Restorer, wants to give detailed attention to any areas of damage that we have experienced in our lives.

Satan is like a vandal who tries to destroy the image of God in the lives of God's creation. The sins of men are his only weapons, because it is only to man that God has given authority on this Earth. Satan might be the instigator of evil ideas, but it's man who is the perpetrator. Satan may have been the one behind the horrific ideas of Adolf Hitler to exterminate the Jews, but Satan could do nothing without Hitler having been his agent, and the perpetrator of those terrible crimes.

PERSONAL NOTES

THE PROCESS OF HEALING

When the Apostle John describes in very simple of terms (1 John 1:9), how the consequences of sin should be dealt with, he says three things must happen for full restoration to take place. He's describing a process:

Firstly: If we confess our sins

Secondly: God is faithful and just and will forgive us our sins

Thirdly: He will cleanse us from all unrighteousness.

John is very clear. Sin doesn't only damage our relationship with God, which then needs restoring through forgiveness, but it also causes damage in us, which then needs cleansing. We need to be healed of the consequences of the sin.

Later on our journey together, we will be looking in much more detail at some of the consequences of breaking God's covenant. When you read through Deuteronomy Chapter 28 and see all the physical consequences of sinful behaviour, it's easy to understand why sinners not only need to be forgiven, but also need to be healed! And if they aren't healed, then the short and long term consequences are serious indeed.

The need for healing isn't just restricted to us. There are also secondary consequences of sin that affect everything under our spiritual authority, including families and land! They all need healing. This principle is clearly implied in one of the most well-known healing promises in the Old Testament. It's when God speaks directly to Solomon in response to his prayer at the dedication of the temple in Jerusalem. This is what God said:

'If my people who are called by my name will humble themselves and pray and seek my face and turn from their wicked ways, then will I hear from Heaven and will forgive their sin and will heal their land' (2 Chronicles 7:14).

This is a wonderful and amazing promise. It spells out so clearly that not only do people need forgiveness for their sin, but they also need healing – and that healing extends to the *'land'*, meaning everything under a person's spiritual authority that has been affected by the consequences of their sin.

PERSONAL NOTES

SIN AND SICKNESS

In the New Testament the Apostle Paul picks up on this vital teaching about the relationship between sin and sickness. In his instructions to the Church at Corinth, about how they should remember the death of Jesus, at the Lord's Supper, he urges people to examine themselves carefully before taking the bread and the wine (1 Corinthians 11:28).

In many of our historic church traditions, which go way back to the very earliest days of the Church, it was normal for people to remind themselves of what all the Ten Commandments actually say, before making a General Confession of their sins. Only then did they feel able to receive the bread and the wine.

The churches of the Outer Hebrides of Scotland still take several days to prepare the hearts of the people for the sacramental act of Holy Communion. It would be considered a grave sin not to examine one's heart most carefully, and deal with all known sin, before receiving the elements of the sacrament – and that needs time.

Paul explains why this sort of confession is so important. It's not just that people need to know they're forgiven of their sin – which they do – but that if they act presumptuously, and take the bread and the wine as if their hearts are right with God, when they aren't, then the personal consequences can be serious. Paul explained it like this: *'whoever eats the bread or drinks the cup of the Lord in an unworthy manner will be guilty of sinning against the body and blood of the Lord'* (1 Corinthians 11:27). It would be like invoking a curse upon oneself through entering into a personal deception in the very process of taking communion. Whenever we cooperate in deception it always gives the enemy a foothold into our lives. This is serious stuff.

Then, in verses 29 and 30, Paul explains further that a man behaving in this way brings *'judgment upon himself'* and as a result *'that is why many among you are weak and sick, and a number of you have fallen asleep'* (died). Paul was under no illusion that unresolved sin issues in anyone's life have a way of manifesting themselves in sickness, and even in death.

In 2 Chronicles 16: 11-14, we learn that King Asa developed a disease in his feet and eventually died. He died because of his sin in depending on a foreign and idolatrous King, instead of trusting in God. We saw how King David was beginning to suffer a string of related symptoms as a result of his adultery. And then in Proverbs 3:7 and 8, we read that

PERSONAL NOTES

when you *'fear the Lord and avoid evil, it will bring health to your body and nourishment to your bones!'* The converse is that unresolved sin can have an unwelcome outworking in our lives.

It seems pretty clear that throughout Scripture we're discovering the same message – ***sin does more than damage our relationship with God. It can also have a consequence in our lives which can cause sickness and which needs healing***.

It's as if there are three dimensions to the consequences of sin – one dimension is the damage to our relationship with God, the second is the damage there may be to our relationship with others – especially those we have sinned against, and, thirdly, the consequential damage there is to ourselves and those who are under our spiritual authority.

In Galatians 6:7-8, Paul uses a picture from agriculture to illustrate his point. He says, *'God cannot be mocked. A man reaps what he sows. The one who sows to please his sinful nature, from that nature will reap destruction.'* Paul says it so very clearly, that it's hard to understand how people can't see his point!

Now, to answer the original question in our title: Yes, we do all need healing, because we're all sinners. We're living in a fallen world and none of us has escaped. When we get to Day 5 of this e will soon need to really understand what confessing sin really means – it's more than just telling God what we've done wrong!

BUT DOES THAT MEAN THAT ALL MY SICKNESS IS DIRECTLY CAUSED BY SIN?

Yes and No!

'Yes', in that if man had not sinned, everything would still be perfect and in the unfallen state. Satan would have no authority on Planet Earth and there would be no sickness and no disease.

'No', in that there are many sicknesses and diseases that are now endemic in the world – meaning that they are rampant across the planet and anyone can get them. They have become part of the human condition. And we all suffer accidents and injuries of varying sorts. As a young man I broke my nose on three occasions when playing field hockey and rugby! Such injuries are not normally related to sin!

While I was away ministering in Rwanda, I was careful to take my

PERSONAL NOTES

anti-malarial pills. If I hadn't taken the pills and a malaria-carrying mosquito had bitten me and I was now suffering from malaria, I would be very angry with myself for not having taken the pills. But I wouldn't be thinking that because I had sinned a mosquito came to get me! The connection between my malaria and sin would only be a very loose connection in the general sense. Neither do I conclude when I catch a cold that this is a direct consequence of my personal sin. It isn't.

But if someone visited a prostitute who is HIV positive and, as a result, they contracted AIDS, there would be a direct link between their own sin and the disease they now had. No wonder Proverbs tells us that avoiding evil is health to one's body!

WHAT ABOUT OTHER PEOPLE'S SIN?

So it now seems clear that we can be personally affected by the consequences of our own sin, but what happens when other people do things that hurt us? Can that also cause us to need healing?

The answer to this question is a definite 'Yes'. For, dealing with our own sin is only one side of the issues of life. Much of the time in our lives we also have to deal with the consequences of what others have done to us. It's not for nothing that Satan is referred to in Scripture as a thief and a robber (John 10:1-10).

When people suffer as a result of their own ungodly choices you could say they are only getting what they asked for! But when people suffer because of what others have done to them, the cruelty of Satan and the horror of sin become much more apparent. People are literally being robbed by Satan of their potential in God – and sometimes they are even being robbed of life itself.

It grieves God greatly to see people suffering unfairly because of what others have done to them. I believe that is why Jesus placed such emphasis in *'the Lord's Prayer'* on choosing to forgive others for what they have done to us. It's only then that we can escape the unfair punishment that Satan loves to load on us. Sadly, the very existence of sin in the world has guaranteed that life is not fair and that some people will suffer more than others.

There's only one place in the world where everything is seen to be fair for every human being – and that's at the foot of the cross. We have all sinned, we all need forgiveness and there are no favours or preferences given. It doesn't matter whether one is a King or a penniless orphan. We're all at the same level, resolving our eternal destiny before our wonderful Saviour, as we receive forgiveness for the sin that separates us from a loving and holy God (Romans 3:23).

The equality and fairness that was handed out to men and women at Calvary was only made possible by the eternal unfairness of what was happening to Jesus. Here, at the cross, the consequences of all of humanity's sin were loaded on the only person ever to walk this planet who didn't deserve ANY of what He was suffering (Isaiah 53).

WHAT MUST I DO TO BE SAVED?

It was in Philippi that the jailer cried out to his prisoners after the earthquake, *'What must I do to be saved?'* Paul and Silas replied, *'Believe on the Lord Jesus Christ, and you will be saved, you and all your household'* (Acts 16:30-31).

The eternal question of a sinner under conviction was answered with the only reply such a sinner would ever want to hear. But in the Greek of the New Testament the words that are used for *'being saved'* and *'being healed'* are similar and they are only translated differently, according to the context of the passage.

Salvation and healing have the same source – the finished work of Jesus on the cross. Isaiah saw this very clearly when he prophesied that both salvation and healing would flow from the death of the sacrificial Lamb of God:

'He was pierced for our transgressions, he was crushed for our iniquities; the punishment that brought us peace was upon Him, and by his wounds (stripes), we are healed' (Isaiah 53:5).

Isaiah's prophecy shows so clearly that both salvation and healing would flow from the completed work of the Messiah.

To receive salvation we receive Him as our Saviour. To receive healing we need the cleansing that the Saviour can bring and which John talked about in 1 John 1:9.

And in the next chapters we will be looking at how you and I can,

PERSONAL NOTES

PERSONAL NOTES

not only rejoice in our salvation, but experience the Saviour also being our Healer.

SUMMARY

While all sickness and disease is ultimately caused by sin, not everything I struggle with in life is a consequence of my sin! The fruit of what Jesus did for each one of us on the cross is seen in both our salvation (restoration of relationship between God and man) and our healing (the restoration of God's order in each one of our lives). Jesus died for both.

PRAYER

Thank You, Lord, for enduring the terrible unfairness of the cross, so that there would be total fairness for every single human being who looks to You for salvation and healing. Help me during this week to be really honest with myself as I continue to walk a personal pilgrimage of hope, healing and restoration. In Jesus' Name, Amen

Stage 5, Chapter 3

GENERATIONAL ISSUES

None of us arrived on the planet without a family history! Every single human being has been parented through many, many generations. When you were conceived, the generational history of your father through his sperm, and the generational history of your mother through her egg, combined to give you an inheritance that has influenced every area of your being.

The Bible pays a lot of attention to generational lines, giving detailed records of families, and sometimes explains how one generation was affected by another. So this is clearly a subject that really matters to God.

PERSONAL NOTES

DOWN THE FAMILY LINE!

We have already established that you, as a human being consist of spirit, soul and body (1 Thessalonians 5:23). We will be returning to look at what this means in more detail in a later unit of *Journey to Freedom*, but for now we simply need to recognise that when God breathed His life into our human spirit at our conception (Genesis 2:7), the living soul and

PERSONAL NOTES

physical body that exploded into being carried with them a picture of our generational history – something which is readily seen and understood in the physical realm on the genetic level. The physical similarity of our genes to those of our parents, brothers and sisters, confirms who we are related to and which family we belong to.

A few years ago I stood in the Huguenot Museum in South Africa looking at pictures of some of my distant French ancestors who established a new life in that far off land. My wife almost burst out laughing as she looked from me to them and back to me again. It was very, very obvious that I was related to them, just by how I looked!

No-one could have doubted that I was a Huguenot, descended from the de Villiers family line. I also recognised that I didn't just carry the visual looks of those amazing people. Something of that same Christian determination had been evident in my own life, driving me on in the vision that God had given me for the ministry.

I remember praying for a lady about some less than savoury aspects of her own character which she was not proud of. She looked at me, somewhat pathetically, and said 'well, we Robinsons are always like this – both my father and my grandfather were just like me'. She seemed resigned to a belief that there was no point in me praying for her, because this was how all Robinsons are and nothing could be changed.

In English we have a saying *'like father, like son'* which simply means that the son is taking after his father – especially in terms of character, gifts and abilities – not just looks. We probably all know of people, even in our own families, who bear a striking resemblance, in looks, character or gifting, to their mother, father, grandmother or grandfather.

I have a friend who plays the flute brilliantly. His father was a great musician who founded an orchestra and he carries the blessing of that generational gifting. Everyone has both strengths and weaknesses in their character or personality. It's not unusual to see the same strengths and the same weaknesses appearing one generation after another down the family line.

A man stood talking to me in the entrance hall at Ellel Grange. He was holding the hand of his six year old son as he confided in me why he had come for personal help. He said, 'I've committed adultery, and my father before me and my grand-father before him – they all committed adultery'.

He then looked from his son to me and back to his son again and then asked a very poignant question, 'What hope is there for him? I don't want him to walk in the same footsteps that I've walked in.'

I was able to give him great encouragement, as I explained how Jesus came to set the captives free and that, at this moment, he, and his whole family line, were in captivity to the enemy's control. He would have to make some choices and deal with the real issues, but if he was willing to walk God's way, then both he and his son could be free forever of this 'curse' on their family line.

At this point I need to explain what I mean, so let's go back to the Word of God and see what the Bible says about this critical issue.

PERSONAL NOTES

THE SINS OF THE FATHERS...

The Ten Commandments are described in Deuteronomy 4:13 as God's Covenant. God's Covenant doesn't refer to an agreement that was made between God and man. It's His gracious provision for mankind, which arises out of His very nature of love. The terms of God's Covenant can never be up for discussion. They can only be accepted or ignored. They can't be changed.

If God's Covenant is accepted and used as the foundation for life, then it will always be a source of God's blessing and loving protection (Deuteronomy 28:1-14). If the Covenant is ignored and rejected, then man has to live with the consequences of making choices based on spiritual ignorance, rebellion and moving outside the boundaries of God's protection (Deuteronomy 28:15-68).

We will be looking at the issues of Covenant much more closely at a later date, but for now it's vital we understand that the content of the Ten Commandments is as unchangeable as the law of gravity. We may not like the law of gravity but, as we have already seen, if we ignore it or fly in the face of it we will always suffer the consequences.

You can't walk off the edge of a cliff without experiencing the effect of gravity. If only the world would realise that the Ten Commandments are just as certain and just as unchangeable. People would then be far more determined to live their lives within God's boundaries, without feeling they were being restricted, and without feeling God didn't understand their personal situation!

PERSONAL NOTES

Jesus said nothing that would undermine the importance of the Ten Commandments. He even went so far as to say that not one word of the Law would pass away until the end of all things, and that whoever practises and teaches them will be great in the Kingdom of Heaven (Matthew 5:17-20). When speaking to the rich young ruler Jesus told him, *'if you want to enter life, obey the commandments'* (Matthew 19:17).

When the Pharisees asked Jesus which was the greatest commandment (Matthew 22:36), Jesus didn't quote one of the Ten Commandments, but gave them two principles. These two principles sum up and embrace everything that is found within the Ten Commandments! When Jesus told them to *'Love the Lord your God with all your heart and with all your soul and with all your mind', followed by 'Love your neighbour as yourself'*, He wasn't saying the old commandments were redundant and these are replacing them!

What Jesus actually said was *'All the Law and the Prophets hang on these two commandments'* (Matthew 22:34-40). He meant that if we truly loved the Lord our God and loved others as ourselves, then we would never want to do things that would take us outside the provisions of the Ten Commandments.

The reason I am emphasising how the importance of the Ten Commandments is stressed in both the Old and the New Testaments, is that some Christians seem to have developed a lack of respect for the Commandments of God. They seem to regard them as merely history! Some have even replaced them with a model of conduct based on a selfish interpretation of 'love', which has become a serious distortion of truth.

As a result, we have Christians who are quite happy to share in faith and worship with believers in Buddhism, Hinduism or Islam, as if these religions worship the same God on an equal footing. And we have people who have tried to rewrite the seventh commandment, *'you shall not commit adultery'* to fit in with their personal sexual desires and relationships! We can't rewrite Scripture to suit ourselves (See: Deuteronomy 4:2, Deuteronomy 12:32, Proverbs 30:5-6 & Revelation 22:18-19) and think there will be no consequence. For, as Paul said to the Galatians, *'God cannot be mocked'*(Galatians 6:7).

The fact is the Ten Commandments are just as important today as they ever were. They are a reflection of the unchangeable nature of God. The fundamental laws of science, which describe the behaviour

PERSONAL NOTES

of the physical universe, can't ever be changed either, because they're a reflection of the nature of matter itself. In the same way, the fundamental laws of the spiritual universe (the Ten Commandments, God's Covenant) can't ever be changed.

We may, mistakenly, think that the Commandments were all swept away with the New Covenant, when Jesus came. But on the contrary, they are unchangeable truth. They're for our good. The Ten Commandments could be seen as the first Handbook for successful human living!

VISITED ON THE CHILDREN

Having now firmly established that the Ten Commandments are relevant for the whole of mankind for the whole of time, I want to draw your attention to one very important detail, of great relevance and significance to our study. Exodus 20:5-6 says:

'For I, the Lord your God, am a jealous God, punishing the children for the sin of the fathers to the third and fourth generation of those who hate me, but showing love to a thousand generations of those who love me and keep my commandments' (Exodus 20:5-6 NIV).

Because of the controversy that can exist around the translation of the first part of this verse, I want to tell you how the King James and the New American Standard versions of the Bible translate the phrase *'punishing the children for the sins of the fathers'*. Instead, they both say *'visiting the iniquity of the fathers upon the children'*.

The difference may seem small, but the impact of this difference is huge. For both Ezekiel and Jeremiah are at pains to say that when it comes to punishment for sin, the sour grapes that the fathers have eaten will not set the children's teeth on edge. Or, as Jeremiah puts it, *'Everyone will die for his own sin'* (Jeremiah 31:30). Ezekiel says *'the soul that sins is the one who will die'* (Ezekiel 18:4) and the son *'will not die for his father's sin. He will surely live'* (Ezekiel 18:17).

It's clear to me in the context of both these passages that the sort of death being talked about is not the physical death that we will all experience, but the punishment of eternal death to the soul. I believe it would be an unfair and an unjust God who punished someone eternally

PERSONAL NOTES

with the consequences of someone else's sin, for which they weren't personally responsible.

But even though it may not be personal punishment for someone else's sin, we can't escape the fact that, in this world, countless millions of people do suffer the consequences of other people's sin. In every single family the children are inheritors of the consequences of the sins of their ancestors.

This is why the translation of this verse is so important. The consequences of the sins of the fathers are undoubtedly visited on the children for at least three or four generations. But *'visiting on'* and *'punishment for'* are not the same thing.

In Nehemiah Chapter 1 we read how Nehemiah is a prisoner of war because his ancestors had sinned. Lamentations 5:7 expresses it this way *'Our ancestors sinned, but now they are gone, and we are suffering for their sins'* (GNB). This is reality.

We all know of people who have suffered the consequences of what their parents, or their more distant ancestors, have done. Maybe even we ourselves have suffered in this way. But suffering as a consequences of the sins of our ancestors is not the same as being punished by God for their sins.

Only this morning a letter came in to Ellel Grange from a lady who was asking for help. She explained how her former drug addict husband had used every bit of his income to feed his habit, rather than feed his family and now their daughter was suffering the consequences of his sin.

A baby born to a prostitute mother, out of a casual sexual relationship with an alcoholic man, will suffer the consequences of the lack of godly parenting. The child may well be far more prone to committing his own similar sins, because of the spiritual influence of the ancestors as well as his learned behaviour from one generation to another.

These are facts of life which we can't ignore. The sins of the 'fathers' truly are visited on the children – and, yes, it could take three or four generations before the consequences of ungodliness are eliminated from the generation line.

Conversely, however, a child born to a godly heritage will inherit and enjoy the fruit of all that is good and godly in the generation line. The spiritual blessings, and the learning by example, coming from one generation to the next, can have a dramatic and life-long effect on the children of such a generation line.

There is a comparative study of the generation lines of two American families. They look at the godly heritage, passed to his descendants by that great evangelist, Jonathan Edwards, and at the heritage of Max Juke, a man who did not know the Lord and lived a pretty ungodly lifestyle. These men were contemporaries. This is a summary of the report:

The study included 1,200 of Max Juke's descendants and nearly 1,400 descendants of Jonathan and Sarah Edwards.
Max Juke's descendants included over 300 convicts, 27 murderers, 190 prostitutes, 509 alcoholics and drug addicts.

Jonathan Edwards' descendants included over 100 clergymen, missionaries and theological professors, 130 lawyers and judges, 99 college professors, 13 university presidents, 60 physicians, 75 Army or Navy officers, 11 congressmen and governors, 3 senators and one Vice-President of the USA – and practically no lawbreakers! Between them they authored 135 books of significance.

This extraordinary comparison graphically illustrates how God has created humanity so that His blessings can come down the generation line, as Exodus 20:6 explains. But individuals in each generation still have to make their own choices of how to live.

The fact that a generation line may be blessed by the Spirit of God, doesn't guarantee that each generation will choose to walk in that blessing. God will never violate His gift of free will to mankind – even to make them good! People have a right to choose to either accept or reject God, no matter how godly their generation line might be. We all have the free will to choose to sin or not to sin. Having a difficult ancestry, does not mean we have no choice about sinning. It may be more difficult to make the right choice, but we still have a choice.

One of the consequences of man choosing to come under Satan's authority at the fall, was that everything God had created within humanity, which was intended to be a blessing, could now be used by Satan for his purposes. So, the capacity for blessing to flow down the generation lines could now be used by Satan to transmit cursing. As a result demonic power, which had entered into a generation line through

PERSONAL NOTES

PERSONAL NOTES

the sins of an ancestor, could pass down that generation line from one generation to another.

I usually illustrate this by likening the spiritual link between one generation and another, to a drain-pipe on the side of a building. All the drain-pipe has to do is transmit whatever liquid is poured in at the top. The drain-pipe has no capacity to reject dirty water and only transmit clean water. It is simply a channel linking the top and the bottom of the pipe.

In just the same way, the linking from one generation to another cannot choose what sort of spiritual power it wants to transmit. It simply passes on whatever is poured in – both the good and the bad.

If God were to make it impossible for evil demonic power to pass down that generational 'drain-pipe', then He would have to block off the drain-pipe altogether, so that neither good nor bad could be transmitted – which would mean that whatever good was in our ancestral line would be denied to us.

So when, in the Ten Commandments, it says that the sins of the fathers will be visited on the children, it simply means that whatever the family line has suffered as a result of the sins of the fathers, will be a spiritual inheritance for the next generation. This is not God punishing one generation for the sins of another. But it's true that what we are and what we do doesn't stop with us – we pass it on!

If a father or a mother rejects the Covenant of God and takes their family into sin and rejects God's Word, then the children will suffer the consequences, often for several generations. Whether or not this is fair isn't the issue. Sin is in the world and the consequences of sin can affect many generations.

SO WHAT CAN I DO? IS THERE ANY HOPE?

'Yes', there is hope and 'Yes', there is something you can do! You can acknowledge the facts of your personal situation, and ask God to remove from you the consequences of the past and establish a new generation line for your future.

The key lessons are found in the book of Nehemiah. In Chapter 1, Nehemiah confesses that both he and his ancestors have sinned (Nehemiah 1:6-7). The day after tomorrow we will be looking more carefully at what confession actually means. Clearly, none of us can repent, for example, for what others have done. Their sin is their responsibility. But we can confess our ancestors' sins, by which I mean, agree that they have sinned.

We can then speak out our forgiveness, and ask God to set us free from the consequences of their sin. Finally, we can take authority over any unclean spirits that have been using the sins of the ancestors, as a vehicle for transmitting their presence and influence from one generation to another.

Later, after Nehemiah had rebuilt the wall, we read of the people rediscovering for themselves what God's Word said. They *'confessed their sins and the sins of the wickedness of their fathers'* (Nehemiah 9:2). They were dealing with the things they themselves had done, and also dealing with what their ancestors had done.

Both steps were vital in order that the people should be free to serve God, unimpeded any more by the spiritual consequences of their generational past. That's the place that I believe God would want us all to be in.

Dealing with the past in this way doesn't change history. It doesn't automatically restore back to you everything that the enemy has stolen. But what it does do is draw a firm spiritual line under the past, so that you're now free to start again with a new, and solid, foundation to your life. As a child of God you are an inheritor of all the blessings that are Jesus's (Ephesians 1:3-14), including His robe of righteousness, His family disposition (He writes His law in our minds and hearts (Jeremiah 31:33)) and His family Spirit – the Holy Spirit, who enables us to walk in His ways. As a member of the family of God you can start rebuilding and begin a new and godly generation line and be a blessing to your children and your children's children. And this was the good news I was able to bring to the man standing in the entrance hall of Ellel Grange with his six year old son.

Under the New Covenant, the authority that Jesus had over the powers of darkness was delegated to His disciples. Now is the time to start living in the fruit of what Jesus did for us on the cross and start saying 'NO' to the enemy as well as 'YES' to Jesus.

My relationship with God should be the most important thing in the world for each one of us. After that, His purpose for my life is more important than anything else on the planet!

PERSONAL NOTES

PERSONAL NOTES

Once we get our relationship with Him right, we can then start to move into the detailed purposes of God for our lives. Satan doesn't want us to know where he has a controlling influence in our lives – but God wants to expose his tactics for what they are, and see His children fulfil their destiny.

SUMMARY

We are all influenced by the generations that have gone before us – by the good and the bad. We can thank God for the good, and we can deal with the bad as we confess what our ancestors have done, and forgive and release them into the freedom of our forgiveness. Then we can deal with the control of the enemy in our lives and start walking towards living in the freedom of the inheritance Jesus won for us on the cross.

PRAYER

Thank You, Jesus, that Your death on the cross was not only sufficient to deal with the consequences of my sin, but that You also want to set me free from the ungodly generational influences on my family lines. Help me, Lord, to put down a new foundation of truth in my life so that I may be a blessing to others. In Jesus' Name, Amen.

Stage 5, Chapter 4

THINGS THAT HAVE HAPPENED TO ME

I pray you are encouraged to realise that, not only does God have a real purpose for your life, but that He is also determined to help you clean up the past so you can look forward to your future! It is out of having a relationship with Him that we grow into living a purposeful life for Him.

Because we live in a fallen world, nothing we experience this side of eternity will ever be perfect – other than, of course, the Lord Jesus Himself. Paul rejoiced to say to his readers in Ephesus, that He has *'blessed us in the heavenly realms with every spiritual blessing in Christ. For He chose us in Him, before the creation of the world, to be holy and blameless in His sight'* (Ephesians 1:3-4).

None of us know yet, from personal experience, what it will be like for us to be totally holy and blameless. That's a joy that awaits us in Heaven. But one of the many miracles of our salvation is that, even at this present time, when Father God looks upon us, He first sees the perfection of His Son. For our only means of access to the Father is through the Son. Seventy two times Paul describes a Christian as being *'in Christ'*. And if

PERSONAL NOTES

PERSONAL NOTES

we are in Him, then we are clothed by Him. ***And His perfection is our clothing, even now!***

But the clothing that is Christ, surrounds a life that has not yet been made perfect – it's a life which Paul also described in other terms when he said, *'Not that I have already obtained all this, or have already been made perfect, but I press on to take hold of that for which Christ Jesus took hold of me'*(Philippians 3:12).

In reality we are people with a carnal nature and a damaged past, en route to eternal citizenship in a Kingdom which we don't deserve to live in, yet by God's grace we will! In the meantime we strive towards this perfection from a position of faith and hope.

JESUS SAID, 'COME, FOLLOW ME'

I often have the privilege of praying with people at meetings and conferences, which means I am able to listen to the stories of what has happened in their lives. Becoming a Christian has given such people a living hope for eternity, but the cry of their heart is for something of God's Kingdom life and dynamic authority to be made manifest in their lives now. When I hear the pain, and even the cruelty, that some have suffered and, on occasions, the depths of sin that people have either committed or been victims of, I marvel all the more at the wonder of the cross. Yes, one day, all the dross of this world, yes everything, will fall away and, praise God, we will enter into our eternal destiny. But first, we have a destiny to fulfil here on earth.

Yet there are many who, without hearing and moving into the truth of this teaching from God's Word, will be trapped by their circumstances and will never see what they dream of and long for. At times like this I can weep at the devastation in the lives of so many of God's children, and long to see the Body of Christ rise up in compassion and mercy, going after the lost sheep and ministering hope to the family of God.

We have already seen that Satan is a destiny robber (John 10:10a), and wants to use every possible hook in our lives to prevent us from realising our potential as citizens of the Kingdom of God! He wants us to look at the mess and give up trying – the very opposite of what Paul was urging us to do, *'to take hold of that for which Christ Jesus took hold of us'* (Philippians 3:12).

PERSONAL NOTES

Christ Jesus took hold of us because He loves us. And He has a purpose for our lives (Jeremiah 29:11, Ephesians 2:10), and right now He wants us to lift up our eyes, see beyond the limitations imposed by Satan's horizons, and step up a gear. Satan, however, wants to tell us that because of our personal failures, God will never be able to use us in the future. He will always want to remind us of all the limitations there are on our lives, because of what others have done to us and what we have done. Satan will always want us to look backwards and downwards.

Jesus, however, says look forward and upwards and *'Come, follow me'*. These are the words He used to call the disciples to follow Him right at the beginning of His ministry (John 1:35-43). But He used them again, after Simon Peter had received some deep personal ministry, to call Simon Peter to serve Him for the rest of his days (John 21:22). This was when the call to follow Jesus touched the very core of who Simon Peter was, and God's potential in him was being unlocked.

From that moment on, the healed Simon Peter was a different man – in stark contrast to the fear which had so gripped him at the questions of a servant girl, he proclaimed with a loud voice, for anyone and everyone to hear, the glorious truths of the Gospel on the Day of Pentecost.

So many folk hear the first call to follow Jesus, at the beginning of their Christian life, but they never get to the place of receiving the healing we all need, and then hearing those loving words again tme and follow Him, into the place of service as a child of the King.

Journey to Freedom is all about getting to that place in God, where He can and does use us in His service, like Simon Peter, for the rest of our days. I pray that this is the place where you want to be, and that you are looking forward to the personal transformation He has for you as we share these precious days together.

OUT OF THE SLOUGH OF DESPOND!

In John Bunyan's amazing book, *Pilgrim's Progress*, one of Christian's early experiences was trying to cross a dangerous piece of wet and muddy ground, a deep mire where he could easily have sunk without trace. There seemed nowhere firm to place his feet and the situation seemed hopeless. This mire was called the Slough of Despond. It was

PERSONAL NOTES

a place filled with fears, and doubts and discouragements! There is a Slough of Despond today, where Satan tries to do everything he can to push you under the mud, so that you're never able to move forward in your pilgrimage.

We're going to take a hard look at ourselves, and see how God wants to lift us out of the 'Slough of Despond'. I want you to ask yourself, 'Is there anything that has happened to me in my past, which is acting like a control or a brake on my growth in God in the future'? We have already seen how we can be affected by the generational influences that have come down our ancestral line. Later we'll be looking at what we ourselves might have done, which has given the enemy rights over our life, things which Satan can still use to hold us in his control and bondage.

We're now going to look at some of the things that might have come against us throughout our life, starting with that moment when we were first conceived and began our journey towards birth, and then continuing through the years of our life right up to this present moment.

FACING MY PAST

In Jonathan Swift's wonderful book, Gulliver's Travels, Gulliver visits a place called Lilliput, where all the people are tiny midgets, when compared with Gulliver's seemingly huge size. To the Lilliputians, Gulliver's a giant, who could do terrible damage in their country, and they have to take action to save their people.

So they wait for Gulliver to fall asleep and then they come to tie him down with their strongest ropes, ropes which, to Gulliver, would be thinner than the finest of strands of cotton! Any one of these 'ropes' he could have broken with a flick of his little finger, but when there were hundreds of these 'ropes' in place, they bound him securely so that he was unable to move. He was a prisoner to a people who were no threat to him, excepting that they had bound him with hundreds of thin strands, which together were too strong for Gulliver to break.

That's a very good picture of how Satan operates in our lives. Very few of the things that happen to us are strong enough in themselves to control our lives, but the combined effect of many things can hold us in bondage. The good news is that there's NOTHING that has happened to us in the past that Jesus can't set us free from in the present! But we have to play our part in the process. Salvation puts us into a restored relationship with God, but it's *healing* which releases us from the chains of bondage.

Here are some of the possible events in a person's life which, if unhealed, could be used by the enemy to hold them from their healing and restoration:

- Being unloved and unwanted by your parents.
- Being the 'wrong sex' as far as your parents were concerned.
- Having brothers or sisters who were seemingly preferred above you.
- Never having your interests, gifts and abilities recognised or encouraged.
- Being squeezed into a parental mould that you didn't fit in.
- Being a victim of cruelty or abuse, sexual or otherwise.
- Being bullied at school, and even in later life.
- Suffering debilitating sicknesses, especially when you were young.
- Having accidents or traumas which caused serious personal suffering.
- Losing a parent, or other close family member or friend, when you were young.
- Suffering deprivation through poverty or parental unemployment.
- Being betrayed in relationships or robbed of goods and things that were precious to you.
- Suffering, as an adult, from poverty, unemployment, accidents, traumas, relationship breakdown, divorce or bereavement?

This is not an exhaustive list. There are many such possible events in a person's life. I'm sure you could add to this list out of your own experience. Experiences like those above have the potential to scar our spirit and soul. A lot depends on how old we were when these things happened to us and the surrounding circumstances of our lives at the time. These and other factors will affect how much damage we received and how much that damage still influences us today.

The great news is that none of these things need remain as curses on our lives – even if many years have passed, Jesus can still set the captives free.

PERSONAL NOTES

PERSONAL NOTES

THERE IS A WAY OUT!

The effect of traumas and painful events varies enormously from one person to the next. If a person is already insecure and fearful and something awful happens, it's likely to have a much deeper and longer-lasting consequence in their life. If someone is surrounded by loving care and comfort at a time when bad things happen, then they are protected from the deeper damage and will not need such deep healing later in life. But often that doesn't happen and the pain can be buried very deeply in a person's innermost being.

Later on in *Journey to Freedom*, we will be looking more specifically at many of these things, especially the consequences of ungodly parenting, abuse and traumas of varying types. But for now I want to encourage you by helping you see that bad though these things can be, they're not impossible hurdles to overcome. I could share with you countless personal stories of healing, touching into every single one of these painful experiences.

Jesus truly is the Good Shepherd! He came in fulfilment of many prophetic words in the Old Testament – including the one in Ezekiel 34 where the prophet Ezekiel was given the tough assignment of prophesying against his own spiritual leaders.

Ezekiel's strongest words of condemnation from the Lord, came because the shepherds of Israel had been caring for themselves and not for the people. They had used the tithes and the offerings to make themselves fat, but had ignored the needs of the hurting and the broken. Ezekiel did not dress up his words in a form that was easy to take! This is what he said:

'You have not strengthened the weak or healed the sick or bound up the injured. You have not brought back the strays or searched for the lost. You have ruled them harshly and brutally. So they were scattered because there was no shepherd and when they were scattered they became food for all the wild animals'(Ezekiel 34:4-5).

In verses 15 and 16 of the same chapter, however, God shows the pain in His heart when the sheep are hurting and have never been healed. Speaking through Ezekiel, He says, *'I myself will tend my sheep... I will search for the lost and bring back the strays. I will bind up the injured and strengthen the weak.'*

This prophetic word about the Messiah was fulfilled when Jesus came and began to heal the hurting and to bind up the broken-hearted. He referred to Himself as the Good Shepherd, and said *'I lay down my life for the sheep'* (John 10:15).

Over nearly twenty five years now I have watched as Jesus, the Good Shepherd, has done exactly as He promised. He has come to the broken lambs. He has cared for the hurting and the abused and He has gently led them in the safety of His loving care and He has set them free from the enemy – the thief who comes *'to steal and to kill and to destroy'* the sheep (John 10:10).

Karen had been given up for adoption by her natural parents. They didn't want her. Eighteen years later she was dying of a viral condition on her kidneys. As she forgave her parents for their sexual sin, a curse was broken upon her. She was amazingly healed and the doctors could no longer find any evidence of the viral condition which, previously, they had said would take her life within twelve months.

John retired early from his successful medical practice. He could no longer hold himself together and became suicidal. As we talked together he shared how his only toy as a child had been smashed by his elder brother. His tears were immediately crushed by an angry father, who then beat him for crying. John had learnt through this terrible experience never to share his emotions – with anyone!

But emotions are part of our God-given expression of life, and without them he was only half the man that God intended and depression had taken over his life. When he was able to forgive his brother and his father, and receive the love of Jesus into his heart, the tears of all the years flowed – and he was healed of his depression!

When people become Christians, their spirits, which were formerly dead to God, burst into new life. They become new creations. But even though everything becomes radically new, becoming a Christian doesn't change any of the details of their personal history.

What God can and does do is to heal us of the consequences of the distress of the past. Satan wants to hang on to the control of those cords around our heart, which make us vulnerable to the powers of darkness. But the heart of Jesus is to see us healed and restored (Isaiah 61:1-3). Little by little, as you grasp hold of these wonderful truths and apply them in your life, you will see God change you from the inside out – forever!

PERSONAL NOTES

PERSONAL NOTES

SUMMARY

None of us have escaped things happening to us that have left a scar on our lives. Satan wants to use all the bad and unhealed things from our past to hold us into his bondage. But Jesus died to set us free and in Him there's real freedom (John 8:36).

PRAYER

Help me, Lord, to identify those experiences which are still painful unhealed memories. I want to bring each one of these to You for healing, so that Satan will never be able to use them against me again. In Jesus' Name, Amen.

Stage 5, Chapter 5

WHAT HAVE I DONE?

No-one likes the idea of swallowing one's pride and confessing sin, but in reality unless we do, we're lost! I could go straight to the key verse in James 5:16, which says *'confess your sins to each other and pray for each other so that you may be healed'*, and simply say, that's what the Bible says so let's get on with it!

Well, we are going to have to look closely at this verse, but unless we really understand what the words 'sin' and 'confession' mean first, we could go through the motions of trying to tell God what we've done wrong, without ever confessing the sin!

If you find that confusing, read on! It took me quite a long time to really understand the difference between giving God a list of things I'd done wrong, and actually confessing my sins. We'll begin by asking ourselves some questions about truth.

PERSONAL NOTES

PERSONAL NOTES

WHAT IS TRUTH?

Have you ever thought that there could be a difference between Truth and Falsehood, and Right and Wrong? They sound as though they ought to mean essentially the same thing – but they don't! They can be very different, according to your circumstances.

Pontius Pilate put to Jesus, the most famous unanswered question ever asked, *'What is truth'* (John 18:38) – not realising that standing right in front of him was THE Man who was the very embodiment of truth. Jesus said, *'I am the way, the truth and the life'* (John 14:6). In Him and in God (for He also said *'I and my Father are one'* (John 10:30)), we have an absolute standard of knowledge, honesty and integrity. In Him, to use just one short word, we have truth – for truth is all three.

When a scientist is looking for the truth about a disease he is researching, he means true knowledge. When a judge asks a witness in a court of law to tell 'the truth, the whole truth and nothing but the truth', he is asking the witness to be honest. When what people say and do is always consistent, and they don't change their story to suit themselves, they are acting with integrity. Integrity is truth unchanging. A person with integrity is the same 'all the way through' – no outside covering 'which looks true', to cover up a heart which is far from true.

Applying these definitions of truth to God, we see that God knows all things – so He doesn't need to speculate about what might be the facts of a situation. What He says is always true. In Revelation 19:11 Jesus is called *'Faithful and True'*.

God fears no-one, so there's never, ever a temptation to deceive anyone else by telling a lie. God is totally consistent with Himself – He's the same all the way through, meaning He has integrity.

He's the ultimate source of all knowledge and all understanding. Nothing is hidden from His eyes. You could say that *'Truth'* is His name! There cannot be any variation in truth – truth is absolute.

WHAT ABOUT RIGHT AND WRONG?

While truth is absolute, right and wrong are relative, and are related directly to where you happen to be and whose authority you're under! If I'm in England it's OK to drive on the left-hand side of the road. It would be wrong to do that in France or America, where everyone drives on the right-hand side of the road. But there's nothing in Scripture to say one is truth and the other error – other than the instruction to obey the governments who have authority in each place.

I heard today about a British woman, in a Middle Eastern State, who has just started a jail sentence for committing adultery. While committing adultery is contrary to God's Covenant for the whole of the human race, it's not against the law in England. What's wrong in one country may well be OK in another country – according to the laws of the land.

In the United States of America, it can be all right to do some things in one State which are illegal in another State. So even within one country there can be variations in what's considered right and what's considered wrong.

A country is defined by the boundaries to an area, over which a government has authority. Within that area of authority the laws of the land determine what's right and what's wrong. It's up to an individual to know what the laws are. It's no defence for drivers to say they were driving within the speed limit of their own country, if they're caught driving at an excess speed on a road in another country.

So, ultimately, what's right and what's wrong legally, is determined by the laws made by the authority you are under.

AND WHAT ABOUT SIN?

Let's, now, take a fresh look at Jesus. Already in *Journey to Freedom* we have clearly understood together that disciples of Jesus are those who not only trust in Jesus to be their Saviour, but who have also invited Jesus to be Lord of their life. They have chosen to come under His authority.

When Isaiah prophesied about the coming of the Messiah, this is what he said:

'For, unto us a child is born, to us a son is given, and the government will be on His shoulders. And He will be called Wonderful Counsellor, Mighty God, Everlasting Father, Prince of Peace. Of the increase of His government and peace, there will be no end. He will reign on David's throne and over His kingdom, establishing and upholding it with justice and righteousness from that time on and forever' (Isaiah 9:6-7).

PERSONAL NOTES

PERSONAL NOTES

Isaiah saw in vision that Jesus would not only be Saviour, but that He was head of an eternal government, with authority over a territory that had no boundaries and no time limits! Then Jesus clearly stated this Himself, when He said that all authority had been given unto Him (Matthew 28:18).

So, what's right and what's wrong for a believer, is not determined by our whereabouts on Planet earth, for the Kingdom of God has no boundaries, but simply by living in accordance with the Truth. If we choose to live in a way that's contrary to the Truth, as illustrated and defined by the life of Him who is Truth, then that action is defined as sin.

Sin, therefore, is simply defined as breaking the laws of God. Conversely, breaking the laws of the land may or may not be sin. It certainly wasn't sin when Daniel chose to break the law of the land that was put in place by Darius the King. The law stated that *'anyone who prays to any god or man during the next thirty days, except to you, O King, shall be thrown into the den of lions'* (Daniel 6:7).

This law, however, didn't cause Daniel to change the habits of a lifetime. *'Three times a day he got down on his knees and prayed, giving thanks to his God, just as he had done before'* (Daniel 6:10). The consequence of Daniel's action was the extraordinary night he had to spend in the lion's den, when the angels shut the mouths of the lions and preserved his life.

From this we can see more clearly that sin isn't defined by the King or the laws of any earthly country. There's a higher authority that matters even more than what's right or wrong, according to the laws of any land. ***Sin is defined as all behaviour – in thought, word or deed – which is in rebellion to the truth – the government of God, as Isaiah described it.***

Just as there are absolutes in the world of science – unchangeable facts and statistics about the universe, such as the lowest possible temperature, known as absolute zero – there are also absolutes in the spiritual realm. When Jesus referred to Himself as being 'THE Truth', He was stating one of those unchangeable absolutes, by which all of humanity will be measured and judged.

We're all sinners who have fallen short of the mark (this is the literal meaning of the Greek word 'to sin') (Romans 3:23). So, it must be obvious that not one of us could ever stand before a holy and righteous

God at the end of time, and claim that we were worthy of entering Heaven's glory. We couldn't justify ourselves before the great Judge on the grounds of our behaviour or life's work.

People may well protest and plead that they are worthy because of their innocence, their good works, their kindness, their generosity or even their attempts to bring peace into the world. They may proclaim their deeds which they consider good, but everything that has ignored the reality of Him who IS truth, will be seen for what it is, a tawdry imitation of righteousness, covering a heart that hasn't submitted to the divine authority of the King of Kings. The pride of man, even in the realms of good works and religion, will try to achieve its own holiness in the sight of God, which is impossible for sinful man (Ephesians 2:8-9).

As I have been writing these words, I have seen afresh how wonderful and amazing our salvation is. All of us will have to face God on that final day of the universe as we await our eternal destiny. But it will only be those who are clothed in the sinless righteousness of Christ who will pass the test and be able to enter Heaven.

However fine we may claim the clothing of our own achievements to be, if we're clothed in our own righteousness, it will simply be seen as filthy rags (Isaiah 64:6, Philippians 3:9), when seen alongside the transcendent glory of the Son of God. Another way of looking at sin is simply to describe it as everything that's done outside of Christ, nothing of which will enter into Heaven's glory. Or, as the old children's hymn by Mary Deck expressed it:

There is a city bright; Closed are its gates to sin; Naught that defileth, Naught that defileth, Can ever enter in.

Oh how precious it is to be in Christ. No wonder Paul rejoiced at the fact that his life was hidden, with Christ, in God! (Colossians 3:3) Our Messiah, Jesus is the only clothing we can wear that will stand the test of the judgment of our hearts in eternity.

The government of the whole universe truly does rest upon His shoulders, and those who believe in Him will be clothed in His righteousness.

PERSONAL NOTES

PERSONAL NOTES

WHAT DOES IT MEAN TO CONFESS SIN?

The word 'confess' in its original context means 'to agree with'. So to confess sin to God is not simply coming to tell Him all the things you have been doing which are wrong, as people might do who 'go to confession'. God is all-knowing, so He's not sitting on His throne waiting to hear from you to find out what you have been doing. He knows that already!

Yes, we do need to own up to those things that are wrong. But what God is waiting for, is for us to come before Him in humility, fully agreeing with what He says about sin. We are to acknowledge our own sins, recognise that we constantly miss the mark (sin), and ask Him for forgiveness. Forgiveness means God releases us from the separation (from Him) caused by our sin, after which God continues His relationship with us as if we hadn't sinned.

Imagine that you stole a huge sum of money from the bank, but then you came to the bank manager, admitted what you had done, and asked him to make good the stolen money out of his own pocket and pay it all back for you. Finally you asked the bank manager to continue in relationship with you as if you had never stolen the money in the first place. And he agreed to! That's what God does when He forgives us!

Oh what a merciful God we have. It's hard to understand why He doesn't wipe us all off the surface of the planet – the only reason He doesn't, is Love. For His love covers a multitude of our sins. He longs for that restoration of relationship with His children even more than we do.

When some people confess sins, they do so knowing what the Bible talks about as being sin – such as breaking the Ten Commandments – and they 'confess' those sins to God, but in their heart of hearts they don't really agree with God, that such things are wrong. Their confession is simply a list of things that God says are wrong and is not a heart owning of the true nature of either sin, or their own personal sins.

Earlier on in *Journey to Freedom* we saw that everything we do in life, whether we are conscious of it or not, is an expression of worship. When we do things that are in accord with the Truth, then we're worshipping God and we benefit from the blessing of His Spirit. But when we do those things which are contrary to the Law of God and are against the Truth, then ultimately we're worshipping the god of this world.

Then, instead of receiving blessing from God, we're in danger of receiving cursing from the enemy. Satan always takes advantage of sin in order to create more pain for God's children. Our sin gives Satan his opportunity.

So, when people persist in sin, it's not surprising that, in addition to breaking relationship with God, sin can do two other things:

- It can take us outside the protection of God (see Psalm 91:1), and
- It can put us in a place of vulnerability to the enemy's attack (Ephesians 4:27).

So, we need to not only ask God for forgiveness for the sin, but also ask Him to cleanse us from the secondary consequences of sin. This is the message of 1 John 1:9 which refers to the need for both forgiveness and cleansing.

So, when we confess we have sinned we need to be specific about our sins. We then need to ask God to set us free from every right given to the enemy in our lives as a result of these sins. This is the process of healing which James talks about in James 5:14-16.

Here, he urges those who are sick to call the elders to come to them, confess all their known sins, ask for anointing with oil and then to pray the prayer of faith for healing the sick. All of these things can be part of the healing process.

The act of confession of sin, one to another, deals with our pride. Pride is the biggest single obstacle to the healing flow of God's Spirit. It was pride that was Satan's primary sin when he was thrown out of Heaven, and mankind has taken on his characteristics. Jesus even said to the Pharisees that their proud and boastful behaviour came from their father, the devil (John 8:44).

SO, WHAT MUST I DO?

I believe that confession from the heart should be part of our normal daily routine of personal discipline before God. We should keep our confession up to date and keep short accounts with God – which means don't dwell on sin but confess it quickly, before it has any opportunity to take root in our lives and create an opportunity for the enemy to cause sickness or invite a spirit of infirmity into our body. Genesis 4:7 refers to

PERSONAL NOTES

PERSONAL NOTES

the consequences of being in rebellion against God as *'sin crouching at the door'*.

To do this:

This is what Isaiah was talking about when he saw Jesus dying and said by prophetic faith, *'by His wounds, we are healed'* (Isaiah 53:5).

- *We first need to humbly come before God and acknowledge that He is Truth and that His understanding of sin is the one we want to agree with.*
- *Then we need to ask the Holy Spirit to shine His light into our lives and expose all darkness, hidden motives as well as obvious sins* (Psalm 139: 23-24).
- *We need to own those things as being our responsibility, and admit that we're without excuse and ask God for forgiveness and cleansing,* as David did in Psalm 51.
- *Finally, we need to receive God's forgiveness in our hearts and, with God's help, to forgive ourselves. If we continue to hold ourselves in unforgiveness, we are saying Jesus' death on the cross wasn't sufficient for us, and putting self in the place of being judge over our own lives!*
- *If we are suffering from a physical illness, from which we do not appear to be recovering naturally, then we need to follow the scriptural injunction of James and call the elders to come, so that we can share with them our confession and be anointed with oil for healing.*

In all the years of ministry that I can look back on, I have seen that there are two primary spiritual issues which people need to face as part of their preparation for receiving God's healing:

They need to unconditionally forgive all those who have hurt them
and

They need to confess those things in their lives which are an offence to the Truth, as seen in the life of Jesus and in the Word of God, and receive His forgiveness.

When people have been faithful and honest in these things, I have seen God bring major healing into their lives.

I will never forget being pressed by the Holy Spirit to teach, without compromise, what the Word of God says about sexual sin. It was a hard message to bring to a well-taught congregation, who I'm sure already knew what the Scripture says. But perhaps they hadn't heard the truth and its consequences spelled out so clearly before.

At the end of that session I invited all those who still had un-confessed sexual sin in their lives to come forward for prayer. There was a long silence, and then it was as if a dam broke when one man came to the front, sobbing into his hands. By the time the meeting was over the majority of the congregation had come to the front to receive prayer.

What was most amazing about that time, was not just the numbers of people who needed to confess sexual sins, but the number of them who then went on to ask for prayer for physical healing, and the amount of healing and deliverance that actually took place.

Jesus, the Healer, was moving among His sheep – confession, repentance and healing were all taking place as God's people got themselves cleaned up in the flow of His love and forgiveness. I have never forgotten the lesson of that day.

LOOKING AHEAD

Later in *Journey to Freedom* we will be looking at the whole area of sexuality, and of how the enemy can use ungodliness in this area to seriously limit our potential in God. We really are on a pilgrimage together, and I pray that as you think carefully through all we have shared together, you will see it as a preparation for all that's to come.

SUMMARY

Confession of sin is much more than telling God what we have done wrong – it's coming to the place of agreeing with God about what He thinks about our sin. When we have reached that understanding, then it's a simple step forward to allow God to expose all darkness in our life so that He may forgive and cleanse us forever.

PRAYER

Help me, Lord, to see more clearly how unconfessed and unforgiven sin stands in the way of my relationship with You. I don't want anything in my past to be a barrier to going on with You in my Christian walk. I pray that You will

PERSONAL NOTES

open my eyes to truly see myself as You see me. Give me the courage to live in the reality of that revelation, by facing the need for confession of sin in my heart. Set me free to serve you in the liberty that flows from the cross. In Jesus' Name, Amen.

STAGE 6

Equipped to Serve

The first and last lesson in leadership
is learning how to serve others

Stage 6, Chapter 1

HEALING FOR DISCIPLES

We are now moving forward in our understanding of what it means for us, as believers, to live as disciples of Jesus Christ. In some of the following teaching units you will recognise topics that we have already referred to. But the Jewish way of teaching, which Jesus, as a Rabbi, undoubtedly used, was to tell the same truth several times, in different ways, so that people would see it from different perspectives. In this way the truths that are learnt earlier gradually become part of who we are. It's like seeing the many different facets of a diamond from different angles.

This is what Jesus was doing when He told so many different parables of the Kingdom in Matthew's Gospel. He was helping us gain a well-rounded understanding of what the Kingdom of God is really like.

So, when in *Journey to Freedom*, you recognise some things that have already been referred to, please don't just rush on, thinking you already know all that! For each time we look at a topic, we will be either seeing it from a different angle or going deeper into our understanding of it.

PERSONAL NOTES

PERSONAL NOTES

BY BLUE GALILEE

I am actually writing this unit of *Journey to Freedom* in Israel, where all the Jewish believers in Jesus, refer to Him by His Hebrew name, Yeshua. It's wonderful to be able to share with many believers here, the amazing truths of the Gospel, in the land where Yeshua Himself walked and taught.

To sense the presence of God, and know His blessing, as we worship the Saviour, our Messiah, with Arab, Jewish and Gentile believers, is an amazing fulfilment of what the Psalmist said in Psalm 133, *'when brothers live together in unity... it is as if the dew of Hermon were falling on Mount Zion. For there the Lord bestows His blessing, even life for evermore.'* I love the older versions of the Bible which translate these words as God *'commands blessing'* in such circumstances, because it gives Him so much joy!

THE FIRST DISCIPLES

It's always such a thrill to be able to walk along the shores of Galilee, where Jesus *'saw Simon and his brother Andrew casting a net into the lake, for they were fishermen'* and said *'Come follow me and I will make you fishers of men'* (Mark 1:16-17)!

With their response to these simple words, a group of young men left behind their work as fishermen and became disciples of Jesus. They took up their new profession as fishers of men! They were ordinary men, who responded to the call of Jesus and from that point on they were known as His disciples. It was only much later that they became known as Apostles.

Not all disciples of Jesus become Apostles, but you can't be an Apostle without first becoming a disciple. An Apostle is someone with a special anointing for leadership and for bringing things into being that God has birthed in their hearts through vision. Apostles cannot be man-made or man-appointed. But when God's anointing is clearly on them, their work can be recognised by others as being apostolic. Apostles have special responsibility for pioneering leadership within the Body of Christ.

A person should become a disciple, the moment they respond to the call of Jesus to follow Him. Sometimes, however, when people respond to the Gospel call for salvation, they only think in terms of going to

Heaven when they die. But being a Christian disciple is much more than that – it's choosing to live with and for the Lord Jesus now, here on Earth!

Choosing to respond to the call to truly follow and serve Jesus, both here on Earth and later in Heaven, doesn't mean that you then get an instant download of all the knowledge and understanding you will need as a disciple! Learning takes time and commitment. Jesus spent three years teaching and training His disciples for the task ahead. For those first disciples it also meant a new career!

PERSONAL NOTES

TRAINING IN LOVE

In many ways, *Journey to Freedom* is a course in discipleship – learning what we all need to know and understand, about walking in the footsteps of Jesus. Yes, it takes time and commitment, but isn't that the least we can do, in response to His incredible commitment to us? He chose to serve mankind by giving His sinless life, so that sinners may come to know Him and have eternal life for themselves.

We often talk affectionately about the 'twelve disciples', but sometimes we forget that being a disciple must also mean coming under authority and discipline. Without discipline we will never fulfil the destiny God has for each one of us.

In Hebrews 12, the writer is trying to help followers of Jesus to see the way forward as disciples. First, he tells them that they must get rid of everything that acts as a brake on their progress. He uses the illustration of a runner, who could never win a race unless he got rid of everything that he was carrying, that could be an obstacle to running. Here are his words: *'Let us throw off everything that hinders and the sin that so easily entangles, and let us run with perseverance the race marked out for us'* (Hebrews 12:1). Training to be a disciple requires determination and a sense of purpose.

Then, later on in the chapter, the writer tells us how important discipline is and that it is a loving father who disciplines his children. Then he says, if we understand that principle for our own children, how much more gladly we should submit to the discipline of our loving Heavenly Father. He says, *'God disciplines us for our good, that we may share in his holiness'* (Hebrews 12:10).

PERSONAL NOTES

What an incredible reward awaits those who gladly seek to rid themselves of everything that stands in the way of their relationship with Father God, as disciples of Jesus – the joy of sharing in the holiness of God. Such discipline *'produces a harvest of righteousness and peace for those who have been trained by it'* (Hebrews 12:11).

When God first gave me the vision for *Journey to Freedom*, I realised that it was for much more than just a training programme in healing, it was for the building up of the Body of Christ, through equipping the saints in how to produce a harvest of righteousness! What an amazing and exciting objective!

EQUIPPED TO SERVE

If disciples are being trained to follow in the footsteps of Jesus, what does this mean in real terms? Surely, it must mean that we will want to follow His example. In his wonderful teaching in the letter to the Philippians, Paul gives an account of what coming to Earth meant for Jesus:

He, *'being in very nature God, did not consider equality with God something to be grasped, but made Himself nothing, taking the very nature of a servant, being made in human likeness. And being found in appearance as a man, He humbled himself and became obedient to death, even death on a cross!'* (Philippians 2:6-8)

This amazing hymn of praise to Jesus, then ends with the declaration that *'God exalted Him to the highest place and gave Him the name that is above every name, that at the name of Jesus every knee should bow, in Heaven and on Earth and under the Earth, and every tongue confess that Jesus Christ is Lord, to the glory of God the Father'* (Philippians 2:9-11).

So, Jesus came TO SERVE others! The word 'minister', means 'servant'. If someone becomes 'a minister of a local congregation' it means that he has been called to serve the people – to love, encourage, teach and heal them and be their Shepherd, their Pastor.

The highest point of Jesus' service to others was when He laid down His life, so that we may rediscover ours. And having served the whole world, in this extraordinary way, it was God who raised Him up to His place in glory. Jesus did not raise Himself up from the dead – Father God did it (Acts 2:24, 10:40, 1 Peter 1:21). And in this we have an important principle. ***It's our responsibility to serve God, in whatever way He leads us***

and whatever the cost. It's God's responsibility to raise us up and reward us (James 4:10).

It's only through serving Him, because we love Him, that we put ourselves in the place of being blessed by the God who is love. Not all the rewards may come in this life, but be assured, the rewards will come. Paul tells us in 1 Corinthians 3:14 that what we offer up to God as the fruit of our life will be tested and each one will receive their reward.

1 Samuel 2:30 says, *'The Lord declares... those who honour me, I will honour'*. This is not just a vague promise that might happen. It's a commitment by God to give blessing to those who honour Him. It's also a declaration of the Lord's faithfulness to the promises He had made.

THE COMMISSION OF A DISCIPLE

When Jesus first sent out His disciples to serve Him (see Luke 9:1-2), He gave them instructions to do three things: **Proclaim the Kingdom of God, Heal the sick and Cast out demons.**

We have already looked at the importance of recognising that, as disciples of Jesus, we are now citizens of a Kingdom – not any of the kingdoms of this world, but of a spiritual kingdom, whose authority exceeds that of Satan, the god of this world. We are like a 'colony of Heaven' living within the confines of an alien land!

God rejoices to bless His Kingdom citizens. He wants to equip them for life, releasing them into their gifting and destiny. But the reality is this – when any of us enter into that Kingdom, we come with the consequences of all the burdens of life, some of our own making, some caused by others and some inherited. In order to fulfil our calling, we need to know the healing and personal restoration that Jesus, the Good Shepherd, would want His sheep to receive.

It's interesting that among the many prophetic words given to Ezekiel by the Sovereign Lord, some of the harshest and strongest words are reserved for the leaders of God's people in Israel, who had responsibility for and authority over the sheep (the people), but used their position irresponsibly and only took care of themselves (Ezekiel 34:2).

God asks, through Ezekiel, *'should not the shepherds take care of the flock?'* (Ezekiel 34:2). They were happy to personally benefit from the

PERSONAL NOTES

PERSONAL NOTES

offerings the people brought but were condemned by God because they had *not 'strengthened the weak or healed the sick or bound up the injured'... or 'brought back the strays or searched for the lost'* (Ezekiel 34:4). Healing of His people was very much on the heart of God then. And God hasn't changed His character or His nature. Healing is still on His heart today.

Later in Ezekiel 34 there is a clear Messianic prophecy about the coming of Jesus, when Ezekiel speaks out words from the heart of God, saying, *'I myself will search for my sheep... I will pasture them... I will tend my sheep... I will search for the lost and bring back the strays... I will bind up the injured and strengthen the weak'* (from Ezekiel 34:11-16).

In these Ezekiel passages God is talking about the healing God wants His people to have in that day, when God's people would one day return to their land (Ezekiel 36:24), something that has been happening in Israel in our own lifetime. God not only wanted to see them return to their own land, but He also prophesied that when they returned to Him, this is where they would also experience His healing.

When Jesus actually came to the Jewish people in Israel, He referred to Himself as the Good Shepherd, who lays down His life for the sheep (John 10:11). But then He said, *'I have other sheep that are not of this sheep pen'* (meaning of Israel), *'I must bring them also. They too will listen to my voice, and there shall be one flock and one shepherd'* (John 10:16).

Here Jesus is painting an incredible picture of Jewish and Gentile believers in Messiah becoming one flock, under the leadership of one Shepherd. This is something that Paul explained in his letter to the Ephesians, when he said that the ultimate purpose of God was *'to create in Himself one new man out of the two'* (Jew and Gentile), *'thus making peace, and in this one body to reconcile both of them to God through the cross... for through Him we both have access to the Father by one Spirit'* (Ephesians 2:15-18).

Later in *Journey to Freedom*, we will take a closer look at God's purposes for Israel, but my reason for drawing your attention to these important scriptures now is simply to say that healing is so clearly on the heart of God for ALL His people – Jew and Gentile. Whichever we are, when we come back to Him, we come with all the consequences of having lived in an alien land. We come without a reliable moral compass and from a place where the Lgod of this world constantly tries to put us into chains of bondage. Jesus said to us all that He had come to set us free from these chains (Luke 4:18, John 10:10).

GETTING READY FOR SERVICE

So His healing is for us all – for you and for me. It's on the heart of God for all believers – without exception, shepherds and sheep, Jew and Gentile. And if we really want to enter into the place of peace with God, through Jesus the Good Shepherd, then giving Him His rightful place in our lives as Lord, Saviour and Healer is essential.

SUMMARY

God has a purpose for each one of our lives. We all need training for the task – training which Jesus gave to the first disciples 'on the job'. But in addition to the training about the work, we need to be personally transformed and equipped for doing this work. This means we must be willing to walk the walk of discipleship and receive the healing we need. Only in this way can we truly set out to serve Him as His disciples.

PRAYER

Thank You, Lord, that you call ordinary men and women to serve You as disciples. Help me to see my life as an opportunity for You to bring healing to others as I seek to serve You as a disciple. In Jesus' Name, Amen.

PERSONAL NOTES

Stage 6, Chapter 2

HEALING FOR THE INNER MAN

PERSONAL NOTES

John was the apple of his parents' eye. They loved God and they loved their son. He was an open faced youth. Everyone loved him. He enjoyed life and was fun to be with.

In his teens he fell in with friends who seemed such cool characters. They took advantage of his generous heart and led him into some very ungodly things. In his twenties, John had become a man of the world. He was no longer the open-faced boy, but was now very worldly-wise and had forgotten God. He was more experienced with women than he should have been. And some of the words that came out of his mouth would have embarrassed his mother and father. In his thirties he had made a small fortune through some very dubious business deals. He had been married, and divorced and was now lonely. The mother of his children couldn't handle his unfaithfulness. In his forties he had lost his fortune, and his family, and could only sustain short-term jobs, in between his bouts of drinking.

In his fifties he came to himself. Mum and Dad were dead by now. He searched out his long-forgotten sister. She hardly recognised him when he stood on her doorstep. The open-face, she had known so well as a child, was gone, and in its

PERSONAL NOTES

place were the scars of a hard and selfish life lived without God, serving only his personal desires.

She wept. He wept. And so began his journey from the island of pain to the harbour of peace. Several weeks later he knelt with his sister and gave his life back to the Lord he knew as a child. She had led the prodigal home to the Saviour. He came, just as he was, to the foot of the cross, and began the journey of recovery as he began to put his life back together.

He could not undo history and change anything from his past, but little by little, the Saviour healed his broken heart and put him back on the road of life. The years that the locust had eaten had taken their toll, but the love of his Saviour brought healing to the damage his heart had sustained. He spent the latter years of his life telling young people of the dangers of false friends and of ignoring God's call on their life. His heart was now firmly anchored in God and He saved many from the traps of the enemy.

This story of John is only a story. But every component of the story is based on the reality of personal ministry experience and is true for someone – maybe, even, for you.

In the past thirty years of my life, I have spoken with hundreds, probably thousands, of people who were in deep need of personal healing. One of the most common things that people say is, 'Why didn't someone teach me about these things when I was young?'

If the heart of man is not securely anchored in God, then it's all too easy to drift across the seas of life until their vessel is ship-wrecked on the rocks of joyless pleasure. But even when that's happened, it's not the end of the road for the believer in God. For He still wants to equip us to serve Him in the best possible way, for however many more years we may have left on the Earth.

THE HEART OF MAN

It's hard to define precisely what the heart of man actually is, but everyone knows what it means to make a decision of the heart! When you talk about someone's heart, you are talking about the very core of their personality, that inner place of their being where the emotions have such influence. It's the place where we think our most private thoughts, where our secret inner motives are rooted and where our decisions are actually made.

PERSONAL NOTES

It's the meeting place of our spirit and our soul, the place where our mind, our emotions and our will converge to determine the issues of life. Above all, it's the place we choose to be responsive to either the sweet influence of the Spirit of God or the dangerous influence of the god of this world, who uses the motives of the heart to further lead our fallen, carnal nature astray.

The Bible has a lot to say about the heart – the inner man. The writer of the Proverbs warns us *'Above all else, guard your heart, for everything you do flows from it'* (Proverbs 4:23). Then, for example, he warns men of the dangers of an adulteress by saying *'Do not let your heart turn to her ways or stray into her paths. Many are the victims she has brought down… her house is a highway to the grave'* (from Proverbs 7:25-27). He is warning about the secondary consequences of following the ungodly desires of the heart – they are serious and dangerous.

Jeremiah described the heart of man as being *'deceitful above all things and beyond cure'* (Jeremiah 17:9). In the next verse we hear that *'the Lord searches the heart and examines the mind, to reward a man according to his conduct, according to what his deeds deserve'*. This must mean that the choices of the heart are within our control, otherwise the idea of a reward according to our conduct would make no sense.

But if God says that the heart of man is *'beyond cure'*, then what do we mean by praying for inner healing? What are we actually praying for? Are we trying to heal something that can't be healed?!

Even the Apostle Paul recognised that there is a problem in this respect. For he admitted his own difficulty in dealing with the motives that were resident in his own sinful nature. *'For I have the desire to do what is good, but I cannot carry it out. For I do not do the good I want to do, but the evil I do not want to do – this I keep on doing'* (Romans 7:18-19).

Then, in verses 22-24 he said, *'For in my inner being I delight in God's law; but I see another law at work in me, waging war against the law of my mind and making me a prisoner of the law of sin at work within me. What a wretched man I am! Who will rescue me from this body that is subject to death?'*

Mercifully, his response to this question is clear and positive, *'Thanks be to God, who delivers me through Jesus Christ our Lord'* (Romans 7:25). There was an answer to Paul's problem and there is a solution for us all. The answer is not a clever argument, but a person – the only person who has ever overcome sin and death. It is only through Jesus that we

PERSONAL NOTES

can enjoy the blessing of living under a higher law – *'the law of the Spirit of life'* which, Paul said, has *'set me free from the law of sin and death'* (Romans 8:2).

LET'S SUMMARISE WHAT ALL THIS MEANS FOR YOU AND FOR ME!

Because of the fall, the heart of every single one of us has acquired a nature which has been corrupted by man's allegiance to the god of this world. We call it the sin nature or the carnal nature. The spirit within our human nature, as originally created in us by God, still craves after Him. But the corruption in our heart, that came through the fall, means that there is a conflicting law also operating in the heart of man. Our carnal nature naturally desires to please our *'father the devil'*, as Jesus described Satan, when He was telling the Pharisees exactly where their ungodly thinking had its origins (John 8: 42-47).

So the constant battle in the heart of every human being, whether or not they are a born again believer, is between the desire to do those things that would please the God who loves and made us, and the desire to please the one who wanted to be above the Almighty and take the worship that was due to God, to himself. In simple terms, the consequence of this is that our carnal nature desires to worship Satan and is intent on influencing us to do things that would please Satan.

When we are convicted of sin by the Holy Spirit, repent and receive Jesus as our Lord and Saviour, we are born again of the Spirit of God. Our human spirit, which had been made dead to God through sin, is restored to having a new and living relationship with Father God. We are then in the position of not having to live according to the demands of *'the sinful nature, but according to the Spirit'* (Romans 8:4).

We can, of course, still make ungodly choices, and sin, by allowing the carnal nature to have its way, but Jesus never came under Satan's control, so His authority is always higher than Satan's and through the power of the Spirit we can resist the Devil and choose to make the right decisions.

As long as we are living on planet Earth we are living in the territory controlled by Satan, the god of this world and we will always, therefore, have a carnal nature. It is only the redeemed, and only when they leave this life and enter Paradise, who will, at the end, lose the carnality of their nature. Nothing in Heaven will be tainted by the sins of mankind. Then we will be totally free of all the consequences of sin. ***There will be no need of the healing ministry in Heaven, for no-one there will be suffering.*** It truly will be Paradise for all believers!

WHO AND WHAT CAN BE HEALED?

So, if the carnal nature can never be cured in this life, what can be healed? The answer is simple – whatever consequential damage there has been, as a result of our own wrong choices or the ways the sins of others have affected us, can be healed. These are our wounds.

There are sins and there are wounds. Scripture tells us to *'crucify the sinful nature, with its passions and desires'* (Galatians 5:24). That means put sinful choices to death – or in even simpler terms, 'say NO to the flesh and the enemy!' ***But we cannot put our wounds to death.*** The wounds are there as a result of our history – no amount of trying to 'crucify' the pain, that we now have as a result of those wounds, will ever work.

To try and do so, is like trying to cure a dandelion problem in a lawn by pulling the flower heads off the plants. All that does is strengthen the roots and make the problem worse. To deal with the dandelions, you have to extract the roots. To deal with the pain of the past the root must be exposed so that the wound can be healed.

You can't change (cure) the fact that we have a carnal nature, but God can heal the damage that the wrong choices of the carnal nature have caused. And under the Lordship of Jesus we can cease to give way to the inner demands that the carnal nature tries to make on our lives. This is the process which the early church fathers referred to as sanctification, which Paul described as *'being transformed into His likeness with ever-increasing glory, which comes from the Lord, who is the Spirit'* (2 Corinthians 3:18).

Jesus' death on the cross dealt with all the consequences of sin – so, in Him, our relationship with Father God can be restored and through Him our wounds can be healed. This is exactly what the prophet Isaiah was talking about in Isaiah 53:5 when, in talking about the Sovereign Lord, the Messiah, he said *'He was pierced for our transgressions... and by His wounds, we are healed.'*

God does not want us to continue suffering because of the wounds

PERSONAL NOTES

PERSONAL NOTES

we have sustained in the battle of life. Jesus sent this very clear message out into our fallen world, by beginning His ministry with healing the sick. This expression of the heart of God for His children is a clear message to mankind, of the love of our Heavenly Father. No wonder He was so upset with the leaders of Israel, in Ezekiel 34, for not bringing God's healing to the hurting. They were not representing the true heart of God to the heart of man.

Many years ago now, the work of Ellel Ministries was described as ***'Bringing the heart of God to the heart of man'***. That phrase has become our most enduring slogan, describing to all who come the nature of God's ministry to a hurting world.

So, in summary, the nature of the heart of man cannot be changed, but all the consequential damage can be healed and in Christ we can have the strength to resist the pressure to sin coming from our carnal nature. And who is this blessing for? For all who come to Him for salvation and healing – for all those who choose to walk in His ways.

AND SO BACK TO JOHN!

In the story above, we saw how a man made wrong choices when faced by temptation – he allowed his carnal nature to lead him astray. When John returned to the Lord, forgiveness was instant and unconditional, but all the damage John had sustained through life was not instantly healed.

Inner healing is a process. The issues have to be faced and dealt with. People need to be forgiven. Sins need to be confessed. The ties to people with whom he had ungodly relationships need to be broken. Healing, and where necessary deliverance, will need to be applied to the wounds.

And little by little the wounds will be healed and John will begin to rediscover who God intended him to be. He will begin to enter into his destiny. And while John's face may still bear the scars of life, the sparkle in his eyes will enliven the creases in his face and he will know the joy of the Lord, which will be his strength.

Yes, he will need to resist the temptations of the flesh in the power of the Spirit of God. And, if at any time he falls back into sin, he will need to come back to God quickly and get his life back on track again. But, I can assure, you that God being his helper, John will once again rejoice in God His Saviour, who has become His Healer and Deliverer as well.

I have seen it happen too many times not to believe that, with God, all things are possible!

And if God can do that for people like John, who have plumbed the depths of sin, then there can be no obstacle to the healing by God of the many much lesser things that also seek to be a barrier to our growth as disciples of Jesus.

SUMMARY

Inner healing, as part of our daily walk with God, is essential, if we are going to grow to maturity as men and women of God. We cannot change our past, but God is able and willing to heal us of the damage that the past has caused.

PRAYER

Thank You, Lord, that you love me so much that you don't want me to remain in bondage to my past. Help me to distinguish between my sins and my wounds so that, with Your help, I can truly crucify the ungodly choices that arise from my carnal nature and be healed of the damage I have suffered because of my past. In Jesus' Name, Amen.

PERSONAL NOTES

Stage 6, Chapter 3

SET FREE TO SERVE

We have now learned together how the carnal nature in the heart of man cannot be healed, but that the damage caused by what has happened to us in the past can be healed. It is obvious that unless we do receive healing for these things, then our potential is limited and our capacity to serve will be restricted. It is a simple fact that a crippled man cannot run to win a race.

We saw how, at the beginning of Hebrews 12, we are urged by the writer to get rid of everything that gets in the way of our ability to run, especially the sin which entangles us in ungodly things (Hebrews 12:1). This whole process could be summarised in the words of verses 12 and 13, which say *'strengthen your feeble arms and weak knees. Make level paths for your feet, so that the lame may not be disabled, but rather healed'*.

It is clear from the context of this passage that the writer is referring primarily to spiritual lameness rather than actual physical conditions. However, I have seen many examples of how, through dealing with the real issues in a person's life, they have then received physical healing.

One couple longed to have a baby, but were unable to conceive. The

PERSONAL NOTES

PERSONAL NOTES

lady had been engaged previously but broke it off when she realized this wasn't the man God wanted her to marry. But this is what that man said, 'If you won't marry me, then you'll never be a mother'. Those words had acted as a curse on her life. When she forgave the man and the power of his words was broken, she was set free and healed. Very shortly after that she conceived her first child!

HEALING THE 'DISABLED'

I often use spontaneous drama, using people from the audience, to teach various points at conferences and church meetings. In one of the most simple, yet most effective dramas, I ask a young man to help me by trying to run a race. The obstacles, however, he has to overcome, are represented by four other people who hang on to his legs and his arms, making it impossible for him to move forward.

One of the hangers-on might represent un-confessed wrong relationships from his past, another the people who have hurt him in the past whom he has never forgiven. A third could be his attempts to dabble in the occult and the fourth might be a dominating mother who still controls him.

With these four 'people' hanging on tight to his legs and arms, I urge him to run, but it's impossible for him to move forward. He remains anchored to the spot by his problems. No amount of extra Bible Study, attending prayer meetings, fasting or anything else will help him run the race more effectively. What needs to happen is that the issues represented by those holding his arms and legs must be addressed and the obstructions removed.

It's easy to see in the drama how when the different issues are dealt with, the man is then set free to run the race of life and be equipped to serve in the Kingdom of God.

This picture, however, is not just an illustrative drama, it is the real life situation for many, many people who are nursing known and, sometimes, unknown issues from their past. The Body of Christ is full of unhealed people, who would love to be able to take a more active role in the Kingdom of God.

The whole purpose behind Journey to Freedom is to equip the saints of God to be warriors for God as disciples of Jesus Christ.

PERSONAL NOTES

THE SWINE FLU HEALTH CHECK!

Shortly before writing this, the governments of many countries began to react to the outbreak of a world-wide pandemic – a flu virus that started its life in Mexico, and was popularly called Swine Flu. I then received a booklet through my letter box from the government, telling me all I needed to know about Swine Flu and what to do if I had any symptoms.

But it was only when I arrived back from one of my teaching trips overseas, and was not feeling very well, that I suddenly thought I had better read what that leaflet said! Because I was now struggling with some flu-like symptoms, that leaflet had now assumed an importance it didn't have previously!

When I found it and read the details, it wasn't particularly helpful. It told me nothing that would help me decide whether or not I had caught the virus. But it did give me an internet address, and told me to go there, online, and check out my symptoms against a series of diagnostic questions that I could answer through my computer. Twenty minutes later it was clear that whatever it was I had come home with, it wasn't swine flu.

But the online check list did help me think through how best to summarise what we have been learning together. And so the next section contains the *Journey to Freedom* Seven Point Health Check!

THE JOURNEY TO FREEDOM SEVEN POINT HEALTH CHECK!

In putting this together, I imagined what questions the writer of the Hebrews might have put on a check list for his 'lame' readers. Or perhaps Paul might have devised for the Galatian or the Ephesian Christians, who were struggling with temptation and the consequences of sin!

All of these are vital questions – even the first one which asks basic questions about whether or not we really know the Lord.

QUESTION 1

Do I know the Lord for myself – or do I only know about Him?

I will never forget the clergyman who came with his wife on a Healing Retreat at Ellel Grange. He had been a minister for thirty-five years, but

PERSONAL NOTES

when he heard the teaching on the first session of the retreat, he realised that there was a major problem in his life. He knew all about Jesus, but as to knowing Jesus personally for himself, that was a very different issue!

Salvation is a gift, received through faith in Jesus Christ, through whom we enter into a living relationship with God. Salvation is not something we can earn or buy (like getting an entrance ticket to Heaven), or something we get as a reward for being religious or putting in years of service in the Church.

Throughout the world-wide work of Ellel Ministries we have now conducted over 3000 Healing Retreats. On almost every single one of these, there have been individuals who came for healing and discovered that the primary healing they needed was to be born again of the Spirit of God. This is like a resurrection from the dead – and there can't be any greater healing need than resurrection!

Only this last week in Israel we met a Russian speaking lady who attended one of our events in Ukraine fifteen years ago. She had come to a healing conference but discovered that salvation was her primary healing need and she was born again. Today, many years later, she is a Pastor's wife in Israel!

If you still have any doubts about whether or not you really know the Lord, may I encourage you to go back to Stage 2 of our journey together and read those units again. If you don't know the Lord, then you can't receive the healing He longs to give to His children.

QUESTION 2

I am trusting Jesus to be my Saviour, so that when I die I can be assured of a place in Heaven, but am I willing for Jesus to be Lord of every area of my life here on Earth?

This is a big and enduring problem. Even though we are living within the limitations of time and space, God has put eternity in the heart of every man and woman (Ecclesiastes 3:11), so that the big question of what happens when we die is never far from the surface of our mind – especially when we are in potentially dangerous circumstances.

When evangelists present Jesus as the key to eternity and the Saviour from death and hell, they are proclaiming truth, but it isn't the whole truth. As a result many people 'go to the front of a meeting' or pray 'the sinner's prayer' only as a means of avoiding hell, should they find, after death, that hell is a real place after all. The important question to ask is not whether or not we are going to Heaven or Hell, but do we love Jesus?

Some of the most challenging words in Scripture come from the lips of Jesus himself, when He says, *'not everyone who says to me Lord, Lord, will enter the Kingdom of Heaven, but only he who does the will of my Father who is in Heaven'* (Matthew 7:21).

Jesus is stating a seldom taught fact – the evidence for our salvation is not shown by whether or not we have a decision card, but whether or not we desire to do the will of Father God here on Earth. Jesus put it very simply when He said, *'If anyone loves me, he will obey my teaching. My father will love him, and we will come to him and make our home with him. He who does not love me will not obey my teaching'* (John 14:23-24).

You can't actually separate love and obedience in the Scripture. It was Jesus' love for mankind that made Him obedient to death on the cross. It should be our love for Him that makes us want to be obedient and serve Him. But if it is evident by the way we live, that we have no interest in loving and obeying God while we are here on Earth, then it is not unreasonable to ask, why should God open the doors of Heaven to us when we die?

The key question arising out of this, in terms of healing, is simply whether or not Jesus is Lord of our lives here and now. Do we love Him enough to want to obey Him, for Him to be Lord of our lives and not just a Saviour who we will suddenly want to depend on when we die? If He's not Lord, then we do not have any authority over the works of darkness in our lives. And we may pray for healing, but we are not in the place where it is possible for us to receive the healing that we are asking for.

QUESTION 3

Have I forgiven all those down my generation line who have done ungodly things which have resulted in me receiving an ungodly inheritance?

It is true that the person we now are, can be seriously influenced by the way others have been before us. One generation after another can be

PERSONAL NOTES

PERSONAL NOTES

influenced by, and even suffer from, the consequences of the sins of the ancestors (Exodus 20:5, Lamentations 5:7).

Where there are known issues, we need to consciously speak out our forgiveness of those ancestors who have given us a bad inheritance. And we then need to forgive, generally, everyone else who has done anything that might have released ungodly spiritual influences into our ancestral line.

When I prayed for James, who at age sixteen had been an epileptic since his earliest days, he was totally healed of the epilepsy. Even though he was unconscious at the time, following a fit, I led him in a prayer in his spirit to forgive everyone on his generation line who had done anything that had made him vulnerable to the condition. Even when a person is unconscious, you can still talk to their spirit, which never goes unconscious.

I then prayed for deliverance and healing and James was totally healed, as was confirmed by the doctors on his next visit to the local hospital. His healing was so profound that the doctors wrote on his medical records that James could never have been an epileptic – even though when I prayed for him he was unconscious, having just had an epileptic fit! It was the act of forgiving his ancestors and then praying for deliverance and healing that released God's healing in James.

QUESTION 4

Have I forgiven my own parents, brothers and sisters for everything I need to in their lives and for anything they did to me, that has left me with lifetime scars?

It's a fact that the people who can hurt us the most are the ones who are closest to us! Parents don't always get everything right and often fall into the trap of treating unfairly, or looking unfavourably on, one of their children – especially if they were wanting a girl and they got a boy, or vice-versa.

Some of the most difficult cases we have to deal with are when the Father or Mother, who should be the ones who were protecting their children, turn out to be cruel and abusive, even sexually abusing their own offspring.

And brothers and sisters can also be very cruel, especially when they become jealous and start punishing one of their number in various ways.

The closer the people are to us, the harder it sometimes is to forgive them. But when Jesus instructed us to forgive all those who have hurt us (Matthew 6:15), He was showing us how we can be set free from the consequences of inner bitterness and un-forgiveness.

QUESTION 5

Have I forgiven all those who have hurt me down the years – from my school days, through youth and college, to work and family life and church life?

Outside the family, there can be many people who have caused us pain in our life. If this is still an issue for you, I suggest you go back and read again the teaching based on 'the Lord's Prayer'.

QUESTION 6

Have I been honest with myself and with God about all the known sins in my own life? Have I confessed them before God and man so that they might be forgiven (1 John 1:9) and healed (James 5:16)?

Am I willing for God to shine His light into every area of my life so that any other darkness, as a result of my own sins, can be exposed and dealt with? It's important we say 'yes' to this question, for often we can be self-deceived and we need to give Jesus our permission to show us whatever we need to know about ourselves (Psalm 139:23-24).

We don't naturally have any desire to face things we thought had been long-forgotten, but sometimes it is those long-forgotten things that the enemy can hang on to, in the secret place of our life. He will want to use such things to maximum effect to keep us bound to the past.

The prophet Isaiah became more aware of the sinfulness of his life, when he had that extraordinary experience of being in the presence and holiness of God (Isaiah 6:5). The closer we get to God, the more aware we become of things that need to be cleansed. This is part of the whole

PERSONAL NOTES

PERSONAL NOTES

process of sanctification through which we are not only being made holy (growing more like God day by day), but receiving our healing as well.

QUESTION 7

Am I willing to serve the Lord all my days, seeking out His best for my life and choosing to serve Him joyfully?

It's easy to think that if we give God the best of our life, we will be depriving ourselves of the pleasures of life! There is a worldly logic about this conclusion, but it's not true. It's another deception of the enemy.

The greatest joy any of us can ever experience is through being fulfilled in God. He has given us gifts and abilities and when we are using these to live in the destiny that He has prepared for us in advance (Ephesians 2:10), we will know the greatest joy. So when we are willing for Him to have His way in our lives we will know the greatest depth of healing and joy any of us can ever experience.

BE SYSTEMATIC

Answering the above questions may not be the solution to every situation you will face in life, but if you deal with all the issues raised by just these seven questions, that in itself is almost sure to be life-transforming. I have seen so often how, when people systematically pray through their lives like this, God brings important things to the surface of their memory that, they suddenly realise, are unresolved issues from the past – things that deep down in their consciousness they may well have been stressed about and wrestling with for years.

In many cases, the consequence could well have been unresolved pain and physical conditions for which you may have been having treatment from your doctor. It always amazes me how often it is that physical symptoms disappear when we resolve the spiritual issues in our lives. We may describe the effect as having been healed, but in reality it is simply the removal of the hidden underlying issues which are eventuality reflected in the body as a pain or physical condition.

PERSONAL NOTES

MORE TO COME

There is much more we need to learn about the nature of man – but all in good time. We will want to see how the mind, the emotions and the will work together in the soul, and how the spirit, the soul and the body operate together, giving us our humanity.

We are taking these steps carefully – one step at a time – so we can really understand the scriptural principles involved and apply them in our lives. This is both for our own benefit and for the sake of others whom God may call us to help along life's journey. This is how the Body of Christ works – helping one another (Ephesians 4:16).

Next we will be looking at how we must always be ready for action as we listen to the Lord and seek to serve Him with everything we are.

SUMMARY

In order to be equipped to serve God, we need to be set free from all the obstacles that are standing in the way of both our healing and our commitment to the Lord. When we choose to obey Him because we love Him, we will be putting ourselves in the place of blessing.

PRAYER

Thank You Lord that Your love for me does not depend on me having a perfect past. Thank You for loving me as I am and for being willing to help me get to the place where I truly fulfil my destiny in You. In Jesus' Name, Amen.

Stage 6, Chapter 4

READY FOR ACTION

PERSONAL NOTES

In recent chapters we have looked at some of the essential stepping stones towards personal transformation. It's vital that we understand, as disciples of Jesus, how we can receive His healing for ourselves and be equipped to serve Him, for we need to be ready at all times for whatever action the Lord calls us to take.

It's no use thinking that when God calls me, I'll get ready then and in the meantime I'll just entertain myself! The fact is, God calls those who have already shown by their heart attitude that they are willing, by preparing themselves as men and women of God in readiness for whatever He may call us to do. That doesn't mean we're not going to have any fun in life – as we will see tomorrow, for the best things in life are always found by being in the place of God's calling.

We may not know what our life's work will turn out to be as we seek to find the destiny God has planned for us. But all God requires of us is to be obedient to Him, one day at a time, and trust Him with the outcome. In my own journey, I knew God was calling me into a healing ministry, but for many years I could only take one step at a time,

PERSONAL NOTES

one day at a time, until the pathway to the work of Ellel Ministries opened up.

And still today my life is like that – one step at a time, one day at a time. When I look back I marvel at God's goodness and faithfulness as I see the way He has safely led me through the enemy's minefield to reach a field of blessing. That doesn't mean there have been no mistakes along the way – there have. One of my own, most important lessons, was realising that even when I make a mistake, ***I'm still loved by God.*** But the sooner I recognise the mistake and get back on track through confession and repentance, the sooner I'll be back in that place of my calling.

The Christian life is never boring! It's an amazing adventure with God. It's an adventure in which God gives us wonderful opportunities to participate in what He's doing. He delegated His authority over the Earth to mankind, and so ***it's through mankind that He normally does His work on Earth.*** This is why He looks for our cooperation to get things done!

St. Teresa of Avila, in the fourteenth century, expressed this principle so well:

"God has no hands but our hands to do his work today; God has no feet but our feet to lead others in his way; God has no voice but our voice to tell others how he died; and, God has no help but our help to lead them to his side."

When it comes to taking action for the Kingdom, God looks for those who are equipped, ready and willing. He looks for those who wait patiently for that divine moment of opportunity, and then spring into action in obedience to their Master.

But none of us can spring into action unless our feet are active, fit and well-shod! I have a friend who struggles because of a problem with his feet. And so he's extremely limited in what he can do. It's the same if our spiritual feet are incapacitated in any way. We're limited in what we can do in the Kingdom of God. Our spiritual feet need to be in good shape and well-shod!

PERSONAL NOTES

WITH FEET SHOD?

So how can we have well-shod feet? In the final chapter of Ephesians, Paul tells us in detail how to defend ourselves against all the spiritual attacks of the enemy. As part of the armour available to a believer he says, *'have your feet fitted with the readiness that comes from the Gospel of peace'*(Ephesians 6:15).

I love the Amplified Version of Ephesians 6:15 in which it says:

'And having shod your feet in preparation, to face the enemy with the firm footed stability, the promptness, and the readiness produced by the good news, of the Gospel of peace'. Then, it cross-references this verse to Isaiah 52:7, where we read those wonderful words:

'How beautiful on the mountains are the feet of those who bring good tidings, who proclaim salvation'

And in Nahum 1:15, we read:

'Look, there on the mountains, the feet of one who brings good news, who proclaims peace'

It's clear from these scriptures that the feet are very important and that they must be well-shod at all times for the work of the Kingdom. There's a sense in which we must never take our shoes off!

If you're a member of the Fire, Ambulance or Police emergency services, you can't be on duty and not have your shoes on. You must always be ready to spring into action. It's no use saying 'just wait a minute while I get my shoes on', when a person's life may be threatened by any delay or a criminal escape being arrested by the Police!

The same principle applies to all the weapons of warfare that Paul describes in Ephesians 6. We should remain spiritually armed at all times – relaxed in God, yes, but ready at all times for a rapid response – just as the emergency services have to be when they're on duty. The only difference between believers and the emergency service personnel is that believers never go off duty!

We may have seasons of our life when we're more relaxed than at others, for we all need rest and recovery, be it on our annual vacation or enjoying a Sabbath rest. But if we think that our vacation, for example, is

PERSONAL NOTES

a time when we can go spiritually off duty, then beware! These can be the seasons of life when the enemy is most actively trying to get us into wrong things and, even, wrong relationships, when we're caught off-guard. Satan never takes a vacation! I'm reminded of the wise, and very true, comment John Bunyan made, when talking about the dangers of being caught off guard and falling into sin: *'One leak will sink a ship!'*

The lesson of the Titanic must never be forgotten. This seemingly unsinkable vessel was steaming in the darkness through a 'minefield' of icebergs. It only took a collision with one iceberg to sink the vessel, with massive loss of life. Instead of being associated with something unsinkable, the very word 'Titanic' has entered the world's vocabulary for the opposite reason. Being caught off guard turned a simple, but catastrophic mistake, into one of the world's greatest peace-time disasters.

Sadly, there have been many Titanics in the history of Christian ministry, some of which have been given huge publicity in recent years by the media, and through which great damage has been done to the Body of Christ. No wonder the Scripture reminds us of the dangers of pride when it says, *'So, if you think you are standing firm'* (on those feet of yours!), *'be careful that you don't fall'* (1 Corinthians 10:12).

While, yes, there is confession, repentance, forgiveness and restoration available for the believer, there are times when the unguarded moment can take a person off course for years, sometimes even a lifetime. Where our feet take us is always of critical importance to God. They can either take us to place of blessing or a place of cursing.

Just the title of Derek Prince's very important book, 'Blessing or Curse, You Can Choose' says it all as he describes the consequences of either remaining in, or going outside of, the provisions of God's Covenant. We will be looking very carefully at how God wants to bless us through His Covenant promises at a later stage.

It's absolutely true that we can't walk anywhere, except on our feet. And wherever our feet go, the rest of our body will follow. The feet can't go one way and the body another. The feet are the agency of the body through which we're taken wherever we choose to go.

It's especially significant that the book of Proverbs includes *'feet that are quick to rush into evil'*(Proverbs 6:18) among the seven things that are detestable to God. We desperately need to put our feet down on safe ground and not let them take us into places of spiritual compromise or sinful activity.

The Psalmist declares that *'Your Word is a lamp to my feet and a light for my path'* (Psalm 119:105). We will do well to always heed the Word of God and let it be a constant light on our path. But for this to be reality in our lives, we need to regularly take in the Scriptures and let them become a bastion of truth in our hearts. If you have any question marks about the importance of obeying God's Word, it may be important for you to read again some of the teaching on *The Bible – My Guide for Life.*

THE GOSPEL OF PEACE

So, let's get back to those shoes we all need to be wearing! Paul tells us that our *'feet must be shod with the readiness that comes from the Gospel of Peace'*. What does this mean?

Firstly we can only know the peace of God for ourselves, which truly does pass all understanding (Philippians 4:7) through knowing God and seeking to bring our lives into line with His truth. We can't know that inner peace which transcends all the issues of life without being in relationship with the God of peace.

If we're going to be the agency of peace for others, we must come to know that peace in our own lives. Otherwise our efforts to tell others about the peace of God, will sound like the man who tells people about how safe the roller-coaster is, but who's too scared to have a ride himself!

In the early days of his ministry, the great evangelist Billy Graham wrote one of those Christian books which will go down in history as a life-changing volume. 'Peace with God' became an instant best-seller and has continued to sell by the thousand ever since and I don't think it's ever been out of print.

It was first published in 1953, just before Billy Graham's momentous evangelistic campaign at the Harringay Arena, in London, in 1954. The book simply explained how every single human being is in need of peace in their heart and the only way to obtain peace is by forgiveness of sin through Jesus Christ.

Mike Martin was a young Cambridge graduate who attended the meetings on one of the nights I went to Harringay with my Dad. I was a ten year old boy at the time. I marvelled at the hundreds of men and

PERSONAL NOTES

PERSONAL NOTES

women who found faith in Jesus Christ, and then peace with God at those meetings. I was deeply impacted by the experience.

We didn't know Mike, but on the way into Harringay Dad responded to a prompting from the Holy Spirit (he was ready for action!) to follow Mike in and pray for him. We sat behind him and Dad prayed! But Mike didn't respond to the Gospel message so, after the meeting, Dad followed him out of the arena and sat next to him on the underground train (even though it was going the opposite direction to our own journey home!) and simply asked him if he had enjoyed the meeting. The man didn't respond, so Dad gave him his card and said 'we'll be praying for you'. With an undecipherable grunt, Mike got off the train at the next stop – and Dad prayed!

Two years later we received a tape-recorded testimony from Mike Martin telling how that simple question, about enjoying the meeting, had prompted him to go back to Harringay the following night and listen once more to Billy Graham. That night, he told us, he gave his life to Christ and found peace with God.

The spiritual shoes Dad was wearing that night were shoes of peace. He was willing to go out of his way – and the wrong direction on the train! – simply because of the prompting of the Spirit to pray for Mike, till he found peace with God. That's something that we should all be ready and willing to do – to share the good news of peace and salvation with whoever God puts across our path. I've never forgotten the lesson. Paul tells us that to take ground from the enemy in this way is a key part of the armoury of the disciple. We must always be ready.

READINESS AT ALL TIMES

In my childhood playing with school-friends, one of the phrases we sometimes used to let everyone know the game was beginning, was 'Action Stations'. That meant we had to be ready. You never know when the Master is going to speak out the equivalent of these words into your Spirit and say 'Action Stations' to you.

What I do know, however, is that if you're not ready when that call comes, you will miss an opportunity to be the feet, the hands or the voice of God in bringing His love into the heart of one of His children. Peter encouraged us to *'always be prepared to give an answer to everyone who asks you to give the reason for the hope that you have. But do this with gentleness and respect'* (1 Peter 3:15).

I pray that this will encourage you to look again at what we were saying in the last section about preparing the ground of our own hearts, in order to be of maximum blessing to others.

PERSONAL NOTES

SUMMARY

Learning how to be ready at all times, for whatever the Lord would want us to do, is foundational training for Christian disciples. None of us is exempt from the responsibility of always being willing to share with others the Gospel of peace.

PRAYER

Help me, Lord, to always be alert to listen to Your voice and respond quickly when You show me those things that You want me to do. I don't want to miss out on being a blessing to others. In Jesus' Name, Amen.

Stage 6, Chapter 5

THE JOY OF SERVING GOD

PERSONAL NOTES

This is a very exciting stage of our journey, focusing our attention on the source of real joy, as we discover that the greatest joy any of us can ever experience is found, first and foremost through knowing God as Father, and then, through that relationship, being in the very centre of His will serving Him.

It is as we allow God to heal our past that we get ourselves more and more in the place where we can both hear His voice clearly and fulfil the destiny that God prepared for us in advance (Ephesians 2:10). If we are not in a right relationship with Father God, then we become wise in our own eyes (Proverbs 3:7) and do our own thing. We can then become the judge of what's right or wrong and we will very quickly start to reap a harvest of unrighteousness, rather than the blessing of God.

An unhealed past – especially one that is unhealed because pride won't face the fact that some of our limitations have been caused by our own sin choices – can be like a pair of spiritual ear plugs, blocking out the gentle voice of the Shepherd, when He is trying to get our attention and

PERSONAL NOTES

lead us into 'green pastures' so that He can restore our soul. I wonder how many 'unrestored souls' there are in the Body of Christ, simply because they are not in a place where they can both hear His voice and then do His will?

THE SOURCE OF JOY

Jonathan Edwards was at the heart of the Great Awakening, one of the most significant moves of the Spirit of God in recorded Christian history. He clearly understood this principle when he said, ***'Christ is not only a remedy for your weariness and trouble, but He will give you an abundance of the contrary, joy and delight.'*** Jonathan Edwards saw Christ as both the source of healing (the remedy for your weariness and trouble) and the fountain of joy.

When Moses struck the rock in the wilderness, the situation was grim and desperate. Without water the children of Israel would die and they were complaining to Moses. Moses was in a tough situation. The people were testing both him and God to the limit. Moses knew that God would not have brought them out of Egypt, just to die in the desert. But the people were not in the same faith position as Moses, who knew also that it was not right to test the Lord in this way. The people were getting ready to stone him (Exodus 17:3-4).

It's always the case when people take their eyes off God, and put them on a man, even a leader as great as Moses, that they will eventually rebel and turn against that leader, because he alone will never be able to fulfil all their expectations. It is only when our eyes are firmly fixed on God, who is the source of life, that the depth of healing He longs to give us can be received. No-one else can be their God! As long as people are looking to men or women to be their source of supply, they will always, eventually, be disappointed.

Moses cried out to God for help and God answered his cry. He told Moses what to do, saying, *'Walk on ahead of the people. Take with you some of the elders of Israel and take in your hand the staff with which you struck the Nile, and go. I will stand there before you by the rock at Horeb. Strike the rock and water will come out of it for the people to drink'* (Exodus 17:5-6).

The rock that Moses struck has always been understood to be a picture of Christ, the Rock, the source of healing and life, the remedy for

PERSONAL NOTES

weariness and trouble. He must always be the one to whom we come. Others may be God's agent, as it were, in the process. But whoever it is that God uses to be His instrument of healing, it's always God, in and through Christ Jesus, who's the source of life and healing. He alone is our source of joy. He's the only one who can keep the spring waters flowing from the very core of our being. This is what Jesus said to the woman at the well:

'Everyone who drinks this water will be thirsty again, but whoever drinks the water I will give him will never thirst. Indeed, the water I will give him will become in him a spring of water welling up to eternal life'(John 4:13 and 14). **This is your source of joy – a spring that never runs dry, whatever the circumstances of life may be.**

JOY AND HAPPINESS

The Bible is full of references to both joy and rejoicing. People who are rejoicing are simply expressing the joy that's flowing from within. Paul urges on his readers by saying *'rejoice in the Lord always. I will say it again: Rejoice'* (Philippians 4:4). Christians have good news in their hearts to rejoice about, and Paul is encouraging them to express that joy and not to keep it hidden!

This is what David was experiencing when the Ark of God was brought back to Jerusalem, and King David was *'leaping and dancing before the Lord'* (2 Samuel 6:16). He couldn't contain his joy, but not everyone was in the same position that David was – and even his wife Michal despised what was happening in David, as he worshipped God with a thankful heart and his joy overflowed!

In those days, the Ark of God represented the presence of God. The Ark returning to Jerusalem is a wonderful Old Testament picture of the presence of God returning to the heart of man, because of Christ. The presence of God in the heart is the source of joy. Joy is an experience that only Christians can truly understand. It's radically different from happiness and can only be reached in and through the presence of God.

A happy person can also be a joyful person, but happiness can be a very superficial experience. It is totally related to circumstances and disconnected from the Christian experience of joy.

For example, on the day I was writing this unit the newspaper had

PERSONAL NOTES

photographs of an elderly couple in the north-west of England who have just won twenty-five million pounds on the lottery. Not surprisingly, their faces looked really happy on the pictures!

But winning the lottery won't change anything on the inside. When the emotion of the moment wears away people will soon discover that their big win hasn't changed them at all. Sometimes the excess of money changes the activities of their life so much, that instead of being happier because of their win, they're less happy than before!

Happiness which is related to circumstances may be wonderful for a season, but it doesn't heal the broken heart. It doesn't cure depression and it certainly doesn't bring the healing that comes about through forgiving others.

Someone with depression might go and enjoy watching his favourite football team play a fantastic match and have a great victory. He would feel so happy that day. But when the feelings of elation wear off, the depression could go even deeper, because the person realises that the experience hasn't made any difference to their underlying condition.

Some people try and gain temporary happiness through alcohol or drugs. But whatever 'happy' feelings they may have during the highs of their experience, when the effects wear off nothing will have changed. Sometimes people discover that when they were high on drugs or intoxicated with alcohol, they did things which they now regret and their subsequent condition is worse than it was before. It may feel great to be happy, but happiness can be a very temporary and unsatisfactory experience.

THE NATURE OF JOY

Joy, on the other hand, is very different from happiness. It's not dependent on circumstances at all. Yes, a joyful person will be even more joyful and feel happy when good things have happened. But a joyful person can still be joyful when good things aren't happening, for joy has its root in the spirit of man, whereas happiness has its root in the soul!

The reason is simple – joy is an outworking of how we are in our inner being, and it's a fruit of being in a right relationship with God. That is why joy is included as one of the fruits that the Holy Spirit develops in our life (Galatians 5:22). This means that people can still

PERSONAL NOTES

know joy in their heart, even when circumstances surrounding them are difficult.

Oswald Chambers was a saintly and much-loved commentator on the Word of God. He died tragically in Egypt of a ruptured appendix when he was a Chaplain in the First World War. One of the most popular devotional books ever published was compiled from his writings and sermons. It was called 'My Utmost for His Highest'. When commenting on joy, Oswald Chambers put it this way: 'The Bible talks plentifully about joy, but it nowhere talks about a "happy Christian." **Happiness depends on what happens; joy does not.** Remember, Jesus Christ had joy, and He prays "that they might have my joy fulfilled in themselves.'

The supreme example of joy in the midst of suffering is expressed by the writer of the letter to the Hebrews when he said that Jesus *'for the joy that was set before Him, endured the cross, scorning the shame, and sat down at the right hand of God'* (Hebrews 12:2).

Jesus' joy was definitely not because He was happy about the coming events of Calvary. His joy came from a far deeper spring than His immediate circumstances. In the very core of His being, He knew that doing what His Father had given Him to do was the only thing that motivated Him. That was the origin of the supreme joy that He knew would be His, even as He endured the cross.

Sir Wilfred Grenfell, that amazing missionary Doctor, who opened up the cold wastes of Labrador to the Gospel at the end of the nineteenth century, said 'Real joy comes not from ease or riches or from praise of men, but from doing something worthwhile.'

Grenfell's life was lived in some of the most arduous of conditions. He was tested to the very limit of his endurance. But what he did, resulted in him experiencing the same sort of joy that motivated Jesus – the fulfilment of what Father God had made him for and given him to do – what joy!

Just for a moment consider what this young man achieved. He went to Oxford University and then trained as a doctor at London University. But while he was there, his life was changed forever through the ministry of that great American evangelist, D.L.Moody.

So instead of entering normal medical practice, Wilfred Grenfell joined the Royal National Mission to Deep-Sea Fishermen and pioneered the development of their first hospital ship. He was following the principle

PERSONAL NOTES

of one step at a time, one day at a time as he sought to follow Jesus into his eventual destiny. These were stepping stones along the way.

This work took him to Labrador in 1892, where he was so greatly shocked by what he later described as 'the poverty and ignorance and semi-starvation among English speaking people of our own race' that he decided to devote the rest of his life to improving the lot of the people of Labrador.

In 1893 he established at Battle Harbour the first hospital of what came to be known as the Labrador Medical Mission. As time went on he not only built other hospitals, but also opened nursing stations, schools, orphanages, and social welfare centres.

When he retired, over forty years later, he had built up an organization that included six hospitals, seven nursing stations, four hospital ships, four boarding schools, fourteen industrial centres, twelve clothing distribution centres, a co-operative lumber mill, and a seaman's institute at St. John's, Newfoundland.

It would be difficult to exaggerate what his lifework meant to the people of Labrador as an example of practical Christianity. It reached all the ethnic groups. His joy was certainly full. There's truly no limit to what one life, totally sold out to Jesus Christ, can actually achieve for the Kingdom of God!

NEHEMIAH'S JOY

Perhaps the most well-known Bible reference to joy comes in the epic saga of how Nehemiah heard the voice of the Lord, while still a prisoner of war and a wine waiter to King Artaxerxes. His grief over the broken down walls and gates of Jerusalem turned to intercession, and as a result he gained permission from the King to return to Jerusalem to rebuild the wall, which he did in the record time of only 52 days, in spite of great opposition.

When the wall was finished, Ezra the scribe (Nehemiah 8:1) brought out the Law of the Lord and read it to the people. The Levites were enrolled to explain its meaning so that the people would understand the Law and know what to do as a result (Nehemiah 8:8).

As a result of hearing and understanding the Law the people came under conviction for their sin and began to weep. The next chapter describes more of what was going on as the people confessed both their sins and the wickedness of their fathers, spending a quarter of the day in confession and worship (Nehemiah 9:2-3)!

This was one of those extraordinary moments in the history of a people of God which turned out to be a day (or several days) of tears of repentance intermingled with tears of joy. For where there is true confession, repentance and forgiveness, there will always be deep-seated joy. Both Ezra and Nehemiah caught the mood of God in what they said to the people:

Ezra: *'This day is sacred to the Lord your God. Do not mourn or weep.'* (Nehemiah 8:9).

Nehemiah: *'Do not grieve, for the joy of the Lord is your strength'* (Nehemiah 8:10).

Finally the people got the message – days of confession and repentance are, ultimately, days of joy, celebration and thanksgiving because the people once again have come close to the heart of God and He's rejoicing with them. *'Then all the people went away to eat and drink, to send portions of food (to those who had nothing prepared) and to celebrate with great joy, because they now understood the words that had been made known to them'* (Nehemiah 8:12).

If you could take before and after group photos of the people on one of our Healing Retreats, you would see the scene in Nehemiah unfolding before your very eyes. The teaching on these retreats so often opens the eyes of the people listening to things they have never understood before. They're then able to deal with their issues and the joy of the Lord in their hearts is the result. The look on their faces tells the whole story.

It's this joy which Nehemiah says is our strength. For it's a joy that no-one and nothing can ever take away. It's not a joy that's dependent on circumstances, it's a joy which radiates from the heart of God and into the heart of man.

Now when the people of God get hold of this message, it's totally life transforming and I would go so far as to say that unless they get hold of this message, they will always be falling short of God's best for their lives.

When we apply the Word of God into our lives we're able to receive

PERSONAL NOTES

PERSONAL NOTES

God's healing for the consequential damage from the things that we have done, and also for the consequences of wounds we have sustained as a result of what others have done to us. The effect is nothing short of miraculous.

TWIN JOYS – DOUBLE STRENGTH

So, there are two joys that God wants us to celebrate. There's the joy that comes from knowing Father God and having His order being established in our lives, through the application of His truth (the Nehemiah joy). Then there's the joy that comes from then getting into the place of serving God, in the ways that He leads us into.

When we know this double joy we can smile through the circumstances around us and rejoice in the Lord always, as Paul told us to do. The joy of the Lord in the hearts of believers produces disciples who are true overcomers – people who face the mountains and don't let them become obstacles, people who see the opposition but don't flinch as they walk through the crowd into their destiny in God.

I pray that as you gradually absorb the truths of God's Word in your daily walk through the pages of *Journey to Freedom*, that you'll not only be able to lift up your eyes and look on the fields which are white for harvest, but that you'll press through in God to take your part in God's team of disciples doing the works of the Kingdom.

SUMMARY

If we're in a place of joy we're also in a place of strength in God. God wants us to experience the joy of relationship with Him and through that relationship know the joy of His healing in our hearts and of serving Him in the fields of the Kingdom of God. The greatest joy any of us can ever have comes through knowing God as Father, and being in the centre of His will for our lives.

PRAYER

Thank you, Lord, that You also rejoice when Your children are able to rejoice. Help me to live in such a way that I won't ever move out of that place where I experience the strengthening of Your joy in my heart every day. In Jesus' Name, Amen.

NOW READ ON...

Congratulations on completing this first and vital step on your personal *Journey to Freedom.* I pray that the foundational truths from God's Word, that we have shared together in ***Building on the Rock***, will become anchored in your spirit, equipping you for your journey of life.

In Book 2, ***God, Me and the Enemy,*** we will learn much more about both the nature and character of God, about ourselves and then about how Satan, the enemy of souls, seeks to undermine our faith and lead us away from the truth. Knowing God as He really is, and understanding the person that we are, are vital to our personal journey of healing and restoration. And the Apostle Paul reminded us of how important it is not to be ignorant of how Satan operates and opposes the life of a believer (2 Corinthians 2:11)

So, may I encourage you now to persevere in your faith with what Paul also said, *"I press on to take hold of that for which Christ Jesus took hold of me"* (Philippians 3:12). God has given each of us a purpose in life and as you continue on your *Journey to Freedom* with Book 2, I pray that you will be strengthened to press on towards this goal.

"Let us throw off everything that hinders and the sin that so easily entangles, and let us run with perseverance the race marked out for us. Let us fix our eyes on Jesus . . . " (Hebrews 12:1-2).

Peter Horrobin

ABOUT THE AUTHOR

Peter Horrobin is the Founder and International Director of Ellel Ministries International, which began in 1986 as a ministry of healing in the north-west of England. The work is now established in over thirty-five different countries.

After graduating from Oxford University with a degree in Chemistry, he spent a number of years in College and University lecturing, before leaving the academic environment for the world of business, where he founded a series of successful publishing and bookselling companies.

In his twenties he started to restore a vintage sports car (an *Alvis Speed 20*) but discovered that its chassis was bent. As he looked at the broken vehicle, wondering if it could ever be repaired, he sensed God asking him a question, *"You could restore this broken car, but I can restore broken lives. Which is more important?"* It was obvious that broken lives were more important than broken cars and so the beginnings of a vision for restoring people was birthed in his heart.

A hallmark of Peter's ministry has been his willingness to step out in faith and see God move to fulfil His promises, often in remarkable ways. His book, *Strands of Destiny*, tells many of the stories of what God has done in the past thirty years and makes an ideal companion volume to the *Journey to Freedom* Series.

In this season of their lives, Peter, and his wife Fiona are concentrating on writing so that all their knowledge and experience can be made permanently available in book form through Sovereign World Ltd.

ABOUT ELLEL MINISTRIES

www.ellel.org

OUR VISION

Ellel Ministries is a non-denominational Christian Mission Organization with a vision to resource and equip the Church by welcoming people, teaching them about the Kingdom of God and healing those in need (Luke 9:11).

OUR MISSION

Our mission is to fulfil the above vision throughout the world, as God opens the doors, in accordance with the Great Commission of Jesus and the calling of the Church to proclaim the Kingdom of God by preaching the good news, healing the broken-hearted and setting the captives free. We are, therefore, committed to evangelism, healing, deliverance, discipleship and training. The particular scriptures on which our mission is founded are **Isaiah 61:1–7; Matthew 28:18–20; Luke 9:1–2; 9:11; Ephesians 4:12; 2 Timothy 2:2.**

OUR BASIS OF FAITH

God is a Trinity. God the Father loves all people. God the Son, Jesus Christ, is Saviour and Healer, Lord and King. God the Holy Spirit indwells Christians and imparts the dynamic power by which they are enabled to continue Christ's ministry. The Bible is the divinely inspired authority in matters of faith, doctrine and conduct, and is the basis for teaching.

Ellel Ministries International
Ellel Grange
Ellel
Lancaster, LA2 0HN
United Kingdom

Further books by Peter Horrobin

STRANDS OF DESTINY

This is Peter Horrobin's personal account of how God envisioned him through the remains of a crashed car, to establish the healing work of Ellel Ministries at Ellel Grange. It will build your faith as you journey with him through the ups and downs of what became a world-wide spiritual adventure.

Paperback 316 pages plus 48 pages of colour photographs, £14.99, ISBN 978-1-85240-835-0

FORGIVENESS – GOD'S MASTER KEY

Forgiveness is key to the restoration of our relationship with God and to healing from the consequences of hurtful, damaging human relationships. This book is one of the most outstanding and concise available on the subject of forgiveness.

Paperback 110 pages, £6.99, ISBN 978-1-85240-502-1

LIVING LIFE GOD'S WAY

'Living Life God's Way' is an immensely readable and practical book. In this revised and updated edition of 'Living the Life – Practical Christianity for the Real World', Peter Horrobin guides you through a landscape of hidden truths. Using real life testimonies, parables and illustrations to unlock some of the most difficult of life's issues that often make us stumble through our Christian walk. This book was written to help new Christians get established in their faith and to provide older Christians with the kind of realistic help that is needed to keep their lives on track with God.

Paperback 222 pages, £10.99, ISBN 978-1-85240-758-2

HEALING THROUGH DELIVERANCE

The Foundation and Practice of Deliverance Ministry

In this comprehensive, practical and ground-breaking volume, Peter draws on this extensive experience to set out a thorough and scriptural foundation for the healing and deliverance ministry—an integral part of fulfilling the Great Commission and a vital key to discipleship. This authoritative handbook will equip you to understand and respond to the call of God to set the captives free. A classic.

Hardback 630 pages, £24.99, ISBN 978-1-85240-498-7

HEALING FROM THE CONSEQUENCES OF ACCIDENT, SHOCK AND TRAUMA

Unhealed trauma is one of the primary reasons why some people do not easily heal from the consequences of accidents or sudden shocks. This ground-breaking book is the culmination of thirty years of experience praying for such people. This foundational teaching has been instrumental in bringing permanent healing to people all over the world.

Paperback 176 pages, £9.99, ISBN 978-1-85240-743-8

The Truth and Freedom Series

All the books in this series have been written by members of the Ellel Ministries Teams. Each one highlights a particular topic that has proved to be of significance in the lives of those who have come on our Healing Retreats. When we get God's truth into our hearts, He ministers His freedom into our lives.

Anger, How do you handle it?
Paperback, 112 pages, Paul and Liz Griffin, ISBN 978-1-85240-450-7

God's Covering, A Place of Healing
Paperback, 192 pages, David Cross, ISBN 978-1-85240-485-7

Healing from the consequences of Accident, Shock and Trauma
Paperback, 176 pages, Peter Horrobin, ISBN 978-1-85240-743-8

Hope and Healing for the Abused
Paperback, 128 pages, Paul and Liz Griffin, ISBN 978-1-85240-480-2

Intercession & Healing, Breaking Through with God
Paperback, 176 pages, Fiona Horrobin, ISBN 978-1-85240-500-7

Rescue from Rejection, Finding Security in God's Loving Acceptance
Paperback, 160 pages, Denise Cross, ISBN 978-1-85240-555-7

Soul Ties, The Unseen Bond in Relationships
Paperback, 128 pages, David Cross, ISBN 978-1-85240-597-7

Stepping Stones to the Father Heart of God
Paperback, 176 pages, Margaret Silvester, ISBN 978-1-85240-623-3

The Dangers of Alternative Ways of Healing, How to Avoid New Age Deceptions
Paperback, 176 pages, David Cross & John Berry, ISBN 978-1-85240-537-3

Trapped by Control, How to Find Freedom
Paperback, 112 pages, David Cross, ISBN 978-1-85240-501-4

ALL THESE BOOKS AND MANY MORE ARE AVAILABLE FROM SOVEREIGN WORLD.